W9-AWM-004

A
SHARE OUR STRENGTH
Book to Fight
Hunger

BROADWAY BOOKS

NEW YORK

COOKING
FROM THE
HEART

---------- 100 ----------

Great American Chefs
Share Recipes
They Cherish

Michael J. Rosen

PRINTED IN THE UNITED STATES OF AMERICA

BROADWAY BOOKS and its logo, a letter B bisected on the diagonal, are trademarks of Random House, Inc.

Visit our website at www.broadwaybooks.com

Book design by Elizabeth Rendfleisch
Illustrated by Agni Saucier

Library of Congress Cataloging-in-Publication Data

Rosen, Michael J., 1954–
Cooking from the heart : 100 great American chefs share recipes they cherish / Michael J. Rosen.
p. cm.
Includes index.
(alk. paper)
1. Cookery. 2. Cooks—United States. I. Title.
TX714 .R6684 2003
641.5—dc21
2002034541

ISBN 0-7679-1371-X

1 3 5 7 9 10 8 6 4 2

Contents

Acknowledgments

In addition to the gratitude that is due each and every chef who has contributed time and creativity not only to this book but to Share Our Strength's ongoing efforts over the years, I would like to express thanks to the following individuals on behalf of myself and Share Our Strength. Special appreciation is extended to Sharon Reiss, who dutifully tested each recipe (while feeding harried friends and neighbors along the way) and provided genial counsel and culinary guidance. Heartfelt thanks are extended to Jennifer Josephy at Broadway Books, who passionately championed this book from the start, as well as to the other enthusiastic supporters at Broadway Books. Likewise, three key people at Share Our Strength assisted in the prodigious task of working with a hundred of the nation's busiest chefs: Catherine Townsend, Debbie Shore, and Pat Nicklin. This is not to overlook the critical participation of so many others at the organization, including Arlison Osborne Hall in the public relations department, as well as Howard Byck, Amy Zganjar, Ashley Graham, and Bill Shore.

Foreword

Most people sense intuitively—modern behavioral science be damned—that we are dual by nature, made up of body and spirit. What has always fascinated me is the way this basic duality gets blurred at the borders, the physical unexpectedly morphing into the spiritual, the senses opening doors to memory, idea, and emotion; these in turn influencing sensory perception. Who has not had the experience of being enchanted by a bottle of wine only to discover, the very next time we order it, that it's not what we remember? What made the first bottle special, of course, was that you drank it in the company of good friends. Or your children were visiting. Or your wife, you realize, has never looked more beautiful than tonight. What you were tasting was the flavor of excitement, of intimacy, of sharing, of joy, of well-being, of love. The grapes were just along for the ride.

In our house, the kitchen has always been the center of things, but more than ever now since our daughters have grown up and moved away. My wife and I eat at the small table there rather than at the big one in the dining room. Most of our friends are roughly the same age, and their kids are grown too, so when they visit our house, or we theirs, we invariably end up in the kitchen. "What can we do to help?" someone will ask after the coats have been hung up. "You can open that bottle of wine you brought," I'll suggest. "Otherwise, relax." Relaxing, actually, is something I've only recently learned to do with dinner guests. Afraid that I would botch the food preparations if I allowed myself to be distracted by conversation, I would always shoo people into the living room, where the chairs were more comfortable, and ignore the fact that the kitchen, with its too-bright yellow light and its stiff-backed chairs, was where people really wanted to be. They prefer swapping lies and truths around the stove as I add chopped prosciutto and diced tomatoes and garlic to half-steamed mussels. They want to be present when I slide those mussels under the broiler for a sizzling finish. Conversation and sizzle. Yum. Later, after the guests have gone home, next to the microwave I'll discover the dish of fresh parsley I chopped and then forgot to add. "Never mind," my wife will say. "They were delicious. The best mussels you've ever cooked." Which is both true and untrue, because I've done a better job of the preparation on other occasions. They just never tasted better.

Throughout his career Dickens wrote about food as an almost spiritual thing, in part, I suspect, because he'd been hungry in his youth (and hunger is not something you ever forget), but also because he believed that food and drink encouraged fellowship, goodwill, tolerance, understanding, and generosity. Scrooge's first act of benevolence after his long night with the fearsome spirits is to purchase a gift of food—the prize turkey he sends to the Cratchits—and his reentry into the world of human feeling is signaled by his joining his nephew's family for their Christmas meal. Dickens's belief in the spiritually restorative powers of food, especially when combined with a good story, is shared by the contributors to this volume, and their gifts of recipe and narrative will warm the heart and tummy.

—Richard Russo
Camden, Maine
September 2003

COOKING
FROM THE
HEART

Introduction

BY WAY OF A BLESSING

Cooking from the Heart is a book of memories, for recipes are simply a kind of memory: an attempt to re-create the taste of some familiar dish . . . a way of passing along a particular method for preparing pie dough or gravy . . . an experiment in recapturing some experience remembered from travels or childhood. A recipe is a memory made indelible.

In this book a hundred of our country's most distinguished, passionate, and *compassionate* chefs share their most beloved dishes with us, recipes that are rich with family tradition. An heirloom dessert, seasonal offering, or cooking method—in every case, the recipe represents something more than a savory experience or a culinary quest. Along with a chef's voice, you'll hear a child's remembrances, a parent's hopes, a partner's aspirations, a grandparent's dreams, a friend's generosity. Aren't the foods that have sustained us, the foods that we offer others, and the foods with which we come to identify ourselves simply a form of love? As chef Craig Shelton says about a soup he learned from his grandmother, ". . . everything that's good about the world derives from love. Foods . . . have been the way I've been able to experience and share much of it."

But this is also a book intended to be filled with *your own* memories, for there's nothing more appealing about someone else's story than its potential to call to mind a story of your own. As I shared time with these chefs over the last year, I invariably found myself recalling my own family's traditions and favorite meals, and I think you'll be doing the same.

Each chef's table—whether oceans, generations, or cultures away—will link with yours as though we were all sitting down to eat at one universal table assembled from each of our individual leaves.

While I've never hunted crayfish in the waterways of rural California as Traci Des Jardins did throughout her childhood, wading barefoot with her many cousins, I do remember my family crossing the shallow creeks of central Ohio, trying one bank after another until we found some sweet spot where my father could hook the bass he prized.

Likewise, my mother wasn't the neighborhood's best pie baker in the way Gale Gand's mother was, rolling out weekly piecrusts with *her* grandmother's rolling pin, but Gale brought to mind those rare pies my mother made with the underripe cherries my father ransomed from our cherry tree before the birds devoured them.

As Mario Batali and Greg Higgins laughingly recounted their childhood roles in family "assembly line" harvests—picking roadside berries or shucking corn for canning chow chow—I was reminded of the endless potatoes I'd grate with my mother and grandmother for the first night of Hanukkah and the huge family supper consisting entirely of latkes.

The flavors, aromas, colors, and textures of the foods we have shared create impressions more profound than mere gustatory recollection. Along with recognizing key sensations—some balance of sweetness and tartness, the "right" size for a dumpling, or the unmistakable crunch of corn bread's crust—come so many associated experiences: where you were, who joined in the meal, what you had been doing just before, as though pulling one container from the crowded larder of your memory forced the entire contents of the shelf to spill onto the counter.

As you read this book and sample the various recipes, perhaps you'll find a new tradition to bring to your circle of friends. Perhaps you'll find yourself searching for heirloom Bavarian molds so you can present wobbling architectural custards to your own grandchildren, much as Stan Frankenthaler's great-grandmother would. Perhaps you'll start packing an extravagant bar of chocolate when you travel, so you can bake

Mary Sue Milliken's Hidden Kisses—a bit of chocolate wrapped in short-bread—to surprise your hosts. Perhaps you'll look at the deluge of mulberries in your backyard a little differently, recalling Seth Bixby Daugherty's crunch recipe that served an entire peace march.

But beyond the pleasures of reading, cooking, and enjoying meals with the dear people in your life, I hope you'll be inspired to share your own strengths, just as the chefs in this book have done, with whatever global or local concern to which you have found some connection. A great portion of this book's profits benefit the antihunger efforts of Share Our Strength, an organization that enlists the talents of individuals, businesses, and corporations in the fight to end a condition of rampant hunger that has never been more urgent than now. Hunger is not a necessary consequence of progress, nor is it a social ill that awaits some scientific breakthrough or legislative act. It requires only our insistence that we, as a nation, will not permit a single citizen to live without the security of a next meal.

On behalf of Share Our Strength's efforts, the committed chefs in this book have hosted fund-raising events, taught nutrition education classes, volunteered hours of labor, donated pounds of food, and enlisted legions of colleagues and supporters. And this book is another outpouring in their valiant ongoing campaign. I speak for all the chefs here when I say that, just as we hope you'll adopt a few of these recipes for your own traditions, we hope you'll add your voice—your own *leaf*—to this one table, where everyone can join in the community of food.

—Michael J. Rosen
Hopewell Springs
Glenford, Ohio

STARTERS

Allen Susser
LOBSTER AND MANGO SUMMER ROLLS

Ming Tsai
PORK AND APPLE POTSTICKERS WITH DIM SUM DIPPER

Susan Spicer
PORK SATÉ WITH INDONESIAN PEANUT SAUCE

Harold Moore
BEEF TATAKI

Anne Kearney
DUCK LIVER MOUSSELINE WITH SWEET AND SOUR PRUNES

Paul Mattison
EGGPLANT RICOTTA MOUSSE

Christine Keff
THAI SQUID SALAD

Guenter Seeger
MATJES HERRING TARTARE

Norman Van Aken
CONCH SALAD WITH SALSA DE VIDA

Jim Barnett
CRAB CAKES WITH FRIED-CORN SAUCE

Tom Douglas
SHRIMP RÉMOULADE ON MOLASSES TOASTS

Chris Schlesinger
GRILLED VIDALIA ONIONS WITH LOBSTER AND TRUFFLE OIL

Allen Susser LOBSTER AND MANGO SUMMER ROLLS

I grew up in Brooklyn, where *mango* meant one of the tropical flavors in the fruit salad. Not exactly an earth-shattering encounter. So nothing prepared me for the experience of mangoes that greeted me in South Miami, where I came to live and work: the whole neighborhood possesses a deep ambrosia when the mango trees bloom, and the varieties of mangoes exceed anything I could have imagined. We have 150 kinds just in this region. In India, where mangoes have been cultivated for four thousand years, there are more than four hundred varieties. Bar none, the mango is the most popular fruit in the world, and every tropical culture uses its native fruit in distinct ways. Cubans love the Toledo mango, the *Vianado*. In Jamaica they prize the Julie or East Indian mango. The Edward, or the Zill, is popular in South Florida.

Since moving here, I have been on a quest to sample as many kinds of mango as I can. Even on my travels I seek out new varieties; I think I'm up to 250 types. Some mangoes have peach and pineapple flavors, a tropical cinnamon aroma, and an aftertaste like pine or dried fruit or lemon. The *Preacho,* a Cuban mango, has a deep floral aroma with a distinct scent of candied orange peel. The *Neillium* is an Indian mango with clove and cinnamon aromas and red-berry, plum, and apricot flavors. The Madame Francis from Haiti has hints of anise, cinnamon, caramel, and fig.

The mango's spectrum of colors is just as astonishing: green, pink, red, orange, red-orange, yellow, canary yellow, crimson, and ruby. And their size can range from the peach-size Cuban mangoes to the cantaloupe-size Mexican Oro mangoes.

When I first opened my restaurant, I placed a little 2 X 1-inch ad in the

LOBSTER AND MANGO
SUMMER ROLLS Serves 4

----

1 tablespoon coarse salt

One 1 1/2-pound live Maine lobster

1 tablespoon fish sauce

1 teaspoon sugar

3 tablespoons fresh lime juice

1 small Thai chile, seeded and minced

12 large Thai basil leaves, chopped

2 fresh cilantro sprigs, chopped

1 cup shredded arugula

1 large ripe mango, peeled, pitted, and julienned

4 rice paper wrappers, 8 inches in diameter

1 Bring a large pot of water to a boil, add the salt, and plunge the lobster into the pot. Cover the pot and boil for 10 minutes. Remove the lobster from the water and transfer it to a platter to cool slightly. Crack the shell and remove the meat from the tail and claws. Freeze or discard the shells. Slice the meat and set aside. (The lobster can be prepared and refrigerated 1 day in advance.)

2 Combine the fish sauce, sugar, lime juice, and chile. Mix in the basil, cilantro, and arugula. Add the mango and toss gently.

3 Fill a shallow dish or pan with warm tap water and spread a cotton cloth on the work surface. Submerge a wrapper in the water for 10 to 30 seconds. Remove it from the water just as it turns limp and carefully spread the soggy wrapper flat onto the cotton cloth. Repeat with each wrapper.

4 Carefully retoss the salad and place a mound of the mixture in the middle of each wrapper. Divide the lobster meat evenly, placing the slices on top of each mound of salad.

5 To make the wrap, roll the bottom of the rice wrapper toward the middle, fold in both sides, and continue to roll toward the free edge. (If the wrapper cracks or doesn't roll easily, use a new wrapper and soak it longer.) ✣ Cut the rolls on a diagonal and place the pieces on small plates, garnished with the remaining salad.

local *Topical News*—"I trade dinner for mangoes. Bring me your backyard fruit"—and it listed my phone number. I've done this every year since, and during the summer I *almost* have more fruit than I can use.

Here's a typical story: A mango tree blooms in December or January, and as the months go on, the fruit forms so that by May or June the mangoes are a pretty good size. Sometime in June the family has its first ripe fruit. Everyone is thrilled. Then, during the next week of ripening fruit, a couple dear friends and relatives receive a perfect mango from the family's very own tree. Then the ripe mangoes fill a basket or a shopping bag that someone takes to work to share. And then two weeks pass, and suddenly they're asking everyone, "Did I give you some of our mangoes yet? Please, take." Then the following week—it's mid-July now—mangoes are dropping from their tree every hour, squirrels are taking bites from them, and their yard's a sticky, rotting mess. That's when they bring us a wheelbarrow full of mangoes. It's a wonderful community connection, and people are so proud to be sharing their fruit with "Chef Allen."

Then, in exchange, we create a full-course dinner for each couple that brings us mangoes, and we include some of their own fruit in the dishes we serve them. For many of our neighbors this is their first truly grand dining experience.

We use the fruit in every possible way: I make mango martinis, mango mojo, mango upside-down cake, mango tarte tatin with ginger, mango chutneys, mango ketchup. I stew them, grate them when they're still green and unripened, grill them, use them in curries and salsas and ice creams. I simply can't exhaust the possibilities.

This particular recipe is a refreshing appetizer that brings mango together with lobster, another resource that's especially sweet and bountiful in summer. I suppose if my restaurant were in Maine, I'd be trading dinners for lobsters. The rice paper makes a simple envelope for this, transparent enough to let the arugula, cilantro, and chopped chiles brighten the flavors of the meat and the mango.

The *New York Times* called chef Allen Susser "the Ponce de León of Florida cooking." His cuisine is a fusion of the world's tropical cultures in a sweet, spicy, and aromatic harmony. Chef Allen's is Miami's premier restaurant, rated number one for food in the 2002 *Zagat Survey*. Allen is the author of *The Great Citrus Book*, *The Great Mango Book*, and *Allen Susser's New World Cuisine and Cookery*.

Ming Tsai PORK AND APPLE POTSTICKERS WITH DIM SUM DIPPER

Being Chinese, I've probably made and eaten more dumplings than any other food. Steamed, boiled, panfried, deep-fried: dumplings have filled my life. I have very distinct memories of sitting with my grandmother and my mother to roll dumpling skins at a large table and help fold them around the fillings. We'd have whole meals based on dumplings: the traditional pork filling (with garlic, ginger, and *shaoxing* wine) and then a filling of *gyou tsai* (garlic chives).

We had a Ping-Pong table in the basement of our home in Dayton, Ohio. Every five years or so my father's three brothers and their families would visit over the Christmas holidays. We'd be ten cousins and four sets of parents talking for hours as we made potstickers around that long green table.

At my grandfather's house we'd have special dumpling nights where I would attempt to outeat my grandfather. I was in third or fourth grade, and I'd manage twenty dumplings. I'd also try to eat more *sambal* or hot sauce than him. It was something of an honor to outdo my grandfather. For Chinese people food *is* culture.

Admittedly, with only two thousand people of Chinese descent in Dayton, we weren't offered much in the way of Asian groceries. Whenever we traveled, we'd fit in a side trip to some city's Chinatown. Toronto's was our favorite. We'd pack our station wagon with cooking tools, Chinese pastries, spices, black bean sauces—

everything we missed. I'm sure we looked like smugglers coming back across the border.

My other grandparents moved to Taipei after the Cultural Revolution, and I'd visit them every summer. Along with improving my Chinese speaking and learning more about our culture, I'd get to eat lots of street food, which included the best potstickers. Plus, there were whole restaurants devoted to dumplings. Going out to dinner always meant a big affair with eight or ten people around a table, ordering hundreds and hundreds of dumplings. We'd start with lighter, steamed dumpings and eventually move on to panfried ones. We'd

PORK AND APPLE POTSTICKERS

Makes 30 to 32 dumplings

----

4 tablespoons (^{1}/2 stick) unsalted butter, softened

^{1}/2 pound ground pork (not too lean)

1 medium green apple, peeled and diced

2 tablespoons finely chopped fresh ginger

1 ^{1}/2 tablespoons finely chopped garlic

1 tablespoon *sambal oelek* (red chile paste, available at Asian markets)

2 tablespoons naturally brewed soy sauce

1 tablespoon toasted sesame oil

2 large eggs

^{1}/2 teaspoon kosher salt

Thirty-two 3^1/2-inch round potsticker wrappers (*sue gow* skins), defrosted in the refrigerator overnight if frozen

2 tablespoons canola oil

1 recipe Dim Sum Dipper

1 To make the filling, knead the butter into the pork in a large bowl until fully incorporated.

2 Add the apple, ginger, garlic, *sambal oelek*, soy sauce, sesame oil, 1 lightly beaten egg, and the salt to the pork mixture. Combine thoroughly.

3 To assemble the potstickers, mix the remaining egg with 2 tablespoons water and set aside. Place 1^1/2 teaspoons of the filling in the center of each wrapper (the edges of the wrappers should stay clean to ensure a proper seal). Fold each wrapper in half to form a half-moon. Seal the top center of each dumpling by pressing between the fingers and, starting at the center, make 3 pleats to the bottom right corner. Repeat pleating process to the bottom left corner. Gently press the dumpling on the work surface to create a flat bottom. Lightly brush the egg wash on the finished dumpling and transfer to a tray lined with parchment

start with lighter shrimp or chicken fillings and move on to spicier ones with pork. And, once again, I had to impress everyone, trying to eat more than any other kid at our table.

The years I didn't journey to Taipei, my whole family vacationed at East Coast Chinese Family Camp. The fathers bunked in one cabin, the mothers in another, and the kids bunked in various buildings according to age. Three or four hundred people from across the country came to share in camp activities like swimming and crafts, as well as games and programs more typical paper. Repeat with the remaining wrappers and filling. Leave space between finished dumplings to prevent them from sticking together.

4 To cook the potstickers, heat a large non-stick skillet over high heat. Add the canola oil and swirl to coat the pan. When the oil shimmers, add the potstickers (flattened bottoms down) in rows of 5. Cook in batches without disturbing until the bottoms are golden brown, 5 to 6 minutes. Add $1/2$ cup water and immediately cover the pan with a lid to avoid spattering. Lift the cover: $1/8$ inch of water should remain in the pan; if not, add a splash. Steam until the potstickers are puffy and firm to the touch, 8 to 10 minutes. If the water evaporates before the potstickers are done, add more water in $1/4$-cup increments. If the potstickers are cooked and some water remains, drain the excess water and return the pan to the burner.

5 Cook the steamed potstickers over high heat for 2 to 3 minutes to recrisp the bottoms. Transfer the potstickers to a platter.

✤ Serve the potstickers with a bowl of the Dim Sum Dipper.

DIM SUM DIPPER Makes 1 cup

$1/3$ cup naturally brewed soy sauce

$1/3$ cup rice wine vinegar

$1/3$ cup $1/8$-inch-thick slices scallion greens

1 tablespoon toasted sesame oil

1 tablespoon sambal oelek (red chile paste, available at Asian markets)

Whisk the ingredients together and store in the refrigerator for up to 2 weeks.

of China. The parents would cook. The kids would clean. (And underlying the whole experience was the hope that your kid would meet and one day marry a nice Chinese kid of the opposite sex.)

One morning we kids would rise early to make a special pancake breakfast for the adults. We'd scrounge around the camp kitchen adding heads of garlic, spicy sauces, anchovies—everything we could find—to the batter. Then we'd fry up the pancakes and rush out into the dining hall to watch our parents and grandparents pour on the maple syrup and eat. But since a typical Chinese breakfast is the previous evening's dinner—marinated meats or fermented tofu, along with the rice porridge—we rarely got the Big Surprise of Disgust we were aiming for.

But the highlight of camp was potsticker night. Throughout the day different families took turns at the five round tables in the dining hall, rolling out the dumpling skins and folding them around one or another filling. We'd crank out something close to six thousand dumplings, stacking them on trays until dinner, when everyone gathered in the dining hall.

This particular dumpling combines an American favorite, apples, with the traditional pork, adding a sweetness and juiciness to the filling. I'm always looking for dumpling innovations (and this one was cooked up with my sous-chef at Blue Ginger, Jon Taylor), even though I've long since given up the need to eat more dumplings than anyone else.

Ming Tsai is the chef-owner of Blue Ginger restaurant in Wellesley, Massachusetts, author of the *Blue Ginger Cookbook*, and Emmy Award–winning television personality whose series *Ming's Quest* appears on the Food Network. He is the recipient of the 2002 Beard Best Chef Award/ Northeast.

Susan Spicer PORK SATÉ WITH INDONESIAN PEANUT SAUCE

Before we moved to New Orleans, we lived in Rijswijk, Holland, from 1957 to 1960. This is one of the dishes my mother learned to cook there, which has become central to our family gatherings.

My dad served in the navy as part of the diplomatic corps, and so my parents often had dinner parties. I was all of five when we moved to Holland, and the sixth of seven kids, so I spent a lot of time in the kitchen with my mother.

My mother is Danish, and even when we lived in Rhode Island, she cooked many unusual things, at least compared to what my friends ate at their houses. But in Holland, because the Dutch had Indonesian colonies, I started to eat even more exotic foods.

Satés were part of the Indonesian feast of many dishes known as *rijsttafel* (Dutch for *rice table,* since rice formed the basis of so many recipes). My parents used to have this delivered to the house, and we'd watch wide-eyed as the delivery guys carried in dish after dish stacked in a tower of round metal containers. This is how we came to understand the local terms *five-boy curry* and *seven-boy curry*, which indicated how

PORK SATÉ Serves 4

1 teaspoon minced garlic

1 teaspoon minced fresh ginger

2 tablespoons vegetable oil

$^1/_4$ cup Indonesian sweet soy sauce
   (preferably Conimex Ketjap Manis,
   available at Asian markets)

1 pound lean boneless pork loin or
   trimmed butt, cut into $^1/_2$-inch cubes

1 recipe Indonesian Peanut Sauce

1 Combine the garlic, ginger, oil, and soy sauce in a medium mixing bowl and add the pork cubes. Stir to coat and marinate in the refrigerator for 2 hours or overnight.

2 Soak 12 wooden skewers in water for at least 30 minutes. Prepare a medium-hot grill or preheat the broiler to high.

3 Thread 3 pieces of pork onto each skewer and grill or broil for 2 to 3 minutes on each side.

✢ Present the skewers on a platter or individual plates with a bowl of warm peanut sauce.

INDONESIAN PEANUT SAUCE
Makes 2 to 3 cups

1 cup smooth or chunky peanut butter

1 teaspoon minced garlic

1 teaspoon sambal oelek (red chile paste,
   available at Asian markets)

$^1/_4$ cup Indonesian sweet soy sauce

1 to 2 cups chicken stock or water

Combine peanut butter, garlic, sambal oelek, and soy sauce in a small saucepan and warm gently. Slowly whisk in the chicken stock, adding a little at a time (the mixture will thicken after each addition). Add stock until the sauce has a creamy consistency.

✢ This sauce can be prepared 1 or 2 days in advance and refrigerated. Rewarm the sauce gently to prevent it from breaking.

Note: The seasonings can be adjusted to your personal taste; we like the sauce a little spicy. I've substituted chicken and even fish for the pork and enjoyed the saté nearly as much. You might also try this sauce as a dip for celery.

many delivery boys it took to carry an order. Inside the metal compartments would be shrimp dishes, curries of different kinds—including a beef curry that my mom learned to cook—rice, condiments, and then the skewered pork pieces with a separate container of peanut sauce.

When we returned to the States, we didn't have teams of delivery boys with their towers of dinner, but my mother had learned to cook some of the Indonesian flavors we'd come to love. She was a very capable cook, and with so many kids she was always preparing meals. Whenever she could, she'd recruit me and my siblings to help, and we'd sit around the table chopping peppers or nuts, frying up onions, sliding the pieces of pork onto the skewers (meat on a stick—how exotic was that!), or stirring the chile paste and thickened soy sauce into the glop of Jif or Skippy peanut butter (and how strange was that!).

Now when we gather as a family at Christmas and other special days, we rarely have turkey or ham. Instead our table is set with rice and curry or *bami goreng*, a noodle dish with cabbage and pork, and these pork satés are always the appetizer. They are, unquestionably, the favorite snack in my family. Before we sit down to eat, my older brother will have sneaked off with a stick of the saté. And one of us will be caught with a finger dipped into the peanut sauce. And I can see us being little kids in Holland, doing the exact same things. Who would want anything to change?

Susan Spicer began her cooking career in New Orleans as an apprentice to chef Daniel Bonnot at the Louis XVI Restaurant. After a four-month "stage" at the Hotel Sofitel in Paris, she returned to New Orleans to open the bistro Savoir Faire in the St. Charles Hotel. Subsequently Susan opened Bistro at Maison de Ville. She is co-owner of Bayona, located in a two-hundred-year-old cottage in the French Quarter; Herbsaint, a bistro-style restaurant; and Cobalt, a regional American restaurant. A Beard Foundation Award–winning chef, Susan has cochaired New Orleans's Taste of the Nation for a dozen years.

Harold Moore BEEF TATAKI

Growing up in New Jersey, I often stayed with my grandmother—especially while my mother attended nursing school. Like most kids, I was probably something of a pain in the neck, which was a particular problem during *The Young and the Restless*, my grandmother's favorite soap.

My grandmother came to America from Tokyo. She met my grandfather because she spoke a little English, which qualified her for a job in the payroll office of the air force. It was a struggle for servicemen to marry local women. The air force just wouldn't permit it. My grandfather was reassigned to Korea for a couple years. But eventually he was allowed to return to Tokyo and they got married. When he finished his tour of

BEEF TATAKI Serves 4

For the marinade

1 cup reduced-sodium soy sauce

1 cup dry sherry

1 whole head garlic

1 thumb-size piece fresh ginger

$1/2$ pound sirloin, cut into 2 thick squares

For the vinaigrette

$1/4$ cup soy sauce

$1/4$ cup fresh lemon juice

$1/4$ cup truffle juice or light chicken or
   vegetable stock

$3/4$ cup extra virgin olive oil

1 teaspoon truffle oil, optional

For serving

1 thumb-size piece fresh ginger, grated

$1/4$ pound enoki mushrooms, gently
   separated

2 shiso leaves, julienned (available at
   Asian markets)

1 scallion, slivered

1 small carrot, julienned

1 For the marinade, pour the soy sauce and sherry into a small saucepan. Cut the garlic head in half across the cloves and smash each half with the flat side of a broad knife.

Add the garlic and ginger to the saucepan and bring to a boil. Remove the pan from the heat and cool.

2 Place the meat in a resealable plastic bag and pour in the cooled marinade. Refrigerate for 24 hours.

3 Remove the meat from the marinade and pat dry. Reserve the bag with the marinade. Heat a cast-iron skillet until very hot. Sear the meat quickly on all sides. The meat should look very dark. (This step will create a lot of smoke.) While the meat is still hot, return it to the reserved marinade and reseal the bag. Refrigerate for 24 hours.

4 To mix the vinaigrette, combine the soy sauce, lemon juice, and truffle juice. Gradually whisk in the olive oil and the truffle oil if desired. Set aside.

5 Remove the meat from the marinade. Slice it $1/8$ inch thick and rub each slice with grated ginger.

✣ Fan the meat slices on each plate. Toss together the mushrooms, shiso, scallion, and carrot in a mixing bowl and dress with 3 tablespoons of the vinaigrette. (Any extra dressing can be used for other salads.) Place a small handful of the salad on top of the arranged meat.

duty, they came to America, finally settling in New Jersey.

At my grandmother's, we had Western and Japanese foods, though any Asian ingredient beyond soy sauce—this was the 1970s—was impossible to find in our area. Monthly care packages arrived from my grandmother's sister in Tokyo. She'd pack boxes with pickled daikon radishes, sushi rice, little red-bean jelly candies, wasabi powder, pickled ginger, and all kinds of things I couldn't imagine how my grand-mother used. One thing she

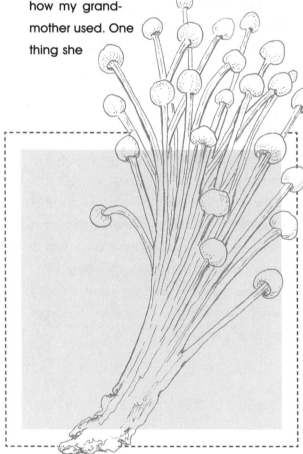

still makes that I love: sushi rolls with pickled ginger and, believe it or not, those Batampte kosher pickles—the half-sour ones—rolled in the rice and nori. Other than these samples of Japanese food, my family ate pretty standard fare like burgers and so forth.

My first real culinary memories are of spending that time with my grandmother, whether washing dishes, setting the table (everyone had to be home for supper), or carrying her basket filled with vegetables from her garden (inside the garden I was too young to do more than trample seedlings and break stems). My grandmother had a small garden, but it was the first time I'd seen someone growing something and bring-ing it into the kitchen and then cooking and serving it. She breaded and fried green tomatoes. She fried zucchini slices seasoned with soy sauce and sesame oil—which is sensational if you haven't tried it. Cooking with her inspired me to work as a chef.

My grandmother's beef tataki is simple. She'd have marinated beef in ginger, garlic, and soy. She'd pat dry the beef and place it in the hot cast-iron skillet, which was so seasoned that nothing stuck to it. The soy would sizzle and caramelize; the meat doesn't burn, but it acquires a charred taste outside, though the inside has a tartare tex-ture. When I came inside from playing and started being "young and restless" myself, my grandmother would hack off a few bits of the beef tataki, chop up some scallions, and set it with a little bowl of soy sauce in front of me. And that would keep me quiet during the rest of the soap.

I hadn't thought about this dish for years, but soon after I started working at Montrachet, a chef from one of Nobu Matsuhisa's restaurants came for dinner, and I was a little nervous figuring out what to prepare for this very accomplished Japanese chef. In a moment of inspiration I took a piece of sirloin, marinated it quickly, and then seared it the way my grandmother did. But I served it with more than just the scallions and soy: I added a julienne of mushrooms, truffle, and lemon juice. It made a delicious *amuse-gueule*, and it made me happy to have brought a bit of my grandmother's legacy to this chef's table.

Harold Moore continues Montrachet's heralded tradition of fine three-star *(New York Times)* contemporary French cuisine in New York City. Harold attended the Culinary Institute of America at Hyde Park. His externship at Restaurant Daniel quickly led to a full-time position there. He worked at Jean Georges, helped to open Vongerichten's Mercer Kitchen, and joined Daniel Boulud once again when he opened Restaurant Daniel. In 2000 Montrachet owner Drew Nieporent put Harold at the helm of his famed TriBeCa restaurant. In 2002 Harold was nominated for the Beard Rising Star Chef Award.

Anne Kearney DUCK LIVER MOUSSELINE WITH SWEET AND SOUR PRUNES

I moved to New Orleans from Cincinnati, where I'd been running a kitchen right out of culinary school. I landed a job at Mr. B's, where I'd fry up three hundred soft-shells and hundreds of orders of craw-fette (a sort of crawfish fettuccine), serving six hundred people at brunch.

I'd heard of a job at Bistro de Ville, a small restaurant with a kitchen at the end of a dank, old alley; at the time, so much of New Orleans seemed held together with a glue gun and a stapler. There were prep tables in the alley, a cooler smaller than my fridge at home, and a chef named John Neal, a skinny, tall, thirtyish boy from Milton, Florida, with straight blond bangs. He was shy, humble, and he couldn't understand why on earth I wanted to work at such a small place.

John had such concentration; his tongue

DUCK LIVER MOUSSELINE

Serves 12 to 14

----

2 cups whole milk

1¹/2 pounds duck livers, any sinew
  removed

2 tablespoons vegetable oil

1¹/2 teaspoons kosher salt

¹/4 teaspoon freshly ground white pepper

2¹/2 ounces (3 to 4 slices) applewood-
  smoked bacon, diced

¹/3 cup minced shallots

1 teaspoon chopped garlic

¹/3 cup brandy

3 anchovy fillets, rinsed

2¹/2 tablespoons Dijon mustard

2 tablespoons capers, rinsed

3 to 6 tablespoons extra virgin olive oil

Warm pumpernickel toasts for serving

1 recipe Sweet and Sour Prunes

1 Pour the milk into a nonreactive mixing bowl, add the cleaned livers, cover with plastic wrap, and refrigerate for 12 hours. Drain the livers in a colander and discard the milk. Rinse well, place the livers on paper towels, and pat dry.

2 Preheat a large sauté pan; add the vegetable oil. Sprinkle the livers with salt and pepper. Place them in the hot oil in batches and sear until crispy on both sides, about 3 minutes total. The livers should be cooked to medium (the interior should be pink). Drain the livers through a strainer and set aside.

3 Wipe the excess oil from the pan, taking care to leave the fond (the caramelized bits) in the pan. Add the bacon, cook over medium heat, and slowly render the fat. Gently stir with a wooden spoon to loosen the fond. When the bacon begins to crisp, add the shallots and garlic. Cook, stirring occasionally, until the shallots become translucent, 3 to 5 minutes. Deglaze the pan with the brandy: slide the pan from the heat and allow the flame to ignite the alcohol's vapors; for electric burners, touch the edge of the pan with a long matchstick. Cook off the alcohol by shaking the pan.

darted across his lips. I was fascinated watching his slender fingers working. He was so unassuming, but he created such confident dishes that never seemed fussed over.

I became John's sous-chef. When John found backing to open his own restaurant, we searched the city together. John settled on 1041 Dumaine Street, a rather dumpy place in a seedy, though safe, neighborhood. The rent was $700 for twenty-four hundred square feet. We opened Peristyle in 1992 with twenty-two seats, and that's where

4 Empty the pan's contents into a food processor fitted with the steel blade. Add the anchovies, mustard, and capers. Cool the mixture for 10 minutes, then process until very smooth. Scrape down the sides at least once. Add the livers while the machine is running. Scrape down the bowl several times during this process. Add the juice from the livers and 3 tablespoons of the olive oil. Taste and adjust the seasonings. If the mousse seems too thick, add 1 to 3 more tablespoons olive oil.

5 Pour into a 3-inch-deep nonreactive storage container. Cool at room temperature for 30 minutes. Cover and refrigerate for 2 hours.

✣ Using 2 small spoons, shape the mousseline into quenelles of about 2 tablespoons each. Place 2 quenelles on each plate with warm pumpernickel slices and a dollop of the Sweet and Sour Prunes. The mousseline and prunes may also be presented in serving bowls, with a separate basket of toasts.

SWEET AND SOUR PRUNES

Makes 4 cups

- -

2 tablespoons olive oil
4 cups thinly sliced yellow onions
2 cups champagne vinegar
10 fresh tarragon sprigs, bundled with
    kitchen twine
1 cinnamon stick
4 whole cloves
2$\frac{1}{2}$ cups sugar
4 cups small pitted prunes, quartered
Pinch of freshly cracked black pepper

1 Heat the oil in a medium saucepan over medium heat and add the onions. Cook for 8 to 10 minutes, until translucent. Add the remaining ingredients and cook over low heat, stirring constantly to avoid burning. Reduce the mixture until very thick.

2 Remove the tarragon, cinnamon stick, and cloves. Refrigerate in an airtight container for up to 10 days.

my real mentorship began. John would send me home with some classic cookbook from his shelves, I'd study the recipes, and then we'd make a given dish with all the proper technique and, well, *discipline* that the dish required. John taught cooking the way you raise a child: share the key values so that later these values can be applied to all kinds of unexpected things. We had such energy together. One of us would imagine a flavor combination, and the two of us would try to bring it to the plate.

We shared many things beyond cooking; gradually, John tired of teaching—or just tired; I didn't know at first, but John had contracted the AIDS virus. Three years later, one week before he died, John was hospitalized.

Despite his passing, Peristyle remained open, and one day I was contacted by the attorney for John's family. One of John's requests was that I be offered the chance to buy his restaurant. Never, at twenty-seven, would I have considered owning a

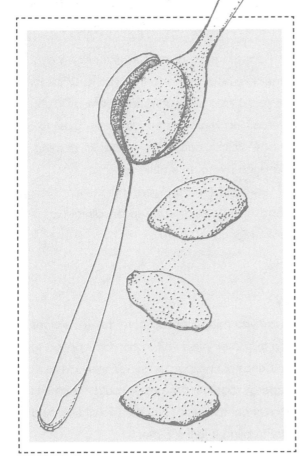

restaurant, especially in such a competitive town. Within five days Peristyle was to go on the public market. I made frantic calls to the small-business administration offices. I hardly knew what to ask. I talked with Emeril, with whom I'd begun working. "Is that really where your heart is?" he asked me. All I knew was that Peristyle couldn't become another gumbo shop. "Yes," I said, and Emeril generously introduced me to his bankers. (By today's standards the restaurant hardly required much investment.)

John's passing left a huge void in my life, but it also replenished it: so many people and opportunities began with John's patience and time, with the legacy of Peristyle.

Perhaps John's most generous gift was teaching me to taste. John made this most delicious duck-liver pâté with prunes, and he always prepared it himself. One day he suddenly assigned me the pâté. I cut shallots, seared livers, deglazed, added capers, anchovies, mustard—I followed his technique precisely. Just before finishing, I asked John to taste it.

"Did you taste it?" he asked me.

"Of course!"

"Did you *really* taste it?" he asked. I stared at him. Then he took a bite, smeared it on the roof of his mouth, sucked in air as if sampling wine, and . . . tasted.

He wanted smokiness but no taste of bacon. He wanted the heightening of flavors that salt creates but no taste of salt. As for the mustard and anchovies, he wanted their presence only to evoke something greater. Tasting alongside John, I learned that a palate didn't simply discern salty, sweet, bitter, and sour. I could taste Provence.

Anne Kearney and her husband, Tom Saud, Jr., have owned and operated Peristyle, in New Orleans, since 1995. Anne received the 2002 Beard Foundation Award for Best Chef in the region.

Paul Mattison EGGPLANT RICOTTA MOUSSE

On a constant quest for inspiration, I often lead culinary tours, and Italy has become my favorite destination. We feature hands-on cooking classes in the morning, take day trips to cheese farms or local wineries, and explore the great ristorantes and trattorias in the evening.

A few visits ago we were near Siena, in the town of Pienza, visiting the marvelous small pecorino producers who make so many distinctive cheeses from sheep's milk simply by aging the cheese (anywhere from three weeks to eight months) and infusing it with herbs, truffles, or ash. And with the by-products of the pecorino, they make ricotta . . . ricotta like you've never had!

One evening our group had dinner at Bodega del Trente. An Italian from Florence and his wife, a French-trained chef, were our hosts. She served rustic Tuscan cuisine with a touch of Paul Bocuse elegance, and he was a charming sommelier with an impressive wine cellar. The meal began with Prosecco, the Italian sparkling wine, and crostini with a duck-liver spread. And then the first course to arrive was an incredible stuffed-eggplant appetizer—the inspiration for this recipe.

You know when you taste something and it reminds you of a flavor from your past or your childhood, and you can't quite put your finger on what that taste is? You think to yourself, "What is that flavor?" and then it hits you. Well, the minute I tasted this layered eggplant dish, I remembered my grandmother and a version of stuffed eggplant she made in her home in upstate New York. It had been ten or fifteen years since I'd tasted her version. (She has since passed away at the age of eighty-seven, after surviving nine bouts with pneumonia. "I'm like a cat," she'd say. "I have nine lives." The tenth bout finally got the best of her.)

My grandmother took care of her garden, she took care of the cooking, and she took

EGGPLANT RICOTTA MOUSSE Serves 8

----

4 eggplants, 2 large and 2 small

2 large eggs

1 cup whole-milk ricotta

1 medium zucchini, halved lengthwise,
    seeded, flesh removed, finely diced,
    and sautéed in 2 teaspoons olive oil

1 ounce fresh basil ($1/2$ cup loosely
    packed leaves), chopped, plus 8 leaves
    for garnish

$1/2$ cup roasted red peppers, diced

Salt and freshly ground black pepper

Vegetable oil for grilling

1 recipe Roasted Red Pepper Coulis

$3/4$ cup shaved pecorino cheese

1 Preheat the oven to 400°F. Line a sheet pan with aluminum foil or parchment paper.

2 Place the 2 large eggplants on the pan and poke each several times with a fork. Bake the eggplants for 20 to 30 minutes or until they have lost their shape and are very tender. Remove from the oven and cool slightly. Peel and discard the skin. Mash or puree the eggplant flesh.

3 Whisk the eggs slightly and fold in the ricotta. Add the zucchini, basil, and roasted red peppers. Fold in the eggplant mixture and season to taste. Cover and refrigerate until needed.

4 Prepare a medium-hot grill. Cut the small eggplants lengthwise into $1/4$-inch-thick slices and season with salt and pepper. Lightly brush each slice with oil and grill until soft, 1 or 2 minutes. Transfer the grilled slices to a tray.

5 To assemble, preheat the oven to 350°F. Lightly spray eight 5-ounce ramekins with vegetable oil. Line the ramekins with the grilled eggplant, overlapping the rims. Fill the center with the mousse and fold over the excess eggplant slice to seal. Place the ramekins in a roasting pan and place in the oven. Fill the pan halfway with boiling water. Bake for 30 minutes.

✣ Ladle one spoonful of the coulis in the center of each plate. Invert the ramekin onto the sauce and lift off the dish. Spoon more coulis around the edge of the mousse. Garnish with a basil leaf and shaved pecorino cheese.

care of me, since my parents split up when I was young. Being a typical Italian grandmother, she made sharing food her mission.

But I learned more than cooking from her. She offered words for the wise on many topics. "Life is like an artichoke," she'd tell me.

"Like with people, you peel away the outer layers—sometimes they are bitter—but you get to the sweet, wonderful heart." She had a great sense of humor and welcomed my friends into her home with open arms and a table full of wonderful flavors. And when they left, her comment was always "She seems very nice—is she Italian?"

So Bodega del Trente brought me all these tastes and memories of cooking with my grandmother, who came from the Bari region of Italy. We made pasta and sausage together and quite often stuffed eggplant. We'd scoop out the flesh of those large purple beauties, stuff them with bread crumbs, cheese, herbs, and sometimes ground meat. Then we'd drench them in olive oil, baste them with red sauce, and roast them to perfection.

My own layered eggplant is a combination of what my grandmother cooked and what Bodega del Trente presented. It's a mousse of pureed eggplant, ricotta, and zucchini stuffed in a mold lined with grilled eggplant strips. I'll admit that when I created this dish for an Italian wine dinner I hosted, I finessed the dish a little more, giving it yet another life. I urge you to do the same.

ROASTED RED PEPPER COULIS
Makes 1 1/4 cups

----

2 tablespoons diced onion

1/2 teaspoon minced garlic

1 cup roasted red peppers

1 cup roasted tomatoes (8 plum
    tomatoes) (see Note)

Salt and freshly cracked black pepper

1 ounce fresh basil (1/2 cup loosely
    packed leaves), chopped

1 Sauté the onion and garlic in a small non-stick skillet with a splash of water (do not burn the garlic). Add the roasted red peppers and tomatoes. Cook together for 5 minutes, stirring regularly.

2 Puree in a blender or food processor. Strain the sauce, season to taste, and add the chopped basil.

÷ The coulis can be prepared 1 day in advance and refrigerated. Gently reheat the sauce as needed.

Note: To roast tomatoes, heat the oven to 350°F. Drizzle the tomatoes with a few drops of olive oil and place on a sheet pan lined with parchment paper. Roast the tomatoes uncovered for 20 to 25 minutes or until the flesh is very soft and the skin separates from the meat of the tomato. Remove from the oven. Cool slightly, peel, and seed the tomatoes.

Christine Keff
THAI SQUID SALAD

Ten years after working—*overworking*—as a chef in New York (I was then at the Four Seasons, having opened three restaurants previously), I said to my partner Tamara, "Let's just pick up and go somewhere totally exotic. How about Indonesia?" And we left. We were up for adventure. We wanted to rough it. (We packed three kinds of olive oil and four different vinegars, so we didn't want to rough it *entirely*.) We traveled all spring and part of summer in a pickup truck around America, and in August we flew to Asia, supposing we might visit Japan, Hong Kong, Thailand, and Malaysia.

In Asia we traveled by train and bus, except for a few large jumps by plane. Tamara had brought along a Polaroid camera, and in the remote villages she took snapshots of people who'd never had their pictures taken before and left them behind as gifts.

I knew nothing about Asian cuisine, but by staying in guest houses and eating at tiny restaurants I learned a little. In Bali we did make some of our own meals: we'd go to the market to shop with a basket and the few words we'd picked up and come home to figure out how to cook whatever it was we ended up buying. One day at the market, a local villager reached into our filled basket and pulled out some green that we'd selected and put it back on the table. She smiled and shook her head; we got the message.

We stayed in Koh Samui, an island in the gulf of Thailand, at a sort of bed and breakfast. Five dollars per night. Bamboo huts. Vacant beach. We found ourselves so caught up with the people and the peacefulness there that we forfeited our plane tickets to Malaysia and stayed three weeks, befriending the young couple who ran the lodging.

Tamara and I would go to the market each day with Bo, and she'd teach us how to prepare and cook whatever she bought. Before

THAI SQUID SALAD Serves 4

- **2 teaspoons salt**
- **1 pound squid bodies, cleaned and cut into 1/4-inch-wide rings**
- **3 garlic cloves, unpeeled**
- **5 dried Thai chiles, coarsely chopped**
- **3 teaspoons fish sauce**
- **3 teaspoons fresh lemon juice**
- **3 medium shallots, thinly sliced**
- **1 teaspoon minced fresh lemongrass**
- **3 fresh mint sprigs, leaves torn into 4 pieces each (stems discarded)**
- **10 fresh cilantro sprigs, 6 coarsely chopped, 4 reserved for garnish**

1 Bring a 2-quart pot of water to a boil, add the salt, and drop in the prepared squid. When the water returns to a boil, immediately remove the squid and place the rings in an ice-water bath to cool. (Even a slightly longer cooking time will toughen the meat.) Once the squid has chilled, remove it from the water and set aside.

2 Heat a cast-iron pan over medium heat, add the unpeeled garlic cloves, and char their skins to a dark toasted color. When the garlic feels soft (about 10 minutes), remove it from the pan. Cool slightly and release the softened cloves.

3 Smash the garlic in a bowl and add the remaining ingredients except garnish. Add the cooked squid rings and toss together. Allow flavors to marry for at least 20 minutes. ❖ Serve the salad on a platter, garnishing with the reserved cilantro sprigs.

long we'd do the shopping on our own, bringing home anything that caught our eye, and Bo would show us what to do with it: she knew—maybe—ten words of English, and we knew even fewer words of Thai. But the preparations were simple: fresh fish to clean, a variety of greens and vegetables to stir-fry, various chiles and curry pastes to concoct, lemongrass and garlic to chop.

When we left, Tamara took a snapshot of us standing outside our hut and presented it to our host Bo.

Nine years later Tamara and I had the chance to return to Thailand. We were leading a culinary tour in Bangkok, and one afternoon we headed toward Koh Samui, this time by plane, landing on the island's new airstrip. We were hoping to find Bo and the serene surroundings we'd so loved. But everything had changed—good for that poor community, sad for the two of us. The beach was full of rich tourists, not backpackers. It had a boardwalk, hotels, shops, concrete bungalows, with air-conditioning . . .

But we found Bo. And she could speak great English! We were able to talk about so many things that we hadn't managed to share nine years earlier. And there, posted on the bulletin board in her kitchen, was the Polaroid of Tamara and me.

This squid salad is one we shared many times with Bo. Similar to Thai beef salad, it possesses those distinctly Thai flavors of garlic and hot Thai chiles, lemongrass and lemon juice, and the intensely salty fish sauce. Ideally this salad cries out for fresh squid, which is almost impossible to find in the States. If you happen to be adventurous, you can come to Puget Sound and jig for them out on the piers, snagging the squid on little hooks. Or you can buy frozen cleaned squid and just imagine yourself on a remote island in the Gulf of Thailand.

Christine Keff trained at New York's Four Seasons Restaurant, Vienna '79, and O'Neill's before opening three other New York City establishments under the Project Management Group. After traveling extensively in Asia, she relocated to the Northwest and worked as executive chef at McCormick and Schmick's and the Hunt Club before opening her own restaurant, Flying Fish. Recognized by the Beard Foundation as the Best Chef in her region, Christine began a second venture in 2000, Fandango, specializing in Latin American dishes. She devotes much of her time to her community through teaching, fund-raising, and mentoring programs.

Guenter Seeger MATJES HERRING TARTARE

My grandmother made Matjes herring every New Year's Eve. She served it with cooked beets and potatoes. It was not just a tradition; it was the way she did things. In the Black Forest of Germany, where our family is from, people cooked in a particular tradition; no one made up dishes to be creative. Northern German cuisine is a distinct thing. And, like most everyone in the village, my family was more or less self-sufficient. We tended a small garden for seasonal produce and looked to the specialty services of our neighbors for other staples. In our town of two thousand people we had three bakeries and two great butcher shops that prepared sausages and beautiful meats. Produce came to a separate market where, every day, you'd pick up your milk and butter.

My family acted as fruit brokers. Strawberries, blackberries, raspberries, and wild blackberries and blueberries from the

MATJES HERRING TARTARE

Serves 4

6 Matjes herring or other small oil-
cured fish, cleaned, pin-boned, tail
removed, and diced ($1^1/2$ to 2
cups)

1 shallot, minced

2 tablespoons minced fresh chives

2 teaspoons peeled and minced fresh
ginger

$1/3$ cup peeled, cored, and diced seedless
cucumber

$1/2$ green apple, peeled, cored, and diced

1 medium ripe tomato, peeled, seeded,
and diced

Juice of $1/2$ lemon

3 to 4 tablespoons extra virgin olive oil

$1/4$ teaspoon freshly ground coriander

$1/2$ teaspoon freshly ground pink
peppercorns

Sea salt

Homemade thin potato chips or
breadsticks, for serving

1 In a small nonreactive bowl, combine the fish, shallot, chives, ginger, cucumber, apple, and tomato. Add the lemon juice and enough olive oil to coat all. (The amount of oil varies with the oil yielded by the fish.)

2 Season with coriander, pink pepper, and salt. Taste and reseason if necessary.

✤ Serve in chilled glass bowls with home-made thin potato chips or breadsticks.

mountains, plum and cherry trees: we grew many of these ourselves, but mostly we would buy blocks of fruit at auctions and transport the produce all over Germany.

On New Year's Eve our whole family would join for a special dinner at eight o'clock: my brother and sisters, my parents, and my grandparents. (We all lived together any-way.) And then, after twelve o'clock struck, my grandmother would serve this salad as a snack amid the New Year's cheers and toasts. And then we kids went to bed.

The Matjes herring comes from the North Sea, and it's been eaten in Scandinavian countries since 3000 B.C. The Scots, too, loved this delicacy and first sold the fish to the Dutch, who devised this method of catching and curing the herring. They take very small fish that have not reached the reproductive stage (*Matjes* means "maiden" in Dutch) and cure the fish in wooden barrels with brown sugar and salt. It's a very exacting process. Each year the first barrel of the new herring is bestowed on Queen Beatrix of Holland.

Over the years I got used to the taste of this New Year's treat. After a few more years, reinventing the dish at various restaurants, I've come to the point where I truly enjoy the taste. At Hoheneck, my restaurant there in Pforzheim at the gateway to the Black Forest, I used to serve the Matjes with marinated vegetables, with lemon and tomato segments, or with root vegetables. Sometimes I mixed it with shallots, sour cream, and dill.

This particular recipe makes an ideal cold first course: the tartness of the lemon and the sweetness of the apples, as well as the ginger and coriander, set off the richly fragrant herring. Don't wait until New Year's Eve to try it.

Guenter Seeger's culinary career spans thirty-six years and much of the globe. Currently chef and owner of Seeger's in Atlanta, Guenter grew up in his parents' wholesale fruit and vegetable business in Baden-Baden, Germany, opened his own first restaurant, Hoheneck, in Pforzheim at the gateway of the Black Forest, and arrived in the United States to be chef at the Regent Hotel in 1984. He later consulted for the Jefferson Hotel in Washington, D.C., before moving to the Ritz-Carlton in Atlanta. He is a Beard Foundation Best Chef/Southeast and a founding force behind the Georgia Organic Growers Association.

Norman Van Aken
CONCH SALAD WITH SALSA DE VIDA

In 1971, in the midst of a winter that it seemed would never end, I stood on the gray corner of a highway in central Illinois. Blasts of wind blew across the emptied cornrows. I turned my backpack to block the bitter gusts, waiting for someone to see my hand-lettered sign "Key West."

My mood lifted with each ride that took me one state farther south. The road grew more lush with every mile. When I finally arrived in Key West, I had no money and no place to stay, but I did know how to cook a little, and I got a job on Duval Street as head chef at a restaurant.

CONCH SALAD Serves 10

1 large cucumber, peeled, seeded, and
  diced
Sea salt
1 small red onion, diced
2 bell peppers, 1 red and 1 yellow, diced
1 1/2 pounds fresh conch, cleaned and
  diced (see Note)
3 garlic cloves, minced
1/4 cup extra virgin olive oil
1/4 cup chopped fresh cilantro leaves
1 recipe Salsa de Vida
Tabasco sauce, optional
Freshly ground black pepper
10 lime wedges for garnish
Chopped chives for garnish
Corn nuts, tortilla chips, or crackers, for
  serving

1 Place the cucumber in a colander over a bowl and sprinkle generously with salt. Rinse well after 10 to 15 minutes and pat dry.

2 Toss the next 6 ingredients with the cucumber in a large mixing bowl. Add the Salsa de Vida and stir to combine. Cover and refrigerate for 2 hours (the citrus juices will "cook" the conch). Taste and add the Tabasco if desired, salt, and pepper.

✛ To serve, place a generous spoonful of the salad in small bowls or plates. Garnish each with a lime wedge and a sprinkling of chives. Accompany with baskets of corn nuts, tortilla chips, or crackers.

Note: If fresh conch is not available, substitute peeled and cleaned fresh shrimp. Dice and blanch the shrimp in boiling water for 20 seconds. Drain and quickly plunge them into ice water to chill. Drain well.

One of my first days there I felt a large shadow slowly block the tropical light that flooded the kitchen—it was like when you're diving in the ocean and a huge fish swims behind you. I froze for a moment. A booming bass voice, singsong with Bahamian inflection, called into the room just as this guy let himself into the kitchen with a big white pickle bucket. *"Hey. Hey.* I'm Frank, the Conch Salad Man. I'll sell you the World's Best Conch Salad, and you can sell it to your customers."

The bucket brimmed with his conch salad. He reached in and handed me a papercupful. I tipped back the mixture of finely diced conch, tomatoes, red onions, Scotch bonnet chiles, bell peppers, celery, citrus juices, and herbs. The flavors of the sea were in there, too. Emptying the cup, I gave this man a closer look now. His black, heavy-framed, saltwater-stained glasses were held to his face with fishing line. His hands were thick and marked from heavy labor. He wore canvas shoes, navy-issue pants, and a white T-shirt. The long gold chain hung around his

SALSA DE VIDA Makes 5 cups

1 large tomato, halved and seeded
1 jalapeño pepper, halved and seeded
2 red bell peppers, halved and seeded
1 small Spanish onion, halved
1 cup fresh lime juice (about 10 limes)
$1/4$ cup fresh lemon juice (about 2 lemons)
$1/2$ cup fresh orange juice
 (about 2 oranges)
1 cup tomato juice
$1/4$ cup sugar
1 teaspoon kosher salt
1 teaspoon black peppercorns, toasted in
 a dry skillet for 2 minutes and ground
Tabasco sauce

1 Preheat the oven to 500°F and line a baking sheet with parchment paper.
2 Place the tomato, jalapeño, bell peppers, and onion cut side down on the pan. Roast until the vegetables are charred, about 30 minutes. Set aside to cool.
3 Peel the skins off the tomatoes and peppers. Put all ingredients in a blender or food processor and puree. Adjust the seasonings. Cover and refrigerate. The salsa can be prepared 1 day in advance.

neck—the only adornment—drew attention to the nasty scar along his collarbones.

He scooped out tastes for each of the other cooks and waiters working nearby. I had never tasted such a thing before.

It was then that I realized that my visitor didn't know that *I* was the chef and that I might be thinking that *I* could *(maybe!)* make my own damn conch salad.

As I came to know this "Conch Salad Man," I came to see that he had one thousand percent confidence that once someone tasted his conch salad, no one else's could possibly do. I like that in a chef.

Key West became my culinary university. The island overflows with honest, in-your-face flavors derived from the Cubans, blacks, Bahamians, and even the wanderers who call Key West their home. I didn't start out to reinvent a cuisine when I came to live here; I came to find a home. In the process I think I found both. See if you don't taste both in this conch salad. —NVA

Norman Van Aken is regarded as the "Father of New World Cuisine," as exemplified by his flagship restaurant, NORMAN'S, located in historic Coral Gables, and his series of innovative cookbooks—*Exotic Fruit Book, Feast of Sunlight, Norman's New World Cuisine,* and *New World Cuisine: Latin America and the Caribbean.* For his

Jim Barnett
CRAB CAKES WITH FRIED-CORN SAUCE

My first memories of fried corn connect to my great-aunt Anne, my grandfather's sister. She was a spinster. When my grandmother died—this is before I was born—she moved in with my grandfather, who owned a rather enormous house. But when he died—I was seven at the time—she moved into a small apartment in downtown Atlanta.

Every year we'd drive from St. Louis to visit her. On the day we arrived, she'd serve us fried chicken, turnip greens (which we called "Georgia spinach," and I loved it), and this fried corn. Sometimes, if dinner wasn't ready, she'd fry up what she called "the chicken gizzards," sautéing the giblets in bacon drippings, and we'd snack on those. I loved this meal so much that, when my great-aunt visited us at Christmas, I always insisted she make us the identical meal (not that corn was even remotely in season in St. Louis).

By the time I knew my great-aunt, she was already very elderly. Her kitchen was tiny, but I always crowded in to watch her cook. She usually found white sweet corn at the open market, which we liked better than the yellow. To make fried corn, she'd shuck the ears—I could help with this—and then she'd take her knife and slice the kernels off the cob into a large bowl—I couldn't help with that. Then she'd scrape the husk with her knife to release this whitish, mushy liquid into a second bowl. This corn juice, a little cream, and butter made the sauce.

When I make fried corn, I use more corn than my great-aunt did; I send some of the kernels through a juicer, which provides a corn "milk" of great flavor, and it also filters out the pithy fibers of the husk that come from scraping.

I've served this fried-corn sauce with salmon, pork, as well as these crab cakes, which I've included here since my memories of crabbing in Charleston, where my mother's sister lived, come from the same time. We'd visit there, too, staying on the beach and jigging for blue crabs off the pilings. I'd tie a chicken neck to a length of string, dunk it up and down in the water, and when a crab finally pinched on the line, I'd swoop a net into the water, bringing the greenish crab with its bright orange and blue pincers into our bucket.

CRAB CAKES Serves 6

----

2 large eggs

2 tablespoons mayonnaise
(not Miracle Whip)

3 slices soft white bread, crusts discarded,
chopped into small pieces

1 teaspoon minced fresh parsley

1 teaspoon minced fresh tarragon,
plus 6 sprigs for garnish

1/2 teaspoon Old Bay Seasoning

1/2 teaspoon sea salt

1/2 teaspoon freshly cracked black pepper

1 pound jumbo lump crabmeat,
picked over

1/2 cup clarified butter or corn oil

3/4 cup panko (Japanese bread crumbs,
available at Asian markets)

1 recipe Fried-Corn Sauce

1 Mix the eggs and mayonnaise together in a nonreactive bowl. Add the next 6 ingredients and blend well. Gently fold in the crabmeat, taking care not to break up the large pieces. Refrigerate for 30 minutes.

2 Heat the butter in a heavy skillet over medium heat.

3 Form the crab mixture into 6 cakes (about 3 ounces each). Lightly coat with the panko and cook until golden brown and heated through, 2 to 3 minutes per side.

✛ Spoon a portion of corn sauce onto warm plates, place a crab cake on top of the sauce, and garnish with a sprig of tarragon.

FRIED-CORN SAUCE Makes 4 cups

----

4 large ears fresh corn, kernels scraped off
the cob (about 4 cups)

1 tablespoon clarified butter

1 slice thick country bacon, minced

2 tablespoons minced red onion

2 tablespoons minced red bell pepper

1/2 cup heavy cream

1 tablespoon cold unsalted butter

Salt and freshly cracked black pepper

1 Juice or puree 2 cups of the kernels. Discard the pulp and set aside the juice.

2 Heat the clarified butter in a heavy skillet and add the bacon. Cook over medium heat until the fat is rendered and the bacon bits are brown. Add the onion and bell pepper and cook for 2 minutes. Add the remaining corn kernels and sauté for 4 to 5 minutes, stirring frequently.

3 Reduce the heat and pour in the corn juice and cream. Simmer until the corn is tender, 5 to 7 minutes. Whisk in the cold butter and adjust the salt and pepper. Keep the sauce warm until ready to serve.

My ancestors in this country date back to the American Revolution. I'm guessing that crabs and corn have been a part of our meals for at least that long.

Jim Barnett is executive chef for Unique Restaurant Corporation, the largest independent restaurant and catering company in southeastern Michigan. He is the culinary force behind fourteen multiconcept restaurants, as well as a bakery that services many of Detroit's best restaurants. For several years Jim has volunteered time in Share Our Strength's Operation Frontline program, guiding single mothers in how to budget their food dollars, helping HIV/AIDS patients prepare foods that fit their dietary needs, and teaching elementary children about better nutrition. He was honored as Share Our Strength's Central Region Chef of the Year in 2001.

Tom Douglas SHRIMP RÉMOULADE ON MOLASSES TOASTS

I was nineteen when I moved from Delaware to Seattle, instantly latching on to the Pike Place Market, which is the heart and soul of Seattle, a neighborhood, a community resource, a place that anchors the city like nowhere I've ever been. That market charged my vision of food and its possibilities.

I grew up with the idea that "fancy" or "gourmet" meant shrimp. When we went out for a really nice dinner as a family, it was for shrimp, or sometimes prime rib. The only other seafood we ate besides bushels of local crabs that we'd get from the Chesapeake, was canned salmon and Mrs. Paul's fish sticks.

There are times when you feel rich in your life, and it's not money in the bank. It's little things that can grant you this feeling of wealth. A full tank of gas in the car can do it. When you buy a case of wine instead of a bottle—even a case of inexpensive wine!—it makes you feel like a success in life. Well, when my father would bring home a five-pound block of shrimp, it felt as if we were rich and throwing this wonderful party.

So shrimp seemed like the perfect dish to offer here, although my folks would never dip their shrimp into a rémoulade. They enjoyed nothing "spicy": a raw onion or a raw pepper couldn't come within a mile of them. My mother's idea of really seasoning a pot roast (serving twelve people) was adding a half-dollar-size ring of onion to the pot. I, on the other hand, love a spicy rémoulade and serve this on many things: fried green

SHRIMP RÉMOULADE ON MOLASSES TOASTS Serves 8 to 10

----

8 tablespoons (1 stick) unsalted butter,
    softened

2 tablespoons molasses

$1/4$ teaspoon chili powder

20 to 24 thin slices white bread, cut into
    2-inch rounds with a cookie cutter

1 pound cooked shrimp, peeled
    and diced

1 cup Rémoulade Sauce, or more to taste

2 tablespoons snipped fresh chives

Lemon wedges for garnish

1 Preheat the oven to 400°F.

2 Combine the butter, molasses, and chili powder. Spread a thin layer of the mixture on each round of bread and transfer them to a baking sheet.

3 Bake for 5 to 8 minutes or until crisp. Remove from the oven and cool.

✛ Combine the shrimp with the Rémoulade Sauce. Mound a spoonful of the coated shrimp on each toast and arrange them on a platter. Sprinkle the toasts with chives and garnish with lemon wedges.

---

tomatoes, as a spicy rouille in a fish chowder, or on this dark molasses toast, which particularly delights me because it recalls those little "party rye" slices that my grandmother always used when she entertained.

Now, my grandmother absolutely loved cooking; it was part of an earlier style of entertaining and sharing food. Not that she made extravagant or complicated foods (her background was Irish), but she appreciated each thing she cooked. She'd slather those presliced loaves with an olive spread she'd make—or remember that pimiento–cream cheese and the container it came in that you'd keep as a juice glass? She loved serving that.

It was my grandmother who taught me to appreciate food and drink. I sipped Jack Daniels with her for the true pleasure of it. I enjoyed Blue Ribbon beer because it went with her crab dip and chips. (My folks didn't drink really, with the exception of spaghetti night, when Mom broke out the Mogen David.)

My grandmother lived three blocks from our house, and by the time I knew her, she spent most of her days baking; a cake or pie was always on the countertop. Her husband had died long before she was even elderly (he was eighteen years her senior), and my mother took inspired care of her.

And so even though I've thrown myself into

RÉMOULADE SAUCE Makes 2 cups

----

2 large egg yolks

2 tablespoons fresh lemon juice

1 tablespoon Creole or whole-grain
   mustard

1 tablespoon ketchup

1 tablespoon Worcestershire sauce

$1^1/_2$ teaspoons red wine vinegar

$1^1/_2$ teaspoons Tabasco sauce

$1^1/_2$ teaspoons chili powder

$^3/_4$ cup peanut or vegetable oil

$^1/_4$ cup finely chopped celery

$^1/_4$ cup finely chopped scallions, both
   white and green parts

2 tablespoons chopped fresh flat-leaf
   parsley

2 tablespoons freshly peeled and grated
   horseradish (grate just before use)

1 teaspoon minced garlic

Kosher salt to taste

1 Place the egg yolks, lemon juice, mustard, ketchup, Worcestershire, vinegar, Tabasco, and chili powder in a food processor and pulse to combine.

2 Add the oil in a steady stream while the processor is running to emulsify the mixture. Add the celery, scallions, parsley, horseradish, garlic and salt. Pulse a few times to incorporate. Pour the sauce into an airtight container and refrigerate up to 1 day in advance.

the bounty of seafood and local produce we have here in Seattle, I cherish the family recipes that my mother gave me (and each of us kids) when we left the house. Each recipe is handwritten on a card and stored in a small box. They're pretty standard, simple recipes, but they are *my* mother's. *Her* chocolate chip cookies. *Her* meat loaf. And these familiar versions will always seem exactly right to me. Everyone has these specific food memories. And now, as someone in his forties, I have come to think of them more fondly than ever.

Three of Seattle's most remarkable restaurants, Dahlia Lounge, Etta's Seafood, and the Palace Kitchen, are owned and operated by chef Tom Douglas and his wife and business partner, Jackie Cross. Starting with the acclaimed Cafe Sport in 1984, Tom has helped to define the Northwest style. Since 1989 their restaurants have won commendations and honors both regionally and internationally, including a Beard Award for Best Chef/Northwest. Tom is the author of *Tom Douglas' Seattle Kitchen* and *Tom and Jackie's Big Dinners*. His program *Spy Chefs* airs on TVFN.

Chris Schlesinger
GRILLED VIDALIA ONIONS WITH LOBSTER AND TRUFFLE OIL

My nephew Tommy has loved cooking with me ever since he turned six years old and we first grilled steaks together. We've had this uncle-nephew cooking thing going on for twelve years now. Our specialties are grilled leg of lamb, pork chops, and any shrimp dish. His folks have a house in Westport, on the southeastern shore of Massachusetts, and Tommy loves everything that has to do with seafood. He's an avid crabber. He's a catch-'em-and-cook-'em kid. And Westport has an abundance of great seafood.

Though I'd spent my childhood in Tidewater, Virginia—another great beach—my time by the water was on a surfboard. In fact, in my twenties, I traveled around quite a bit surfing that endless summer. I lived in Hawaii and Barbados. I blew off college and started working as a cook.

(By the way, for my generation, becoming a chef was not a promising career. Cooking was something you either loved or didn't, since being a line cook is really closer to construction work; and back then, the job had no glamour or prestige.)

Here in Westport, I've thrown myself into fishing—I go after bluefish, fluke, and striped bass and also the great shellfish here, like bay scallops, littleneck clams, oysters, and, of course, lobsters. I'd never been lobstering before, but it turns out not to be all that hard—just rather smelly. You go buy traps and throw them in the water where everyone else has their traps, and then you hop in the boat so you can pull them out every now and then and see if there's a lobster inside.

Tommy and I go out in the mornings, not particularly early, with bait bags—frozen fish heads and skeletons, pretty fragrant. Tommy drives us out in a small eighteen-foot powerboat, and I get to stuff the wire cages. But the first trick is just finding the pots, *our* pots, even though we've painted them blue and green with bright orange polka dots. One of us steers, and the other one grabs the pot's buoy as we glide past.

We time ourselves for each pot. The clock starts as soon as you grab the buoy, which, depending on the water condition, can take some time. Then you haul the pot into the boat, reach in and pull out the lobster (if you're lucky), gauge it to make certain it's legal size, clear the rest of the pot (there's usually some surprise inside like a scup, baby black bass, starfish—no telling what), and then you throw another sack of bait

GRILLED VIDALIA ONIONS WITH LOBSTER AND TRUFFLE OIL Serves 4

----

2 medium Vidalia onions

3 tablespoons olive oil

Kosher salt and freshly cracked black pepper

Juice of 1 lemon

$1/4$ cup finely chopped fresh chervil leaves, plus 4 whole sprigs

$1/2$ pound cooked lobster meat, coarsely diced

2 tablespoons white truffle oil

1 Prepare the grill, allowing time for the coals to hold a medium-hot temperature (you should be able to hold your hand over the coals for a count of 4 seconds).

2 Cut the onions into 1-inch-thick slices, keeping each piece intact.

3 Rub the onion disks with the olive oil, salt, and pepper. Grill the slices until golden brown (slightly charred but not burned), about 5 minutes per side. They will become translucent. Remove the slices from the grill.

4 Gently toss the grilled onions, lemon juice, and chopped chervil together in a mixing bowl. Adjust the seasonings as necessary.

✤ Arrange the onions on 4 plates, place the lobster meat on top, and drizzle with the truffle oil. Garnish each with a chervil sprig.

into the trap and toss the pot back in the water. Our best time ever: 1 minute and 37 seconds; that *could* be the current world record. On a good day, since we're licensed for only ten pots, we haul in five or six pound-and-a-half lobsters, maybe a two-pounder. So that means most of the time most of the pots are empty and we've just enjoyed a nice long boat ride together.

Back at home, Tommy and I will boil them, grill them, or give them to neighbors. And this dish, which uses the plucked-out lobster meat, is a dish we cooked up together. I love the combination that pairs the mellow lobster with the earthy truffle oil and the humble, sweet, smoky onion. A nice little appetizer or a great lunch with green salad on the side.

Currently Chris Schlesinger owns two immensely popular restaurants in Massachusetts: East Coast Grill in Cambridge and Back Eddy in Westport. He is the coauthor, with John Willoughby, of eight cookbooks, including *License to Grill*, *Thrill of the Grill*, *Big Flavors of the Hot Sun*, and, most recently, *Let the Flames Begin*.

BRUNCH AND
LIGHTER DISHES

Ann Cashion
SOUTHWESTERN EGGS BENEDICT

Dean Fearing
LOBSTER TACO WITH YELLOW TOMATO SALSA AND JÍCAMA SLAW

Marty Blitz
YUCA CHORIZO KNISH WITH CILANTRO CREMA

Oliver Saucy
CLASSIC SWISS FONDUE

Bruce Hildreth
TWO BLINTZES

Marc Vetri
CRESPELLE OF MOUNTAIN TALEGGIO AND PROSCIUTTO

Robert Del Grande
AN INDULGENCE OF DOUGHNUTS

Andrew Carmellini
POTICA YEAST CAKE

Ann Cashion
SOUTHWESTERN EGGS BENEDICT

When I was developing the brunch menu for a new Tex-Mex restaurant here in D.C., my mother came for a visit from our family home in Mississippi. It was a weekend, I was under so much pressure to design this new menu, and I neglected her the whole time. I felt awful about this. She planned to drop by the restaurant on Sunday morning before heading to the airport. And that morning I woke with a completely realized food vision in my head: how I could please my mother and also create the centerpiece for this brunch menu.

When my mother arrived, I served her a quesadilla filled with Canadian bacon, topped with two poached eggs, and covered with a hollandaise enlivened with chopped jalapeño and cilantro. She was the first person ever to eat what came to be the restaurant's signature brunch item. She was just so pleased. It was a moment of resolution and peace, a still moment. And the dish has stayed and stayed on our menu.

When people ask how I created that dish, I tell them, "I dreamed it." But there is more to the story.

When I was in high school, my mother took us to New York City to visit my uncle Joe. This was a very big deal; I'd never been outside of the South really. And Manhattan was so much to take in. We ate out every night, and I saw a world of cuisine there that was so broad and deep. (I mean Jackson, Mississippi, didn't have ethnic restaurants.) We went to Luchow's, the first German food I'd ever had. Then a Japanese restaurant and an Armenian restaurant and a beautiful Middle Eastern restaurant. I went to the Metropolitan Museum and MOMA, and I was utterly blown away by the artwork; I took Polaroid snapshots of my favorite works of art. (I think I still have them.)

And then one evening I remember sitting in Uncle Joe's apartment and seeing Neil Armstrong hop out of the spaceship and walk on the moon. A man was walking on the moon! That astonishing walk was the symbol of my own voyage to New York: I was walking on a whole new world.

Our last meal in Manhattan was at the Edwardian Room in the Plaza Hotel. The room was so grand, we were dressed up, and it felt like a holiday, like Easter. And I ordered Eggs Benedict for the first time. I was delirious with pleasure. Even the eggs were so dramatically poached, with a whorl of white at the peak from being lowered into the center of swirling, boiling water.

Back in Jackson, I insisted my mother learn to prepare Eggs Benedict (even without the

SOUTHWESTERN EGGS BENEDICT Serves 4

$^1/_2$ cup grated Monterey Jack cheese

$^1/_4$ cup sour cream

8 small flour tortillas

12 slices Canadian bacon

4 tablespoons ($^1/_2$ stick) clarified butter

8 large eggs

2 teaspoons cider vinegar

Pinch of salt

1 recipe Southwestern Hollandaise

1 Mix the cheese and sour cream together to form a paste. Spread a thin layer of the mixture on each tortilla. Place 3 slices of bacon on 4 of the tortillas and top with the other prepared tortillas.

2 Heat a heavy sauté pan over medium-high heat and add 1 tablespoon clarified butter. Slide 1 quesadilla into the skillet and cook each side for 2 to 3 minutes or until golden brown. Repeat the process with the remaining 3, placing them on a tray and setting in a warm oven.

3 Boil water in a large saucepan. Gently place the eggs (in the shells) in the boiling water for a count of 30 seconds. Remove the eggs from the water (this precooking helps the egg maintain its shape while being poached).

4 Bring 6 cups of water to a boil in a deep 10-inch skillet. Lower the heat and bring to a simmer. Add the vinegar and salt. Crack each egg and gently release it into the pan. Spoon water over the eggs to keep them covered. Cook for 1 to 1$^1/_2$ minutes. (Alternately, cover the pot as soon as the eggs are placed in the simmering water and remove the pan from the heat, allowing the eggs to sit for 4 to 5 minutes before removing them with a slotted spoon.)

✢ Arrange the quesadillas on warm plates. Place 2 eggs on top. Stir the jalapeño peppers and cilantro into the hollandaise and spoon over the eggs.

fancy swirl). And she did just that: she was an accomplished cook, since we had all our meals at home. Hers was basic cooking, and sauces certainly weren't her style. And yet she taught herself to make an excellent hollandaise for this dish. It didn't take her long, and she got such a charge out of mastering the suspension of oil in the yolks. Then, for years after that, she made us Eggs Benedict after Sunday church.

And so twenty-five years later, in a quiet moment before opening the restaurant, I was able to return a little of the gift my mother had given me.

SOUTHWESTERN HOLLANDAISE

Makes about 1 cup

1/2 pound (2 sticks) unsalted butter

1/4 cup dry white wine

1 tablespoon fresh lemon juice

3 large egg yolks

1/2 teaspoon salt

2 jalapeño peppers, minced

2 tablespoons fresh cilantro leaves, chopped

1 To make the sauce, melt the butter in a small saucepan and keep warm.

2 In a small saucepan, reduce the white wine to 1 tablespoon and combine with the lemon juice.

3 Whisk the egg yolks and salt together. Add the wine and lemon juice and combine well.

4 Beat the egg mixture over low heat or in a double boiler until thickened. Gradually whisk in the melted butter, 2 tablespoons at a time, mixing well after each addition. Cover the top of the sauce with plastic wrap to prevent a skin from forming. Keep the sauce warm over a bath of hot water. Just before serving, add the jalapeño peppers and cilantro.

A 1976 graduate of Harvard University, Ann Cashion continued to pursue doctoral work in English literature at Stanford University before devoting herself to culinary work. For the past twenty-three years, Ann has worked in restaurants both here and abroad. She began her career in the San Francisco Bay Area before apprenticing at Francesco Ricchi's trattoria near Florence, Italy. She has opened several restaurants, including Austin Grill, Jaleo, and Cashion's Eat Place in Washington, D.C., where she serves as executive chef. With her partner John Fulchino, Ann opened Johnny's Half Shell on Dupont Circle in 1999.

Dean Fearing LOBSTER TACO WITH YELLOW TOMATO SALSA AND JÍCAMA SLAW

My dad ran a hotel in Ashland, Kentucky. In 1965 he joined with Holiday Inns, and it was policy then that the general manager live in the hotel. So from sixth grade on, that's where we lived. He was supposed to have five meals a week in the main dining room, so most days we'd gather at five-thirty at a big round table in the dining room and order from the menu. So there we were, eating pretty formal food most evenings. Surf and turf was a favorite, and that was my first taste of lobster.

LOBSTER TACO Serves 6

Salt

Three 1-pound live lobsters

Six 6-inch fresh flour tortillas

1 tablespoon olive oil

**1 cup spinach leaves, cut into a fine
julienne**

1 cup grated jalapeño Jack cheese

1 recipe Yellow Tomato Salsa

1 recipe Jícama Slaw

1 Preheat the oven to 350°F.

2 Bring water to boil in a large stockpot. Add
1 tablespoon salt and the lobsters. Cook for
7 to 8 minutes or until done.

3 Remove the lobsters from the water and
cool slightly. Twist the tail off the body and
pick out the meat, being careful not to
shred it. Cut the tail meat into thin medal-
lions. Reserve the claws for another use.

4 Wrap the tortillas tightly in aluminum foil
and place in the oven for 8 minutes.
Remove from the oven and keep warm.

5 Heat the oil in a medium sauté pan over
medium heat. Add the lobster and season
with a dash of salt. Cook until the meat is just
heated through, about 1 minute. Add the
spinach and cook for about 30 seconds or
until wilted.

6 Remove the pan from the heat and add
the grated cheese. Stir until the cheese
melts.

✣ Spoon equal portions of the lobster mixture into the center of the warm tortillas. Roll
each tortilla into a cylinder shape and
place on a warm plate. Serve with 2 heaping spoonfuls of Yellow Tomato Salsa around
the tacos and garnish with a small mound of
Jícama Slaw.

As my brother and I got older, we'd pitch
in around the hotel kitchen, standing in for
staff that didn't show. Basically we were
thrown into the food business. And we had
some sense of pride: we wanted to be good
and well liked, not just the brats whose dad
worked at the hotel.

When my family settled down in Louisville,
my brother and I set our hearts on starting a
rock band, giving up the restaurant work.
But my father arranged for me to speak with
Harvey Colgin, a retired corporate chef who
had moved to Louisville after a lifetime of
cooking, including a long apprenticeship
with Escoffier himself in the early 1920s. He
took me under his wing for two years, so I

guess that makes me a second-generation Escoffier-trained chef. Eventually I enrolled at the Culinary Institute of America.

As for my first taste of Mexican food, which is so central to my life in Texas now, when we moved to Louisville, my brother found Porcano's, the only Mexican restaurant around. It had been there forever (probably since the fifties). We had no Latin population in Louisville—not even in the kitchen of Porcano's, which was run by little gray-haired ladies. But they served fantastic tacos and enchiladas, and we ate there constantly until the owner died and it closed.

So now I try to capture something of those foods I loved growing up in the dishes I create at my restaurant. I want to spin tradition into something unconventional and modern. For instance, I take a down-home dish such as chicken-fried steak and prepare duck that way and then make it into a salad with roasted parsnips. In my version of tacos, I use yellow tomatoes instead of red in the salsa, which is hardly native to a Mexican kitchen. And instead of using an inexpensive cut of meat for a taco's filling, I use lobster. I love the soft, simple, and homemade tortilla and how it contrasts with the lavishly rich lobster.

I first made these tacos some twenty years ago at the Mansion on Turtle Creek. We had a strict, polished French maître d', Jean-Pierre. We were a very established, classic French restaurant, and there I was, a young chef, thinking to add a stamp of southwestern cuisine to our dining experience. A scary thing to try in 1986. I went to the captains' meeting at 5:45 with the night's special: lobster tacos. Well, I thought Jean-Pierre would fall over dead. "Chef, chef," he fumed, "we can't serve a cheap dish like a taco here!

YELLOW TOMATO SALSA
Makes 3 cups

----

2 pints yellow cherry tomatoes or 1 pound
  yellow tomatoes, cut into wedges
1 tablespoon maple syrup if tomatoes
  are not sweet enough
2 small onions, minced
2 garlic cloves, minced
1 jalapeño pepper, minced
1 tablespoon minced fresh cilantro
2 to 3 tablespoons fresh lime juice
Salt to taste

1 Place the tomatoes in a food processor and pulse until well chopped. (Do not puree.) Add maple syrup, if necessary.
2 Mix the remaining ingredients together in a bowl. Add the tomatoes. Taste and adjust seasonings. Do not make this salsa in advance.

Our guests can go to a Mexican diner down the street and get this for two dollars!" Jean-Pierre only got worse as the restaurant began to fill.

But by 7:30 the thirty orders of tacos I'd made up were gone. Jean-Pierre ran back to the kitchen, fuming: "We need more of those tacos! How can you be out?" First I had infuriated him with the very idea of this dish, and then I did it a second time by not having enough of it!

But after that, we gradually added more American touches to our French-inspired cuisine. This lobster taco sums up the casualness and the elegance that I try for with my recipes.

Dean Fearing is chef of Rosewood Hotels & Resorts' the Mansion on Turtle Creek in Dallas. Often regarded as the "Father of Southwestern Cuisine," Dean was at the forefront of developing the new cuisine when he joined the Mansion in 1985. A Beard Award–winning chef, Dean has hosted two cooking shows, TVFN's *Entertaining at Home with Dean Fearing* and *Dean's Cuisine*, and authored two cookbooks, *The Mansion on Turtle Creek Cookbook* and *Dean Fearing's Southwest Cuisine: Blending Asia and the Americas*. Dean also plays progressive Texas country music with his group, the Barbwires.

JÍCAMA SLAW Makes about 7 cups

2 small jícamas, peeled and julienned

4 small bell peppers, 2 red and 2 yellow, julienned

2 small zucchini, julienned (use only the green skin with about $1/4$ inch of the flesh)

2 small carrots, peeled and julienned

$1/4$ cup extra virgin olive oil

2 to 3 tablespoons fresh lime juice

$1/2$ teaspoon salt

$1/3$ teaspoon cayenne pepper, or to taste

Mix together all ingredients in a medium bowl. Adjust seasoning if necessary.

Marty Blitz
YUCA CHORIZO KNISH WITH CILANTRO CREMA

I was born in Brooklyn, and my *bubbe* lived right by the Brooklyn Bridge, so I could walk over to Coney Island and spend the day on the beach. I'd hang out with my cousin, who'd have come down from Queens, and we'd swim, wander the boardwalk, watch the old folks play cards, and eat. We ate three things, and we were devoted to them: Italian ices (lemon was my favorite); a slice of pizza—straight up, just cheese; and knishes. We'd buy them either

YUCA CHORIZO KNISH
WITH CILANTRO CREMA

Makes 12 to 14 knishes

$^1/_2$ pound yuca (cassava), peeled, fiber
    removed, and cut into 1-inch pieces
1 pound Yukon Gold potatoes, peeled
    and cut into 1-inch pieces
Salt and freshly ground black pepper
2 large egg yolks
1 tablespoon olive oil
1 teaspoon minced garlic
1 small onion, minced
1 jalapeño pepper, minced
2 tablespoons chopped red bell pepper
$^1/_2$ cup finely chopped chorizo sausage
1 cup grated manchego cheese
1 cup sour cream
$^1/_4$ cup finely chopped fresh cilantro
1 cup vegetable oil, approximately
1 cup all-purpose flour

I Place the yuca and potatoes in a large pot and cover with water. Add 1 tablespoon salt and cook over medium heat, at a simmer, until tender. Strain and mash with a potato masher until the mixture is very smooth. Add the egg yolks and mix well. Set aside.

2 Heat the olive oil in a sauté pan over medium heat. Add the garlic, onion, jalapeño, and red pepper. Sauté until the vegetables are soft, about 5 minutes. Add the chorizo and cook for 2 minutes more. Remove from the heat and fold into the yuca mixture. Add the cheese and stir to incorporate. Season with salt and pepper to taste. Chill for at least 1 hour.

3 To prepare the cilantro crema, blend the sour cream and chopped cilantro. Season with salt and pepper, cover, and set aside or refrigerate. The crema can be prepared several hours in advance.

4 Pour the vegetable oil into a nonstick sauté pan to a depth of $^1/_4$ inch. Turn the heat to medium-high; allow the oil to get very hot.

5 Place the flour in a shallow pan or plate. Divide the knish mixture into 12 to 14 patties and dust each one with flour. Place the knishes into the hot oil in batches and sauté until golden brown on each side. Drain the knishes on paper towels.

✣ Arrange the warm knishes on a heated serving platter. Serve with cilantro crema.

from the carts up by the parking lots or from one of the vendors who'd walk the beach with a cooler/hot box slung around his neck.

There was nothing like potato knishes—a cross between a baked potato and a wonderful square of stuffing—wrapped in wax paper, with a little sand on them eventually. We devoured them (always two apiece) with a can of Tab.

When my family moved to Detroit, I began working at a Benny's Deli. I was fourteen. I ended up working at six other delis there: Irving's, Katz's, the Stage Deli, the Bread Basket, the Pickle Barrel, and Deli Unique—all traditional, kosher-style delis.

Knishes in Detroit could be potato but also ground meat or spinach filled (like a Jewish spanakopita) or stuffed with some other vegetable. And knishes were topped with brown gravy or mustard or sour cream.

The cooks at nearly every one of these places were huge ladies. Rarely were they Jewish. They'd cook up all the salads and spreads and desserts, and when I tried to watch how they made some of the dishes I loved—like the knishes, which were all made by hand—they'd shoo me away as if everything were some great secret.

Here at Mise en Place, in Tampa, you can't help thinking of fusion when you're cooking: our community is southern *and* Latino *and* Caribbean. So our "New World bistro food" takes inspiration from all these cuisines. It seemed only natural to take the knish, a staple of my own Jewish, Brooklyn heritage, and translate it as well.

Now, I know some people are shocked at seeing the word *knish* next to the word

yuca—let alone when that's followed by the word *chorizo!* (At one point I was surprised that knishes could be filled with spinach and ladled with brown gravy!) But after you give up your expectations of what a knish is supposed to be, I bet you'll love these.

If a person is willing to say that he has a favorite tuber, then mine is the yuca. It lends a density to the knish with its natural starch, while the potato lightens the texture a bit. (When you use only potatoes, you need flour to keep the knish together.) We've done lobster knishes and smoked salmon knishes. We've taken the other traditional Jewish foods like blintzes and created a version with a saffron, shrimp, and mascarpone filling. We've taken the blintz batter and added curry to do up a funkier Caribbean blintz. It's a treat to take something of my own, somewhat lost culture and renew it here in the wider world of Florida.

Marty Blitz is chef of Mise en Place, an urban bistro with a sixteen-year uptown reputation, rated number one by Zagat's for food in Central Florida/Gulf Coast Restaurants. Marty is a Beard Foundation Rising Star and regularly serves on the Florida Culinary Cuisine Council, an organization established to "preserve, protect, enhance, and expand" Florida's regional culinary style. Marty and his

Oliver Saucy
CLASSIC SWISS FONDUE

My father is from Switzerland, where I spent my first six years living at a castle in the Black Forest. (It had been refurbished as a resort, and my dad was the food and beverage manager.) The castle still had the gun emplacements and the oil drums on the roof for pouring the boiling oil on the attackers. It was a tourist destination with a chapel and restaurants—but it also happened to be where we lived. (Imagine being a kid *living* in a Grimm's fairy tale!)

When we moved to the States, I was six, and my father took a teaching position at the Culinary Institute in Hyde Park while I set up a weather station in our backyard; I was going to be a weatherman. But a few things persuaded me to change my mind; eleven years later, I enrolled at the Culinary Institute.

This fondue is one of my father's specialties. When we'd come in from a day of skiing or when his brothers were visiting (they also moved here from Switzerland), he'd prepare fondue. It's a celebratory dish: a family treat we'd have a few times a year. Everyone would gather around the fondue pot, which has a whole bottle of wine in it, and you drink the same kind and the same amount of wine along with it. (When you're a kid, just having three or four pieces of bread brings on a little buzz.)

The fondue is a whole meal, a ritual, really. You have the great bread for dipping. You start with a small salad and continue dipping into the fondue, which gets thicker since the bread draws the liquid from the melted cheese. Then you follow this with kirschwasser—also from the Black Forest—which is reported to help with digestion. And

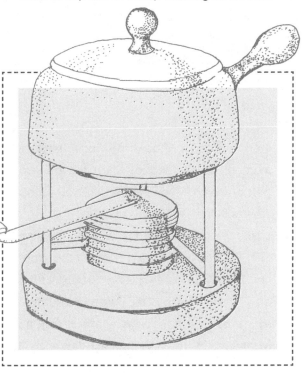

CLASSIC SWISS FONDUE

Serves 4 to 6 as a main course,
8 to 10 as an appetizer

----

2 loaves sourdough bread

**1 1/4 pounds Emmenthaler Swiss cheese,
grated, at room temperature**

**3/4 to 1 pound Gruyère cheese, grated,
at room temperature**

2 tablespoons all-purpose flour

2 garlic cloves

**1 bottle aromatic white wine such as
Sauvignon Blanc or Viognier**

1 or 2 bay leaves

2 dashes Tabasco sauce, or to taste

1 Cut the bread into bite-size cubes, place in a basket or bowl, and set aside.

2 Combine the cheeses in a large mixing bowl and toss with the flour. (Flour keeps the cheese from clumping together and will create a smooth texture when melted.)

3 Slice the garlic cloves in half and rub the inside of the pot with the cut side of the cloves. Leave the cloves in the pot and add the wine; add 1 or 2 bay leaves, and Tabasco to taste. Cook over medium-high heat until the liquid just reaches a simmer, stirring occasionally, 4 to 5 minutes.

4 Remove the garlic cloves and bay leaves. Add the cheese to the hot liquid and stir constantly over medium-high heat until all the cheese melts. Remove the pot from the direct heat; continue to stir to bring the fondue together. It should have the consistency of soup; it will thicken further as it cools.

✤ To serve, pour the mixture into a fondue pot set over a medium flame. Skewer the bread pieces and dip into the fondue.

---

then hot tea. Finally, the most special moment of the fondue: when the cheese gets a little brown on the bottom, you scoop it out with the last pieces of bread.

Since you just bring the wine to the simmer, the cooking doesn't burn off the alcohol. The wine comes shining through in this dish—the warmed aromas are so perfumy—so the beauty of the wine is everything. It's two-thirds of the ingredients! Recently I made the dish with friends who have a wine shop, and they brought a lovely Spottswoode Sauvignon Blanc that created a fantastic fondue. But you can make it with any aromatic white wine you enjoy.

It is true: fondue can be temperamental. This is not the béchamel cheese soup you find at chain restaurants. In fact, some American versions of the Swiss cheeses won't work because the oil will separate out; you need authentic Swiss cheeses. You also need a quality fondue pot; cheap tin pots tend to burn whatever's inside. When I got married, my dad mail-ordered us a present from Switzerland: a ceramic pot that's $^3/_4$ inch thick and distributes the heat very evenly. Even though I live in Florida, where there's no chance of a perfect snowfall for skiing, I love to gather friends around our fondue pot. There's still something childlike, or maybe fairy-tale-like, about dunking bread crusts into this cauldron of heady spirits.

Oliver Saucy is culinary director and co-owner of Darrel & Oliver's Cafe Maxx in Pompano Beach, East City Grill in Weston, and East City Grill of Birmingham, Alabama. A Culinary Institute of America graduate and Beard Award recipient, Oliver is continually recognized as a pioneer in the celebration of South Florida's distinctive regional cuisine. His restaurants are always among the top-rated establishments in Florida, as cited by the *Zagat Survey*, *Mobile Travel Guide*, *Gourmet*, *Bon Appétit*, *Wine Spectator*, and the *Miami Herald*.

Bruce Hildreth
TWO BLINTZES

I had never eaten a blintz before 1982, when my wife and I celebrated our first anniversary. Anne's grandmother Pearl bought us a bottle of Schramsberg champagne and invited us to her apartment for a blintz tutorial.

Grandma Pearl was not overbearing, but she did have opinions. She'd told Anne, "Don't worry about starting a family too soon; have fun first." And she knew her granddaughter didn't cook. So the year we married, I was working as a sous-chef—I hadn't been to the CIA yet—and she decided that since I was "the chef" in the family, I should carry on her blintz recipe and the family tradition. Pearl was Jewish, though her daughter, Anne's mother, had married a nice Irish Catholic. Anne hadn't been reared with much of either religion's practices. Grandma Pearl figured blintzes were part of Anne's heritage that ought to be preserved, so for our first anniversary Anne and I arrived at Pearl's apartment for my blintz lesson.

All of four-foot-nine, Pearl walked everywhere and worked until the day she died, or nearly, at eighty-nine. So here was this tiny woman in a kitchen that was equally tiny, demonstrating the right consistency for the

CHEESE BLINTZES Makes 2 dozen

----

1 pound dry farmer's cheese, crumbled

1 large egg

1 tablespoon sugar

3 to 4 tablespoons unsalted butter, melted

1 recipe Blintz Crêpes

1 recipe Quick Fruit Topping

Sour cream, optional

1 Combine the farmer's cheese, egg, and sugar in the bowl of an electric mixer with a paddle attachment. Blend on low speed until incorporated. Add 1 tablespoon melted butter and blend well. Cover and refrigerate. This can be prepared 1 day in advance.

2 To assemble, lay out several crêpes, spongy side up, and place 2 tablespoons of filling in the center of each crêpe. Fold the edge closest to you over the filling, then fold in the edges from either side and roll forward to form a cylinder. Transfer to a tray, seam side down. Repeat with the remaining crêpes. In an airtight container, the blintzes can be refrigerated for 1 day or frozen for several weeks.

3 To serve the blintzes, melt 1 tablespoon of the remaining butter in a large nonstick skillet over medium-high heat. Add 8 to 10 blintzes, seam side down, and cook until golden brown, about 2 minutes. Turn and brown the second side, another 2 minutes. Transfer the cooked blintzes to a tray and keep warm. Repeat the process with the remaining blintzes.

✣ Arrange the blintzes on a warm serving platter or individual plates. Just before serving, spoon the Quick Fruit Topping and the sour cream if desired over the center of each.

---

batter and how to tilt the blintz pan so the batter coats the surface quickly. She explained about the right kind of farmer's cheese to use (she preferred the wetter cheese, which you have to drain, while the "Baltic style" is drier and more crumbly).

After she made the first few blintzes, she handed me the pan with periodic warnings: "Now, don't let their bottoms brown, or the blintzes will be too brittle when it comes time to roll them up." "Don't put too much batter in the pan." "Use your fingers; go ahead." At some point I must have passed the test.

I made the rest of the blintzes, and we had them topped with jam and sour cream alongside the champagne. And the blintzes were fantastic. They're really just a nice conveyance for butter, and since my family's of

WILD MUSHROOM BLINTZES

Makes 2 dozen

----

1 ounce dried porcini

3 to 4 tablespoons unsalted butter

$1/4$ cup chopped shallots

$1/2$ teaspoon minced fresh rosemary

$1/2$ teaspoon minced fresh thyme

$1/4$ cup reserved mushroom liquor

1 pound dry farmer's cheese, crumbled

1 large egg

2 teaspoons sugar

Freshly ground pepper

1 recipe Blintz Crêpes

1 recipe Wild Mushroom Sauce

1 Soak the mushrooms in 1 cup hot (not boiling) water for 30 minutes or until soft. Gently lift the mushrooms from the water, leaving the sediment in the bottom of the bowl. Squeeze the mushrooms dry over a cup to catch the juices (liquor). Pour the soaking liquid from the bowl through a coffee filter. Combine and reserve all of the juices.

2 Mince the rehydrated mushrooms. Melt 1 tablespoon butter in a skillet over medium heat. Add the shallots and cook until translucent, 2 to 3 minutes. Add the mushrooms, rosemary, and thyme. Cook, stirring constantly, for 3 minutes. Add $1/4$ cup of the mushroom liquor and cook until most of the liquid has evaporated and the mushrooms are just moist, about 2 minutes. Remove from the heat and cool.

3 Place the farmer's cheese, egg, and sugar in the bowl of an electric mixer with the paddle attachment and mix on low speed to blend. Add the cooled mushrooms and mix until just incorporated. Add pepper to taste. Cover the filling with plastic wrap and refrigerate. This can be done 1 day in advance.

4 Follow steps 2 and 3 in the Cheese Blintz recipe to fill and cook the crêpes. Top with the Wild Mushroom Sauce rather than the Quick Fruit Topping.

English descent—we're notorious butter lovers—I took to blintzes immediately.

After Pearl died, Anne and I were given her blintz pan. (Anne's sister has Pearl's handwritten blintz recipe, with its grease stains and frayed edges; it's framed in her kitchen.) It's just a five-inch skillet with a wooden handle, but it made the size blintzes she wanted, and the heavy aluminum heats evenly. We also got a few pieces of Pearl's furniture that we cherish: our youngest son, Casey, sleeps in her bed; and we've adapted her peculiar Art Deco coffee table (that served as her desk in her real estate agency) into a dog

BLINTZ CRÊPES Makes 2 dozen

1 cup whole milk
4 large eggs
1 cup all-purpose flour
1 teaspoon salt
Unsalted butter for cooking crêpes

1 Blend the milk and eggs in a food processor or blender. Add the flour and salt and mix again until smooth. Strain the batter into a bowl, cover, and refrigerate for at least 1 hour.

2 Heat an 8-inch nonstick pan over medium heat. Add 1 teaspoon butter and melt. Wipe the pan with a paper towel to remove most of the melted butter. Pour 1 ounce (about $1/8$ cup) batter into the skillet and swirl the pan quickly to distribute the batter and form a thin, uniform crêpe. (If the skillet is sizzling, the pan is too hot.) Cook the batter until the edges are dry and the top surface is slightly spongy rather than sticky, 20 to 30 seconds. Gently slide the crêpe out of the pan, dry side down. Repeat the process until all the batter is used, wipe the pan after each crêpe with the buttery paper towel, or add butter if necessary. The crêpes can be stacked.

QUICK FRUIT TOPPING Makes 2 cups

6 tablespoons unsalted butter
3 cups sliced fresh strawberries
   or whole berries

Melt the butter in a skillet over medium heat. Add the fruit and cook until soft, 2 to 3 minutes. Pour over the cooked blintzes.

WILD MUSHROOM SAUCE
Makes $2 1/4$ cups

6 tablespoons unsalted butter
6 cups sliced shiitake mushrooms or
   favorite wild mushroom(s)
3 tablespoons brandy
$1/2$ cup mushroom liquor, reserved from
   the filling
$1 1/2$ cups crème fraîche or 2 cups heavy
   cream
Salt and freshly ground black pepper

Melt the butter in a medium skillet over medium heat. Add the mushrooms and sauté until soft, about 4 minutes. Add the brandy (it might ignite) and mushroom liquor and cook until the mushrooms are dry and the liquid has nearly evaporated, about 3 minutes. Add the crème fraîche and stir to incorporate. (If using heavy cream, reduce the sauce for several minutes to reach the desired consistency.) Season to taste. Pour the sauce over mushroom-filled blintzes.

kennel for our two golden retrievers. (Pearl would be delighted.)

So now I cook the blintzes, not only because I am the professional cook in the family but also because I really do love cooking for family gatherings. I often double the batter so I can put any extra blintzes in the freezer. They reheat beautifully.

The batter and the cheese filling are strictly Pearl's. The wild mushroom filling is my own improvisation; I like having a savory version. Indeed, I never saw Grandma Pearl so much as look on a wild mushroom; she was not the sort of grandmother who'd appear at the screen door with an apron full of wild mushrooms she'd just gathered. It may not be "kosher" in her book, but it's a nice option for a dinner appetizer or an early-afternoon brunch.

Bruce Hildreth is proprietor and chef of Tapatio, a Caribbean-rim restaurant in the Columbus Arts District, which he opened in 1992. Consistently ranked among the top ten restaurants in Columbus, Ohio, Tapatio participates actively in community philanthropic efforts. Bruce graduated from the Culinary Institute of America and has worked for twenty-five years in the culinary field.

Marc Vetri CRESPELLE OF MOUNTAIN TALEGGIO AND PROSCIUTTO

In my midtwenties I spent two years working at Taverna Del Colleoni, a renowned restaurant in Bergamo, in the north of Italy. Among the discoveries I made during this great apprenticeship was Taleggio, a raw cow's milk cheese that's unique to the Lombardy area. I believe there are only four places that can officially produce Taleggio, because this cheese requires the right air and moisture, as well as a specific curing and aging process.

The rarest variety is *Taleggio di monte* ("from the mountain"), which has been made in a specific place and in a specific way since the tenth century. Like Parma ham, it achieves its perfection because of how the surrounding mountains and sea air dry the cheese. Much of it is still made in the caves of Valtellina at the foothills of the Alps. When the milk from the local cows is salted or brined, and cured in these caves, the rind takes on a certain kind of mold that's yellow or pinkish, and the cheese develops very few holes, a straw-white color, and a tangy, meaty flavor that deepens with aging.

At the Taverna, I ate Taleggio every day. It was always on the menu as well, often served in this rustic appetizer, a crespelle,

CRESPELLE OF MOUNTAIN TALEGGIO AND PROSCIUTTO

Makes 12 filled crêpes

---

2 large eggs

1 cup all-purpose flour

$^{1}/_{2}$ cup whole milk

2 tablespoons grapeseed oil or corn oil,
  plus a few drops for the pan

Pinch of salt

Pinch of freshly ground white pepper

Pinch of freshly grated nutmeg

$^{3}/_{4}$ pound Taleggio cheese

12 slices prosciutto or favorite
  cooked ham

$^{1}/_{4}$ pound Parmesan cheese, freshly
  grated (1 cup)

4 tablespoons ($^{1}/_{2}$ stick) unsalted butter

1 To make the crêpe batter, whisk together the eggs and flour in a medium mixing bowl until almost smooth. Gradually add the milk, whisking until the batter is smooth. Pour the oil into the batter in a thin stream, stirring constantly. Add the salt, pepper, and nutmeg. Cover and allow the batter to rest for 1 hour at room temperature.

2 Heat an 8-inch nonstick pan over medium-low heat. Place a few drops of oil in the pan and spread it across the bottom with a brush or paper towel. Add a small ladle of batter (2 tablespoons) to the hot pan and swirl the pan to coat the bottom with the batter. Cook until the edges of the crêpe are golden brown. Flip to the other side with a rubber spatula and cook for 30 seconds. Slide the crêpe out of the pan to cool. Continue the process until all the batter is gone; the recipe should make 12 crêpes. The crêpes can be made ahead of time and stacked between sheets of wax or parchment paper.

3 Preheat the oven to 450°F. Line a baking sheet with parchment paper.

4 Place 6 crêpes on a work surface. Carefully slice the Taleggio cheese into 12 equal portions and place the pieces on one half of each crêpe. Layer a piece of prosciutto on top of the cheese. Fold over the crêpe to cover, creating a half moon. Now fold in the opposite, perpendicular direction, making a V with a curved top (the folded crêpe is now a quarter of its original size). Place the crespelle on the baking sheet and sprinkle with Parmesan cheese. Dot each with a small piece of butter. Repeat with the remaining 6 crêpes.

5 Bake until just brown on top, 3 to 4 minutes.

which is like a folded crêpe, surrounding the cheese and, perhaps, another ingredient.

These crespelle were a versatile way the restaurant served many special ingredients: when porcini season arrived, we would slice the mushrooms and tuck them inside. We would make crespelle filled with onion marmalade and drizzled with truffle oil. They could be the envelope for a fish mousse or the first vegetables of a season like radicchio or fava beans. We'd stuff these crêpes with a cheese and vegetable mixture.

Not only did I come to love the Taleggio, but the first time I helped to cook the crespelle with ham as well—we used both cooked ham and the cured prosciutto—it brought me back to my own American version of this: the ham and cheese sandwich I wished my mother would have packed in my lunch box every day—except ten times better. What a remarkable pleasure when a familiar sensation returns to you when you're far away from home or from childhood and the place where you remember the flavor.

After graduating from Drexel University in business, Marc Vetri moved to California to study jazz guitar but ended up cooking with Wolfgang Puck at Granita. Marc spent two years in Italy studying with Pieroangelo Cornaro at Taverna Del Colleoni, preparing prosciutto, making wine, and pressing olive oil. His culinary career includes opening a restaurant in Juneau, Alaska, for Princess Cruise Lines and a stint as executive chef at Bella Blu, before opening Vetri's in 1988. In 2001 Marc was named one of America's Ten Best New Chefs by *Food & Wine*.

Robert Del Grande
AN INDULGENCE OF DOUGHNUTS

Here's what I tell people: If you eat doughnuts only when you make them yourself, you'll be having the right amount of doughnuts in your life. Homemade doughnuts have celebration built into them. They can be a big deal, a treat. I know, when you think of making doughnuts, you imagine your grandmother doing this, but there's no reason you can't make doughnuts yourself. There's no real magic to it, but there's a genuine magic in eating them. It's like going back to a starting point, making a connection with a simple, earnest food.

I suppose my love of doughnuts began in childhood—where else? On Sundays, in San Francisco, my brother and sister and I would go to church, and afterward we'd walk to a

BUTTERMILK DOUGHNUTS

Makes twelve to fourteen doughnuts,
about 2¹/₄ inches in diameter

----

¹/₂ **cup buttermilk**

2 large eggs

¹/₂ **teaspoon vanilla extract**

1³/₄ **cups all-purpose flour, plus additional**
    flour for rolling

1 cup granulated sugar

1 teaspoon baking powder

¹/₄ **teaspoon baking soda**

¹/₂ **teaspoon salt**

2 tablespoons unsalted butter, melted

2 quarts peanut oil

¹/₂ **cup confectioners' sugar**

1 In a small mixing bowl, whisk together the buttermilk, eggs, and vanilla. Set aside.

2 Combine 1¹/₂ cups of the flour, ¹/₂ cup of the granulated sugar, the baking powder, baking soda, and salt in a separate mixing bowl. Add the buttermilk mixture and melted butter and stir to combine. (The dough will be very sticky.) Allow 5 minutes for the dough to rise.

3 Preheat the peanut oil to 365°F in a heavy deep pot.

4 Sprinkle 2 tablespoons of the remaining flour on the work surface and 2 tablespoons over the dough itself. Turn the dough onto the work surface and coat the outside of the dough with the flour. Flour your hands and gently press the dough into a 9 X 7-inch rectangle ³/₄ inch thick. Cut the doughnuts with a 1³/₄-inch round cookie cutter. Open a hole in the middle of each doughnut with the tip of a knife. Dust your fingertip with flour and increase the opening of the hole. (Doughnuts may also be cut into small rectangles using a knife.)

5 Check the temperature of the oil and fry the doughnuts in small batches for 45 to 50 seconds. Turn the doughnuts when the dough expands and splits at the top, and cook for an additional 45 to 50 seconds. Transfer the cooked doughnuts to paper towels and cool slightly.

6 Combine the remaining ¹/₂ cup granulated sugar and the confectioners' sugar in a bowl. Toss the warm doughnuts in the sugar mixture one at a time.

✛ The doughnuts are best eaten warm.

doughnut shop. We had a mission: we were going to get the doughnuts for our breakfast. We'd stare into the glass cases at all the doughnuts shingled there, weighing the possibilities: glazed doughnuts, old-fashioned buttermilk ones, twisted ones, and those

VARIATION: SOUR CREAM DOUGHNUTS

Substitute 1 cup thick sour cream for the $^1/_2$ cup buttermilk.

VARIATION: CHOCOLATE DOUGHNUTS

Decrease the flour quantity to 1 cup plus 2 tablespoons and add $^1/_2$ cup unsweetened cocoa powder; sift to combine. Add 2 tablespoons cocoa to the sugar-coating mixture.

VARIATION: POLENTA
AND RICOTTA DOUGHNUTS

With the simple addition of lemon zest or fennel seeds, this recipe can create two distinct flavors. Divide the cooked polenta into two portions, adding one optional ingredient to each, creating both varieties.

1 cup whole milk

$^1/_2$ cup polenta (coarse cornmeal)

1 cup ricotta cheese

2 large eggs

$^1/_4$ teaspoon vanilla extract

1$^3/_4$ cups all-purpose flour, plus additional flour for rolling

1 cup granulated sugar

1 teaspoon baking powder

$^1/_4$ teaspoon baking soda

$^1/_2$ teaspoon salt

2 tablespoons unsalted butter, melted, or olive oil

$^1/_2$ teaspoon freshly grated lemon zest or crushed fennel seeds, optional

2 quarts peanut oil

$^1/_2$ cup confectioners' sugar

1 Simmer the milk in a large heavy pot. Whisk in the polenta and mix well. Reduce the heat to low and stir until the mixture is very thick, 5 to 6 minutes. Scrape the polenta into a bowl and cool for 5 minutes. Stir in the ricotta, eggs, and vanilla. Mix until smooth.

2 Combine 1$^1/_2$ cups of the flour, $^1/_2$ cup of the granulated sugar, the baking powder, baking soda, and salt in a mixing bowl. Add the polenta mixture, melted butter, and the lemon zest or fennel seeds if desired. Stir to combine. (The dough will be very sticky.) Allow 2 minutes for the dough to rise.

✤ Follow steps 3 through 6 in the Buttermilk doughnut recipe.

crullers (always wondering how they'd done that!). Even now, when I think about which variety of doughnuts I'd choose, it would be the same ones. All these years pass, and you still haven't changed your mind—that's the power of these simple tastes.

When we'd walk in the door, my parents would have breakfast on the table, and we'd present the box of doughnuts as if it were a real accomplishment.

Sunday, for someone who loves breakfast, is the most luxurious: eggs and bacon . . . and then doughnuts. Of course, we probably had some prohibition about eating them beforehand. So eating them was also part anticipation and part fulfillment!

Even now, when I make doughnuts for my family or guests, we have breakfast first. I make the dough, cut out the doughnuts, but I won't fry them up. I let the oil heat during breakfast and then, in an instant, fry the waiting rings of dough. I recruit my daughters or one of the guests to help roll the hot doughnuts in the powdered sugar. And then there's coffee and these hot, fragrant, crispy doughnuts at the perfect moment.

More often than not, we make these baking powder doughnuts since they can be put together at the last minute, unlike yeast doughnuts, which do require forethought. And the basic recipe is so easy, I'm always tempted to look at my shelves and think about more variations: swapping yogurt for sour cream, adding fennel or lemon zest. Once in a while I'll fill the doughnuts with some great jam, just poking the stem of a spoon into a doughnut and then using the spoon itself to slide in a bit of jam. In any case, you should treat yourself. Your grandmother knew what she was doing.

Robert Del Grande achieved considerable renown as executive chef and partner of the celebrated Café Annie in Houston. A Beard Award–winning chef, Robert also holds a B.S. in chemistry and biology and a Ph.D. in biochemistry. In 1981 he began cooking at Café Annie and subsequently revised the culinary landscape with flavors of the Southwest. He is now president of Express Foods Group LLC, the home office for Café Express (self-serve cafés), Rio Rancho (rustic cowboy cuisine), and Taco Milagro (handmade food and tequila bar).

Andrew Carmellini
POTICA YEAST CAKE

Baking played a central part in my childhood in Cleveland. My mother is an excellent baker, and her pastries, breads, and desserts reflect her Polish ancestry as well as some Italian dishes from my father's family. This potica (it's pronounced paw-TEET-za) was the centerpiece for most religious holidays. (My mom's side of the family convened for holidays; my father's side was so large it took a lot to bring us all together.) It's a wonderful yeast dough, filled with nuts and rolled like a jelly roll, but then two rolls are baked together, rising one on top of the other, so that each slice is a double whorl. It's my mother's dish of dishes, and she always has to make five or six cakes so that each of us can take a potica home.

I also baked when I was very young. I was a hyperactive kid, and my mom read somewhere that certain activities could be particularly helpful: cooking was one thing that would supposedly concentrate my energy. When I was very little, I remember I had a box of polenta and measuring cups, and though I don't remember how I could have found this all that much fun, I'd play with these pots and pans, measuring the cornmeal, for hours.

But later I'd make real things like meringue cookies as well as a whole range of invented cookies. I don't remember how many of them were any good, but I did like experimenting. One week I'd make pinwheel cakes, another week layered cakes, and then I'd try different toppings and frostings. Eventually I'd try to master one thing, like a Black Forest cake, and then go on to the German chocolate cake or pies.

Actually, our newspaper in Cleveland, *The Plain Dealer,* sponsored a Junior Chef Club in the fall of 1978. Every week for six weeks they printed two easy kid-appealing recipes. I asked the library at the newspaper to unearth a few clippings. There were recipes for appetizers, salads, main dishes, and desserts—for instance, Onion Dip, made with cream cheese, yogurt, a package of onion soup mix, and parsley. Or Quick Heavenly Hash, "one dessert that will go down easy after any meal, whether it's holiday time or not," which was basically fruit cocktail, apples, whipped topping, marshmallows, and walnuts. (Neither dish has found a place here at Café Boulud.) Kids were supposed to make each recipe on their own and then send in a coupon, signed by a parent, "certifying" that the dish

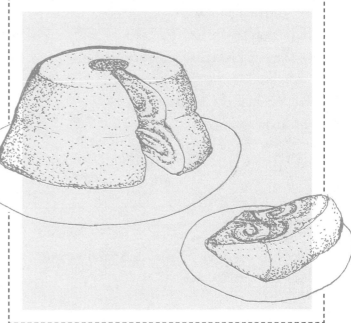

POTICA YEAST CAKE

Makes 1 cake

For the cake

Two $1/4$-ounce envelopes active dry
  yeast

3 tablespoons granulated sugar

8 tablespoons (1 stick) unsalted butter,
  melted

$1/2$ cup unsweetened applesauce

$1/2$ cup whole milk

3 large egg yolks, beaten

3 cups all-purpose flour, plus extra flour for
  rolling

$1/4$ teaspoon salt

Confectioners' sugar for garnish

For the filling

$1/4$ cup whole milk

1 cup plus 3 tablespoons granulated
  sugar

$3/4$ cup pitted dates, coarsely chopped

1 teaspoon ground cinnamon

$1 1/2$ cups ground walnuts

3 large egg whites

1 Dissolve the yeast in $1/4$ cup lukewarm water. Stir in 1 tablespoon of the granulated sugar and allow the yeast to soften for several minutes.

2 In a mixing bowl, combine the butter, applesauce, and milk. Stir in the egg yolks. Add the dissolved yeast to the butter mixture and stir well.

3 Combine the 3 cups flour, the remaining 2 tablespoons sugar, and the salt in an electric mixer. Pour in the liquid mixture and beat well. The dough will be sticky.

4 Cover the bowl with plastic wrap and refrigerate for a minimum of 4 hours or overnight; this will make the dough more pliable and easy to roll out.

5 For the filling, combine the milk, 3 tablespoons of the granulated sugar, and the dates in a small saucepan. Heat over low heat for 5 minutes. Smash the softened dates with a fork or potato masher. Stir in the cinnamon and walnuts and mix well to form a thick paste. Cover with plastic wrap and allow to cool.

6 To finish the filling, beat the egg whites

had been made and that the junior chef had abided by such rules as always cleaning up, using pot holders, and taking care when handling knives.

You had to keep a notebook to write down how the recipe turned out, how your family liked it, and what you'd do differently next time. After a few months of submitting your until frothy and add the remaining cup of sugar, 1 tablespoon at a time, to form a thick meringue. Fold in the date mixture and set aside.

7 Preheat the oven to 350°F and grease an angel food cake pan.

8 Divide the cold dough into 2 equal pieces. Roll one piece of dough into a 20-inch square on a floured surface. Carefully spread half of the date mixture over the entire surface of the dough. Roll the dough up like a jelly roll and pinch the seam and the ends.

9 Place the roll in the bottom of the prepared pan, forming a ring. Pinch the two ends together. Repeat the process with the remaining piece of dough and place that roll on top of the first.

10 Immediately place in the oven for 60 to 65 minutes or until a skewer poked in the middle of the cake comes out clean. Immediately remove the cake from the pan and place upside down on a cooling rack.

✤ When cool, transfer the potica to a plate or cake stand and dust with confectioners' sugar.

twelve division) or a "buffet scrambled egg sandwich" (the twelve-to-sixteen division) in front of the judges. Finally the newspaper gave out certificates and prizes, including movie tickets and cookbooks.

I'm not sure I ever finished the course or received the certificate, but I do have vivid memories of baking alongside my mother, as well as her potica recipe, which is still the key to our family gatherings.

Andrew Carmellini grew up in Cleveland, Ohio. He attended the Culinary Institute of America, interning at some of New York's best restaurants. After a part-time job at the governor's mansion in Albany, Andrew met (through Governor Cuomo's wife) restaurateur Tony May, who orchestrated a six-month traveling apprenticeship through Italy's top kitchens, culminating in a *commis* position at the San Domenico in Imola. When Andrew returned to America, he worked at New York's San Domenico, Lespinasse, and Le Cirque 2000. Since 1998 Andrew has been executive chef at Café Boulud.

"lessons," you were eligible to be a finalist. Based on the notebooks and an essay you were supposed to write, six junior chefs were selected to cook an omelet (the eight-to-

SOUPS AND STEWS

Ella Brennan and Ti Adelaide Martin
SOFT-SHELL CRAB SOUP

Daniel Boulud
MUSSEL AND SAFFRON VELOUTÉ WITH PARSLEY-GARLIC GRATIN

Douglas Rodriguez
BLACK BEAN SOUP WITH BASIL-GLAZED PLANTAINS

Sheila Lukins
AROMATIC BUTTERNUT SQUASH SOUP

Marcus Samuelsson
CHILLED POTATO AND CHIVE SOUP WITH GINGERED POTATO SALAD

Jerry Traunfeld
SALT CREEK OYSTER STEW

Craig Shelton
SOUPE DE POISSON

Alice Waters
SOUPE AU PISTOU

Susan Goss
SOUP BEANS, CORN BREAD, AND WILTED FIELD GREENS

Mary Sue Milliken
CHICKEN MEATBALL SOUP

Michael Chiarello
OLD HEN PASTINA BRODO

Hiro Sone
NIKU-JAGA

Claud Mann
POSOLE DE PERLITA

Ella Brennan and
Ti Adelaide Martin
SOFT-SHELL CRAB SOUP

As Ella Brennan's daughter, my memories of cooking aren't at home; they're at our family's restaurant, Commander's Palace. Brennan kids are always running around the kitchen. When my brother Alex and I and my cousins Dickie and Lally weren't in school, we were at the restaurant. We did a little dishwashing. We'd let out the live turtles that would be waiting for the stockpot. I'd mark the previous days' menus with a rubber stamp, "Souvenir."

The soft-shells would be there in their crates, a dozen or more shallow boxes stacked on the floor. And here we were, the boss's kids, and a chef would say, "Hey, bring me one of those crates," and someone would carry over a box, very gently. We were taught such great respect for food.

Then a chef might say, "Here, you two snip the faces off these crabs," and we'd join in, cleaning the crabs for frying. My mom and her sisters would be hovering nearby—"You all be careful, don't cut off too much"—because if you make too large a cut, the hole can fill with oil and the crab can pop when it's frying.

My parents exposed us to all kinds of eating, and being restaurant kids, we prided ourselves on enjoying it all. "We're having cow tongue poor boys for lunch," my mom would say, and we'd say "Great," though none of our friends ate anything at all. We had contests to see who would eat the biggest raw oyster.

My parents instilled confidence in us as well. Even when we were little bitty kids, Mom would say, "Go over to table forty-four and say 'hi.' " "But I don't know them," I'd protest, and she'd say, "Well, go on over and introduce yourself." We just don't know a stranger in our family.

Most everything about growing up touched on food. We took cooking lessons, including a crêpes class from Roy Gust, whose family owned the venerable restaurant Antoine's. Before my first real dance—I must have been twelve—I cooked steak Diane and bananas Foster. It couldn't have been simpler, but it sure impressed our friends.

And we spent weekends and vacations at our cabins on the Mississippi Gulf Coast, about an hour from New Orleans. We'd be fifty-some people there crabbing in the bog that was our backyard. Some days we'd fill three garbage cans with the blue crabs using nets baited with chicken necks. We'd find soft-shells, too, which are the same blue crab, just molting. Once one sheds its shell, the tender crab fills up with water, and it's a

SOFT-SHELL CRAB SOUP

Serves 4

----

5 tablespoons unsalted butter

$\frac{1}{2}$ cup chopped onion (1 small onion)

$\frac{1}{2}$ cup chopped celery (2 ribs)

1 tablespoon minced garlic (3 cloves)

1 teaspoon saffron threads

2 medium to large live soft-shell crabs, cleaned (ask your fishmonger to do this for you), claws removed and reserved for garnish

$\frac{1}{2}$ cup dry white wine

3 cups heavy cream

2 large egg yolks

Salt and freshly ground black pepper

$\frac{1}{4}$ pound lump crabmeat

1 small bunch watercress, cleaned, thick stems removed

1 Melt 3 tablespoons of the butter in a heavy medium-sized pot over medium heat. Add the onion, celery, and garlic. Cook, stirring, until the vegetables are translucent but not browned, about 3 minutes.

2 Mix in the saffron and cook for 2 minutes. Add the crabs and cook until they turn red, about 3 minutes. Pour in the wine and reduce the liquid for 1 minute. Add the cream and bring to a boil, then lower the heat and simmer for 3 to 4 minutes.

3 Puree the entire pot's contents in a blender or a food processor until smooth, about 4 minutes. Strain the soup through a fine sieve, pushing on the solids to release their juices.

4 Mix the egg yolks together in a bowl. Whisk in 1 cup of the hot soup to temper the yolks, then add the warmed yolks to the remaining soup.

5 Strain the soup back into the pot and adjust the seasonings. Keep the soup warm.

6 Melt the remaining butter in a small sauté pan and add the lump crabmeat and claws. Heat through. The claws should turn bright red.

✤ To serve, divide the crabmeat and claws among 4 warm bowls, add a few sprigs of watercress, and ladle the soup over the top.

third again as big within an hour. Nothing's more amazing to see than that.

So soft-shells have always played a big part in my life. People call the restaurant every day: "Do you have soft-shells?" And if we say no, they'll hang up and then call back the next day with the same question. Or when folks sit down to order, the first thing they ask is if we have a soft-shell special. We're crazy for crabs down here, maybe because you can get them only when you get them. They're a delicacy you just look forward to. But soft-shells never used to be a fine-dining food: they were what you cooked at home—like crawfish, which was never a restaurant dish. Redfish, too, was thought of as a trash fish down here till we started blackening it. But that's what Mom did and what my cousin and I like to do at Commander's Palace: look back in history and bring those good foods forward.

This crab soup is quintessentially Creole, and it's made with female crabs, when possible, since they have the fat, where the flavor is. And that makes this soup even richer. With such concentrated flavor, a demitasse is just enough—it sort of stamps "Souvenir" right across your taste buds, so you won't forget it.

Ella Brennan has worked in the restaurant business since 1944, when she opened Commander's Palace in her hometown of New Orleans. Commander's Palace was named 1996's Outstanding Restaurant in America by the Beard Foundation. Ella, dubbed the "Queen of Creole Cuisine" by *People* magazine, along with her sister Dottie Brennan, Dottie's son Brad, niece Lally Brennan, daughter Ti Adelaide Martin, at Commander's Palace, and son Alex Brennan Martin, at Brennan's of Houston, continue to celebrate the possibilities of Creole cuisine. Ti has, likewise, extended the Brennan family vision, opening Palace Café, chosen by *Esquire* as one of America's top new restaurants, and Foodies Kitchen. She coauthored *Commander's Kitchen* with the late Jamie Shannon.

Daniel Boulud MUSSEL AND SAFFRON VELOUTÉ WITH PARSLEY-GARLIC GRATIN

This soup is inspired by the memory of a wonderful recipe we made while I was a young apprentice in Lyon doing a "stage" with Paul Bocuse. This was the dawn of nouvelle cuisine in France, and he was making a special mussel soup that arose from his sense of creativity rather than from his sense of Lyonnaise tradition. This was revolutionary, really. In contrast to a traditional velouté, which would be thickened with flour and cream, this version was lighter. It was also much more intensely flavored with the sweetness of the vegetables (a julienne of leeks, carrots, celery, fennel, and tomatoes) and the brininess of the mussels. And the finished soup had a brilliant, golden broth from the saffron and the touch of cream. It was

MUSSEL AND SAFFRON VELOUTÉ WITH PARSLEY-GARLIC GRATIN Serves 4

For the mussels and the cooking broth

1 tablespoon unsalted butter

2 medium shallots, thinly sliced, rinsed, and dried

2 pounds mussels, scrubbed

1$^1/_2$ cups dry white wine

Freshly ground white pepper

1 For the mussels, melt the butter in a Dutch oven or a large casserole over medium heat. Add the shallots and cook until translucent, about 5 minutes. Add the mussels and turn the heat to high. Pour in the white wine and a pinch of pepper. Cover with a lid and cook, shaking the pan to help the mussels cook evenly, just until the mussels open, 3 to 4 minutes.

2 Drain the mussels through a strainer lined with a double layer of cheesecloth placed over a bowl. Reserve the cooking liquid (2 cups) for the soup base. The broth can be refrigerated in an airtight container for 1 to 2 days or frozen for several weeks.

3 Remove the mussels from the shells, discard any black fiber or shallots attached to the meat, and set the mussels aside. They can be refrigerated in an airtight container for 1 day.

For the parsley-garlic gratin

$^3/_4$ cup fresh bread crumbs

10 tablespoons unsalted butter, softened

2 tablespoons chopped fresh flat-leaf parsley

4 garlic cloves, minced

1 tablespoon finely chopped toasted almonds

1 tablespoon finely chopped high-quality ham

Salt and freshly ground white pepper

4 Mix the gratin ingredients together and place on a piece of plastic wrap. Cover with a second sheet and form a 4-inch square. Place it on a tray and freeze for 30 minutes. Remove from the freezer and cut into 4 squares. Refrigerate for up to 1 to 2 days in advance.

To complete the dish

2 tablespoons unsalted butter

2 tablespoons extra virgin olive oil

2 medium onions, thinly sliced

1 fennel bulb, trimmed and thinly sliced

2 celery ribs, peeled, trimmed, and thinly sliced

1 medium leek, white and light green parts only, thinly sliced, washed, and dried

1 carrot, thinly sliced

3 large ripe beefsteak tomatoes, peeled, seeded, and chopped

1 large pinch of saffron threads

1 bouquet garni (1 teaspoon each fennel seeds, coriander seeds, and white peppercorns, 1 bay leaf, 2 fresh thyme sprigs, 4 fresh flat-leaf parsley sprigs, all tied in cheesecloth)

1 cup heavy cream

2 cups mussel broth (reserved from cooking the mussels)

1 quart unsalted chicken stock or reduced-sodium store-bought chicken broth

Salt and freshly ground white pepper, optional

5 To complete the dish, melt 1 tablespoon of the butter and the olive oil in a large pot over medium-high heat. Add the onions and cook, stirring often, until translucent, 5 to 7 minutes. Add the fennel, celery, leek, carrot, and tomatoes and cook until the vegetables are tender, 15 minutes. Add the saffron, bouquet garni, cream, mussel broth, and chicken stock. Taste and season with salt and pepper if necessary. Bring to a boil, reduce to a simmer, and cook for 20 minutes. Skim the stock often to remove impurities that rise to the surface during the cooking.

6 Cool the soup slightly and transfer the liquid and vegetables, in small batches, to a blender or a food processor. Puree the soup and pass it through a fine-mesh strainer, pressing the solids to release all of the liquid. Taste and correct the seasonings if necessary. The soup can be cooled and refrigerated in an airtight container for up to 4 days or frozen for 1 month. Bring to a boil before serving.

7 Preheat the broiler to high. With the remaining tablespoon of butter, grease 4 small shallow gratin dishes. (If you have ovenproof soup bowls, use these.) Place the mussels in the center of the dishes, forming a circle 2 inches in diameter. Cover the mussels with a square of parsley-garlic gratin and broil for 2 to 4 minutes. Watch carefully: remove the dishes as soon as the tops turn golden brown.

✢ With a large spatula, slide one mussel gratin into the center of 4 warmed bowls. Ladle the hot soup around the mussels and serve immediately. (If you broiled the gratin in ovenproof bowls, ladle the soup directly into these, being cautious of the bowls' heat.)

an elegant dish, with the broth ladled separately from a tureen, and I've remembered this dish for some twenty-five years.

Just this year I thought about creating my own version, and I wanted the mussels to have a little crust, the way escargots baked with bread crumbs, smoked ham, and herbs can develop a crispness. And I thought a crust would work with this soup the way a crouton or a toast is often presented with a soup. Besides the nice texture, the gratin crust keeps the mussels moist and the soup warm, providing an earthiness to the whole dish.

Before working with Bocuse, I'd enjoyed many great mussel dishes. Often on Fridays, at home in Lyon, my mother would prepare *moules poulette,* a simple simmering of the shellfish with cream, shallots, and herbs that's finished with egg yolks and cream. And then, at other restaurants where I trained, mussels were so inexpensive they were purchased just for their juice, for making stocks and sauces—the mussel meat was often served to the staff.

So mussels remain one of my favorite kinds of seafood, especially in winter. They're both sweet and briny, and so often they're the sort of dish you can eat with your fingers: just plucking out the freshly steamed mussels involves you more intimately. In this soup,

however, you'll want a spoon—and seconds, probably, and maybe even a trip to Lyon.

After training under France's most renowned chefs, Daniel Boulud worked as chef to the European Commission in Washington, D.C. He joined the opening brigades for New York's Polo Lounge and Le Régence restaurants and was Le Cirque's executive chef from 1986 to 1992, during which time it was chosen as the most highly rated in the country. In 1993 Daniel Boulud opened his eponymous restaurant, Daniel, which has received accolades including Mobil's prestigious five-star award, four stars in the *New York Times*, and Zagat's top food rating. Daniel's other restaurants include Café Boulud and DB Bistro Moderne, as well as Feast and Fêtes Catering. He is the author of three cookbooks and a monthly column in *Elle Décor.*

Douglas Rodriguez BLACK BEAN SOUP WITH BASIL-GLAZED PLANTAINS

Though my parents both emigrated from Cuba, I grew up in New York City, on the Upper West Side in a fairly Latin

BLACK BEAN SOUP Serves 8 to 10

----

1 pound dried black beans

2 bay leaves

1 cup extra virgin olive oil

2 large red bell peppers, chopped

2 medium onions, chopped

8 garlic cloves, minced

1 tablespoon ground cumin

2 tablespoons dried oregano

2 tablespoons chopped fresh oregano leaves

1 1/2 tablespoons sugar

2 tablespoons salt

1 red onion, diced, for garnish

1 cup sour cream for garnish

1 recipe Basil-Glazed Plantains

1 Place the beans in a large nonreactive pan. Cover with 3 quarts cold water and add the bay leaves. Bring to a boil, then reduce to a simmer. Cook the beans for 2 1/2 to 3 hours, stirring frequently and adding more water as necessary to keep the beans covered at all times.

2 Heat the oil in a large skillet. Add the bell peppers and onions and sauté over medium-high heat until translucent, about 15 minutes. Add the garlic, cumin, and dried and fresh oregano and sauté for 2 more minutes. Remove from the heat and cool slightly. Transfer the onion mixture to a blender and puree until smooth. Set aside.

3 When the beans are almost tender, add the onion puree, sugar, and salt and continue to cook until just tender, 20 to 30 minutes. Taste and adjust the seasonings.

✣ To serve, ladle the hot soup into warm bowls and garnish with a sprinkling of red onion and a dollop of sour cream. Serve with the Basil-Glazed Plantains.

neighborhood. We ate Cuban food exclusively. Once in a while my mother would fiddle around with a lasagne or she'd venture into Tuna Helper—but even that she'd serve with plantains. She'd concoct something like *spaghetti con pollo ragu* (pasta with stewed chicken), but there would be a side of plantains. Whether sautéed or fried, sweet or salty, pretty much every meal had plantains. Plantains and rice and beans. To my father, dinner wasn't dinner without rice and beans.

My mother's black bean soup is a family heirloom, a fine recipe that's been passed along for more than a century. It's what I grew up eating. Because this dish is so simple—and it's vegetarian as well—great-

BASIL-GLAZED PLANTAINS Serves 8

$^1/_2$ cup balsamic vinegar

$^1/_2$ pound (2 sticks) unsalted butter, softened

3 tablespoons honey

2 tablespoons chopped fresh basil

1 teaspoon salt

4 sweet yellow (neither too green nor too ripe) plantains, unpeeled

1 Prepare a medium-hot fire in the grill.

2 Reduce the vinegar to $^1/_4$ cup over medium-high heat and cool slightly.

3 Combine the vinegar reduction with the butter, honey, basil, and salt. Beat vigorously until smooth.

4 Place the plantain with its least curved side against the table. With a small paring knife, make a shallow cut from tip to tip along the curved edge that faces up. Repeat the process, making a second cut $^1/_2$ inch away from the first. Remove the $^1/_2$-inch strip of peel. Use your fingers to gently loosen the skin from the sides of each plantain (the plantain remains in the skin).

5 Spread the butter inside the pocket you've created, covering as much of the plantain as you can while still leaving the skin intact.

6 Place the plantains, cut side up, on the outer perimeter of the grill to receive indirect heat. Watch carefully for the first 15 minutes of cooking (they should not catch fire). Grill for 50 to 60 minutes, basting with the remaining butter. The cooked flesh should be soft.

⁙ Place the whole plantains on a platter and scoop out the glazed fruit into individual portions.

quality olive oil is crucial: the best you can buy makes all the difference. No matter how many dishes I've created using black beans, this is the only black bean soup I make. I don't tinker with it. I don't try to enhance it. This is a dish that taught me something profound about cooking.

I got my first cookbook when I was twelve years old. It was called *Cooking with Bacardi Rum.* I bought the book at a rummage sale at my elementary school. I remember dabbling in several recipes from that book, including a favorite, Welsh Rarebit—a nice soupy plate of cheese.

But an even bigger influence than this book was Julia Child. My brothers and cousins were all older—they were in their early teens—and they wanted to watch cartoons on Saturday mornings. I was maybe seven or eight, and I wanted to watch Julia Child on PBS. I had to wrestle them to change the channel.

When my cooking career started, I began to cook my mother's black bean soup. It was a dish with more legacy and confidence than I certainly had as a new chef. And black beans, along with plantains, were another theme I kept repeating as I began my journey to invent something using my memories of Cuban foods in a new way.

Just a final note. One day I was at Yucca, another restaurant I owned for a while at the El San Juan Hotel in Puerto Rico. I began talking to a customer about my cookbook collection, and for some reason I mentioned my Bacardi cookbook. It turned out she was a great friend of the author; she arranged a chance for us to meet, and I had the author sign his book for me. That's almost a metaphor for something I love about cooking: how things keep returning and reconnecting. Foods can do that.

Douglas Rodriguez is the creator of Nuevo Latino cuisine. The son of Cuban immigrants, Douglas began his career in Miami, returned to New York to open Patria in 1994, and currently is executive chef/owner of both Chicama and Pipa in Manhattan and Alma de Cuba in Philadelphia. *Newsweek* chose Douglas as one of the hundred Americans who will most influence our country in this millennium. The author of *Nuevo Latino, Latin Ladles,* and *Latin Flavors of the Grill,* and a new book on seviche, Douglas also hosts a cooking and travel program on PBS.

Sheila Lukins AROMATIC BUTTERNUT SQUASH SOUP

I have always hosted everyone in my family for Thanksgiving. As relatives have married over the years, the dinner party expands. I seat eight at my dining room table and maybe twenty guests at two ten-foot rented tables that travel down the long hallway. (It's actually long enough that I could have banquets and serve mead!) But the whole idea of Thanksgiving is to have as many people as necessary: no one should be alone. I'm always ready to set another place at the table.

AROMATIC BUTTERNUT SQUASH SOUP Serves 10 to 12

----

3 butternut squash, 2 pounds each, halved lengthwise and seeded

3 medium carrots, cut into thirds

2 medium red onions, thinly sliced

10 cups chicken or strong vegetable stock

6 tablespoons unsalted butter

1/4 cup plus 2 tablespoons packed dark brown sugar

1/2 teaspoon ground ginger

1/2 teaspoon ground mace

Salt and freshly ground black pepper

1/2 cup fresh orange juice

Crème fraîche for garnish

1 Preheat the oven to 350°F. Place the squash halves, skin side down, in a shallow roasting pan. Arrange the carrots and onions around the squash and pour 2 cups of broth into the pan. Place 1 tablespoon each of butter and brown sugar in the center cavities of each squash half. Cover the pan with parchment paper and then with aluminum foil. Bake for 2 hours.

2 Remove the pan from the oven, uncover the squash, and cool slightly. Scoop the squash pulp into a large heavy pan and discard the skin. Add the carrots, onions, and cooking liquid from the roasting pan. Add the remaining 8 cups of broth, as well as the ginger, mace, and salt and pepper to taste. Bring to a boil, lower the heat, and simmer, partially covered, for 20 minutes.

3 Cool the soup slightly and puree, either with a submersible hand blender or in small batches in a food processor or blender. Return the puree to the pot and stir in the orange juice; taste and adjust the seasonings.

✤ To serve, heat the soup thoroughly and ladle into warm bowls. Dollop with crème fraîche.

Thanksgiving's our indigenous holiday, America's own tradition, and to me it's a time to go all out. But it's also time for traditional foods; remember, no one wants cilantro at Thanksgiving! A little variation is great, but the foods need to be familiar—almost heirlooms.

For instance, I love making stuffing, and even though I vary it every year—instead of corn bread with Italian sausage, I'll use well-spiced turkey sausage or I'll switch from raisins and prunes to dried cherries—the feel of the dish is what I've loved ever since my entire family convened at my cousin's house in New Jersey. We were from Philadelphia, and their house was the middle ground for our spread-out family. The turkey was cooked at their house, and the out-of-town relatives brought the rest of the dishes.

Today I do most of the holiday cooking, starting at five in the morning, when I put the two eighteen-pound turkeys into the oven. (I do assign my niece Marci her sweet potatoes. And my niece Sheri brings little pumpkin or zucchini breads. Oh, and I can't resist buying those giant cherry pies from William Greenberg, the most wonderful bakery here in Manhattan.) I cook up big bowls of apple compote, fresh whole cranberry sauce, and this wonderfully unusual soup as a first course.

The key to this soup is to roast the vegetables. That intensifies and sweetens all the rich, deep flavors of the squash. Then aromatic spices—those "apple pie spices" like mace and ginger—capture the very essence of Thanksgiving in this soup. Red onion adds a bit of sweetness and color, as does the brown sugar, and the addition of orange juice at the very end brings back a certain brightness. There's both sweet and savory in this luscious soup, and the crème fraîche contributes just the right tartness.

While it serves a big crowd, it also works for another favorite Thanksgiving tradition: next-day leftovers.

A native of Philadelphia, Sheila Lukins has studied both here and abroad in the culinary arts as well as the visual arts. The author of *U.S.A. Cookbook*, Sheila is a chef, food writer, and cooking teacher, whose contributions to the food world have been celebrated by numerous awards and citations. Her five earlier books, which include *The Silver Palate Cookbook* and *The New Basics*, have sold more than six million copies. In fall 2003 she releases her sixth cookbook with Workman Publishing. Since 1986 she has been food editor at *PARADE* magazine.

Marcus Samuelsson
CHILLED POTATO AND CHIVE SOUP WITH GINGERED POTATO SALAD

On the west coast of Sweden, chives grow like weeds in that cold, salty, hilly terrain. These chives are not necessarily the kind a chef would want since they're a little tough and strong. But when I grew up, my father's side of the family had a home in the fishing village of Smogen, and the entire hillside during those summers was covered with the wild chive's green stems and purple flowers. They made a vast field of color against the blue sky and the dark sea's water. When you brushed the thin spears

CHILLED POTATO AND CHIVE SOUP Serves 4

---

4 medium Yukon Gold potatoes, peeled
   and quartered

1 quart chicken stock

2 garlic cloves

1 cup finely chopped fresh chives

2 fresh tarragon sprigs, stems removed,
   leaves finely chopped

Juice of 1 small lime

Salt and freshly ground white pepper

1/2 cup sour cream

1 recipe Gingered Potato Salad

1 Place the potatoes, stock, and garlic in a medium pot over medium heat and simmer until the potatoes are very soft, 30 to 35 minutes.

2 Puree the soup in small batches in a blender (or use a submersible blender); add the chives, tarragon, and lime juice to the soup while it is being pureed.

3 Season to taste with salt and pepper. Whisk in the sour cream. Chill the soup for several hours.

✤ To serve, place a quarter of the potato salad in the center of each chilled bowl and ladle the soup around the salad.

GINGERED POTATO SALAD

Makes 3 cups

1/2 cup olive oil

1 tablespoon mustard seeds

8 medium thin-skinned new potatoes,
   boiled, peeled, and cut into 1/4-inch
   slices (3 cups)

2 tablespoons Dijon mustard

2 tablespoons fresh lime juice

2 tablespoons balsamic vinegar

Salt and freshly ground black pepper

1 tablespoon freshly grated horseradish,
   optional

2 tablespoons pickled ginger, finely
   chopped

1 Heat the oil in a deep skillet, add the mustard seeds, and simmer over low heat for 1 hour. Remove from the heat and cool completely.

2 Place the sliced potatoes in a large mixing bowl. Place the mustard in a small mixing bowl and whisk in the cooled oil and mustard seeds. Add the lime juice, vinegar, salt and pepper to taste, and the horseradish, if desired; stir to incorporate. Toss the potatoes with the dressing and the pickled ginger. (Do not refrigerate or make ahead of time, since cold diminishes the salad's flavors.)

walking past, the chives released their slightly pungent onion scent.

This was the main onion we had in that region and the only fresh herb. Not a lot of things can withstand that cold and salt. We ate Matjes herring or mackerel garnished with those chives. Chives appeared in our fish soups and on the eel and fish we smoked in big barrels.

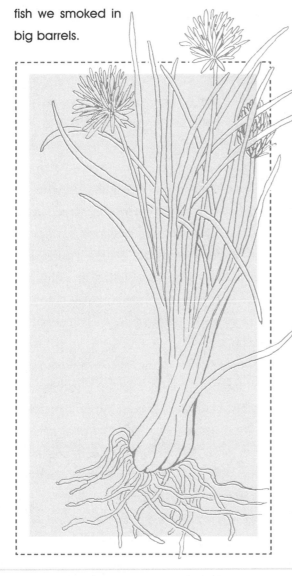

The culture of that fishing village centered on the basic things in life. Everyone had a high level of consciousness about the relationship between work and food and providing for a family. And even though we often ate lobster, crab, and herring—luxury foods!—we never considered them luxuries. We were simply eating what was available to us in Smogen.

In contrast to our season at the fishing village, where nearly everything was caught or cultivated and eaten right away, our time in Gothenburg—a major city where my mother's family is from—was more about making provisions for the longer, colder months ahead.

My mother's family had gardens. My grandmother, in particular, tended a large patch where she grew everything: red currants, strawberries, carrots, red onions, plums—it was always the season for something, and we'd be picking and then pickling or preserving whatever was ready. Pantry cooking is so important in Sweden. On our shelves we'd have jars of herring, pickled onions, apple jams, and every other sort of jam from lingonberry to blackberry, and even beverages like apple lemonade, a kind of cider that can be bottled.

So as we moved from the country to the city, our way of cooking shifted too. Summers were about simple, quick-to-prepare meals: a piece of fish, a soup, potatoes from a nearby farmer. The other three seasons, in the city, called for more elaborate preparations, involving longer, slower cooking times and a greater use of condiments and previously prepared items.

When I started cooking, I had in the back of my mind this idea of creating recipes that could include those chives since they are such a landmark of my homeland. Potatoes, sour cream, chives: as I work in my kitchen today, I long to bring some of the clarity of those simple ingredients—and that simpler way of life—to the dishes I prepare.

Marcus Samuelsson is executive chef and co-owner of three-star Aquavit, a modern Scandinavian restaurant in mid-town Manhattan. Marcus also oversees Aquavit's Minneapolis location and AQ Cafe in Manhattan's Scandinavia House. He was named a Rising Star Chef by the Beard Foundation in 1999.

Jerry Traunfeld SALT CREEK OYSTER STEW

My partner, Stephen, and I hadn't had days off together for years, and we suddenly managed to schedule a week-end. We hadn't been camping for maybe twenty years, and there's nothing like trekking three miles up a mountain for being alone and just forgetting the world. But since we had only a single weekend, we thought we'd try car camping: we'd drive to some great spot, pitch a tent, and then hike from there.

So we pack our gear and our dogs, Lulu and Ruggles, stuff a cooler with basic cook-ing provisions, and set off for the Olympic Peninsula.

Knowing that the line at the ferry during summer can be very long, we arrive an hour early. And the line is huge. We wait. The ferry loads. The last car on is two cars ahead of us. We wait another hour.

When we finally arrive at the peninsula, I realize we haven't filled the gas tank. But we figure another station is bound to appear. Of course, when the fuel gauge light illumi-nates, there's no gas station in sight. The stress inside the car mounts. We're riding on the tank's last fumes when we find an open station.

Shortly thereafter Lulu throws up in the car.

At the campgrounds all the good spots— the ones that don't border the parking lot or the outhouses—are taken. But after circling for a while we manage to find one fairly large, secluded site, which, once we unpack, we see is officially *two* sites. Two tiny sites. There's no room for a second tent,

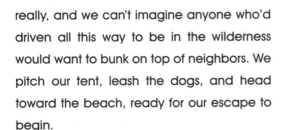

SALT CREEK OYSTER STEW

Serves 2

----

2 tablespoons unsalted butter

$1/2$ leek, white part only, washed and thinly sliced (1 cup)

1 tablespoon finely chopped fresh ginger

$1/4$ cup dry white wine

$1/2$ cup heavy cream

10 ounces freshly shucked extra-small oysters

$1/2$ teaspoon sea salt

1 tablespoon coarsely chopped fresh tarragon

1 tablespoon fresh lemon juice

Crusty French bread, for serving

Melt the butter in a medium nonreactive saucepan over medium heat. Add the leek and cook until translucent, about 3 minutes. Add the ginger and cook for 1 minute. Pour in the wine and simmer for 30 seconds. Add the cream and bring to a simmer. Add the oysters and heat gently until firm and warmed through, about 3 minutes. Add the salt, tarragon, and lemon juice. Taste and reseason if necessary.

✢ To serve, spoon the oysters and sauce into 2 warmed bowls, with crusty French bread on the side.

really, and we can't imagine anyone who'd driven all this way to be in the wilderness would want to bunk on top of neighbors. We pitch our tent, leash the dogs, and head toward the beach, ready for our escape to begin.

The moment we return, a beat-up van stops beside our tent and starts backing in, right into the adjoining slip of a space. We cannot believe this. There isn't room for a van, let alone a tent!

Out pops Mom and Dad . . . and their kid. Then a second kid. Then another. It's like the circus clowns climbing out of the tiny car:

kids keep squirming out of the van. There are seven children.

Trying to be polite, we suggest that there must be other spots where they wouldn't feel so crowded. The kids are already mobbing our dogs. We gesture at the sliver of space where a tent might go. "There's just no room," we shrug; it's not our fault the campground subdivided such a meager space.

"That's okay. We don't have a tent," they reply. "We're sleeping in the van." And then out comes a playpen, opened not two feet from our tent, and an eighth child, a screaming baby, to go in it.

I am now beside myself. I offer to buy this site from them, to give them money for another site.

It's getting dark. Clouds have blown in. Hell-bent on having our weekend together, Stephen and I take down our tent, shove the gear into the car, and drive off in search of another site.

Amazingly, we find one. Someone vacated an even nicer campsite on a cliff overlooking the water. We can't believe our luck. So we unpack and pitch the tent again as the clouds blacken. As the wind blows colder and stronger.

The moment it starts raining, we first-time car campers understand why this site was abandoned: it offers absolutely no protection from the elements. We are now freezing.

On the drive over, we'd stopped at a tiny store and bought a jar of freshly shucked oysters. And even though it's raining and our teeth are chattering, I pull together dinner: oysters stewed with ginger and tarragon, bread, wine. We're now so . . . hungry is the least of it, that we dive into dinner. The oysters are so delicious, so unexpected, such an about-face after all the aggravation, that by the second glass of wine we're laughing about the ridiculous day. We're together. We're huddled by the fire. And it is, despite the rain, a beautiful spot from which to lose the world.

As executive chef of The Herbfarm in Woodinville, Washington, Jerry Traunfeld received the Beard Foundation Award for Best Chef in his region. He is the author of *The Herbfarm Cookbook*, winner of an International Association of Culinary Professionals Award, and is working on a second book of herb-inspired recipes. Featured in many magazines for his expertise in the area of culinary herbs, Jerry has appeared on numerous television programs and as a regular guest on public radio's *The Splendid Table*.

Craig Shelton
SOUPE DE POISSON

This soup blends childhood experiences with my more modern and scientific thinking about cooking. While I grew up in the States, my sister and I spent many summers and holidays in Paris and in the Cognac region of France, where my grandmother ran a restaurant. This beautiful, dark, flavorful fish soup is a traditional French delight she always prepared for us during our visits.

Her son, my uncle Jean-Marc, was the big brother I never had. And whenever we spent time in France, he took me under his wing

SOUPE DE POISSON Serves 6

----

1 tablespoon olive oil

2¹/₂ shallots, chopped

¹/₂ medium onion, chopped

10 large garlic cloves, minced

1 leek, chopped (³/₄ cup)

¹/₂ fennel bulb, chopped (³/₄ cup)

Pinch of saffron threads

2 tomatoes, peeled and quartered

2 tablespoons tomato paste

1 teaspoon salt

¹/₂ teaspoon freshly ground white pepper

1 teaspoon cayenne pepper

1²/₃ cups dry white wine

6 cups Fish Fumet

**1 bouquet garni (2 pieces outer leaves of
  a leek, 3 celery heart ribs, 1 bay leaf,
  3 fresh thyme sprigs, 5 parsley stems,
  and one 3-inch piece of orange peel,
  wrapped in cheesecloth and tied with
  kitchen twine)**

**3³/₄ pounds fish fillet scraps (sea robins,
  wolffish, monkfish, conger, halibut,
  snapper, black sea bass, etc.)**

Twelve ¹/₂-inch baguette slices

1 recipe Spiced Aioli

**¹/₄ pound Cantal or Gruyère cheese,
  grated**

1 Heat the oil in a large heavy pot and add the shallots, onion, garlic, leek, and fennel. Cook until translucent, about 8 minutes. Increase the heat to high and caramelize the vegetables.

2 Reduce the heat to medium and add the saffron, tomatoes, tomato paste, salt, white pepper, and cayenne and cook for 10 minutes, stirring often. Add the wine, bring to a boil, and cook for 5 minutes. Add the fish fumet and bouquet garni. Lower the heat and simmer, uncovered, for 1¹/₂ hours.

3 Add the fish fillet scraps, bring to a slight simmer, and cook for 2 minutes. Remove the pot from the heat and allow to rest for 30 minutes.

4 Pass the soup through a food mill and then through a coarse chinois or large-mesh strainer. Reserve the fish pulp.

5 Reseason the soup if necessary. Add fish pulp (up to 1 cup) to make the soup thicker. Pick out any small bones before adding the pulp back to the soup.

6 Preheat the broiler. Toast the baguette slices lightly on each side under the broiler. Spread each crouton with 2 teaspoons Spiced Aioli and sprinkle with cheese. Briefly broil again to melt the cheese.

✛ Reheat the soup and ladle it into warm bowls. Float one or two croutons on top.

FISH FUMET Makes 6 cups

1/4 cup vegetable oil

1 large shallot, sliced

1 small onion, sliced

5 to 6 large mushrooms, sliced

2 pounds fish bones and heads, rinsed for
    10 minutes in running cold water

1/2 cup dry white wine

1 teaspoon sea salt

1 bouquet garni (3 fresh thyme sprigs,
    3 celery heart ribs, 5 parsley stems,
    2 green outer leaves of a leek, tied
    with kitchen twine)

Heat the oil in a large saucepan over medium heat. Add the shallot, onion, and mushrooms and cook until translucent, about 5 minutes. Add the fish bones and heads and cook for 5 minutes; shake the pan to keep bones and vegetables from sticking. Add the wine and salt, bring to a boil, and boil for 1 minute. Lower the heat, add 6 cups cold water and the bouquet garni, and bring to a simmer. Cook at a low simmer for 20 minutes. Remove from the heat and rest for 10 minutes. Strain the fumet. This can be prepared 1 or 2 days in advance. Store in an airtight container in the refrigerator. Frozen, it will keep for a month.

SPICED AIOLI Makes 1 cup

----

10 to 12 garlic cloves, minced

1 large egg yolk

1/2 teaspoon salt

Pinch each of saffron threads, cayenne
    pepper, and smoked paprika

1 cup olive oil

2 tablespoons fresh lemon juice

In a small nonreactive bowl, whisk together the garlic, egg yolk, salt, saffron, cayenne, and paprika. While stirring constantly, pour in the oil in a slow, steady stream to create a thick emulsion. Add drops of lemon juice and up to 2 tablespoons of water to keep the sauce from separating. Cover and refrigerate until ready to serve. (If the sauce breaks, start with a clean bowl and 1 additional egg yolk and slowly whisk in the broken sauce. You may need additional tablespoons of olive oil as well.) The aioli can be refrigerated in an airtight container for up to 2 days.

and introduced me to nearly everything: how to order in a restaurant, how to catch a fish. (Later he also taught me how to meet a woman.) He was a total connoisseur, utterly charming.

When we went fishing, we didn't really

catch much, but we did manage to take a slew of Jean-Marc's ancient bamboo rods and tangle them in the trees all along the riverbank.

My grandmother might have made this soupe de poisson with fish we'd caught. Instead she would go to the market and buy rockfish or rascasse, conger eel, rouget, and local crabs. It all went into one pot and simmered along with all the carefully measured ingredients. And then after everything cooked for a few hours, she'd pass the soup through a food mill.

Now, this recipe differs from my grandmother's preparation in that I've reconsidered each part of the cooking process. Why throw the fish in at the beginning? You don't need to poach a fish for four or five hours—it will taste like burlap going down the throat. So we put the flesh of the fish into the soup during the last minutes of the cooking. (And we don't just gut the fish, we clean it completely—no gills, eyes, or blood lines to cloud the flavor or the color.) That way when we puree the soup it's simply marvelous fresh fish that's being tasted. Wine, too, comes *after* the vegetables have released their flavors. So I like to work with the original concept and ingredients but rebuild each element along very rigorous ideals. Ingredients that need several hours to reach their peak go in first, while aromatic things go in only once the soup is removed from the heat. Sure, it's more labor, but it creates a soup with higher brilliance and color and a cleaner texture and flavor. And labor is just another way of expressing love.

I read something recently that suggested there are only two emotions—love and fear—and everything else is just a subsidiary of these. I do understand—and not simply because of all the great love and great laughter that filled my grandmother's restaurant—that everything that's good about the world derives from love. Foods like this soup have been the way I've been able to experience and share much of it.

Craig Shelton, a dual citizen of the United States and France, has trained with many of the finest chefs of Europe, such as Jöel Robuchon, Paul Haeberlin, and Gaston Le Nôtre. He has worked at many top American restaurants, including Ma Maison, La Côte Basque, Le Bernardin, the Rainbow Room, Le Chantilly, and Bouley. Craig is currently chef at the Ryland Inn in Whitehouse, New Jersey, one of *Gourmet* magazine's Top 10 Country Restaurants in America. When not cooking, Craig tends the several-acre vegetable and herb garden on the grounds of the inn.

Alice Waters
SOUPE AU PISTOU

Several years ago a close friend of mine, Susie Buell, asked me to plan a menu for a fund-raising dinner she was hosting at her home in San Francisco. Susie is an energetic Democratic supporter, and the dinner was for none other than President Clinton. For such a grand occasion I put a good deal of thought into creating something elegant and impressive. I faced a dilemma, though. We didn't know exactly when the president would arrive, and I was certain he would make his entrance the moment everyone else was ready for dessert. What we needed was something flexible enough to reheat.

For inspiration I often turn to the wonderful meals I've enjoyed with old friends at Domaine Tempier, a winery in the Bandol region of southern France. Back in the early 1970s I was introduced to Lulu and Lucien Peyraud, the proprietors of the winery, by our mutual friend Richard Olney. Cooking together in her beautiful kitchen, Lulu and I forged a lifelong friendship. She showed me so much about food and how effortless sharing a meal with friends can be; she always manages to cook in a way that allows her to be at the table, enjoying her guests. Lulu is simply not a last-minute cook; she prepares what she needs ahead of time, allowing for the kind of flexibility that we needed for the president's dinner.

Lulu is famous for her incredible seafood and lamb dishes. In her version of one of my favorites, the classic Provençale *soupe au pistou,* Lulu includes the bone from a leg of lamb to give the stock an utterly rich flavor. Although pistou is a peasant soup at heart, I knew that if we served it in huge flat bowls, the soup would be striking with its gorgeous, bright summer vegetables.

When the night arrived, we started the meal with some anchovy and olive toasts and served local salmon with a lemon vinaigrette before bringing the soup to the table. To each bowl we added a spoonful of pistou to enliven every bite with basil and garlic. It was absolutely beautiful and deliciously fragrant. Breaking from Lulu's recipe, we also stripped the meat from the lamb bone and added it back into the soup, making the dish still more elegant. And to bring the dish full circle, we served bottles of Bandol from Domaine Tempier itself.

As it happened, I was too nervous to sit and eat with the president, who did, in fact, come a little late (and loved the soup). But still later in the evening, once the guests had left the dining room, the cooks and I warmed

SOUPE AU PISTOU Serves 6 to 8

For the lamb shanks

2 lamb shanks

Salt and freshly cracked black pepper

1 medium onion, quartered

1 carrot, quartered

1 celery rib, quartered

4 fresh thyme sprigs

For the soup

Salt and freshly cracked black pepper

1 pound fresh shell beans (cranberry, borlotto, dragon tongue), shelled (1 cup)

1 onion, quartered

1 bouquet garni (2 fresh thyme sprigs, 6 parsley stems, 12 cracked black peppercorns, 1 bay leaf, wrapped in cheesecloth or put into a tea infuser)

2 tomatoes, peeled, seeded, and chopped, juices reserved

1 pound green beans, cut into $3/4$-inch pieces

2 green zucchini, cut into $3/4$-inch cubes

2 yellow summer squash, cut into $3/4$-inch cubes

$1/4$ pound orzo, conchiglie, or orecchiette pasta

1 recipe Pistou (recipe follows)

Grated Parmigiano-Reggiano cheese for garnish

1 Season the lamb shanks with salt and pepper, cover loosely with plastic wrap, and set aside for 1 hour at room temperature or overnight in the refrigerator.

2 Place the shanks in a medium pot, barely cover with cold water, and slowly bring to a boil. Skim off the impurities that rise to the surface, then add the remaining ingredients. Return to a boil and reduce the heat. Simmer for $1^1/2$ to 2 hours or until the shank meat is very tender (falls off the bone when poked with a fork). Cool the shanks in the broth, uncovered.

3 To prepare the soup, add 6 cups water, 1 tablespoon salt, the shell beans, onion, and bouquet garni to a medium soup pot and simmer for 30 minutes. The beans should be tender but not falling apart.

4 Drain and reserve the cooking liquid ($3^1/2$ cups). Remove and discard the onion pieces and bouquet garni. Return the bean broth to the pan along with the reserved tomato juices and bring to a boil. Season with salt. Add the green beans. When the broth returns to a simmer, add the zucchini and the yellow squash. Bring the broth back to a simmer and add the cooked shell beans and diced tomatoes. Simmer gently for 10 minutes. Add the pasta and simmer for an additional 10 minutes. Taste the soup and adjust the seasoning. *(continued)*

5 Remove the lamb shanks from the broth. Strain the lamb broth, discard the vegetables, and reserve. Remove the meat from the bones and cut it into small bits. Add the meat and 2 cups of the reserved broth to the soup. Allow the soup to sit for 1 hour to allow the flavors to develop.

✤ Reheat the soup and ladle it into warmed bowls. Bring the pistou to the table in the mortar and offer generous spoonfuls with each bowl. Sprinkle the soup with grated cheese.

PISTOU Makes 1 1/4 cups

3 garlic cloves

2 cups fresh basil leaves, roughly chopped

1/3 cup grated Parmigiano-Reggiano cheese

1/2 cup extra virgin olive oil

Pound the garlic cloves to a puree in a mortar. Add the basil and pound to create a paste. Add the cheese and then the olive oil, stirring to combine.

up a bowl for ourselves. Even though it had waited for hours, after reheating the *soupe au pistou* was simply delicious.

Alice Waters is the owner of Chez Panisse in Berkeley, California. Over the last three decades Chez Panisse has cultivated a network of local farmers who share the restaurant's commitment to sustainable agriculture. In 2001 Chez Panisse was named best restaurant in the United States by *Gourmet* magazine. Alice Waters initiated the Edible Schoolyard project in 1995, which incorporates her ideas about food and culture into the public school curriculum. She is the author of eight books, the most recent of which is *Chez Panisse Fruit.*

Susan Goss SOUP BEANS, CORN BREAD, AND WILTED FIELD GREENS

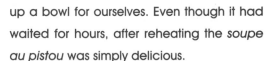

Most of my early memories come from my great-grandmother's house—it's the place that embodies my childhood. And most of what I remember is eating, waiting to eat, or the lingering smells of what had been eaten: an odor of dark brown spices, a yeasty smell, and something older, maybe, more tangy, like cabbage—all welcoming.

In the winter, GG—that's what we called her—made us gingerbread men. They were enormous. (Or maybe they really weren't.) We'd hold them in our mittens and nibble them on her porch. I didn't like the red hots

BRAISED WHITE BEANS WITH SMOKED PORK HOCKS

Serves 8

For the beans

2 cups dried white navy beans

1 small carrot, cut into thirds

1 celery rib, cut into thirds

1 small red onion, quartered

2 fresh parsley sprigs

1 large bay leaf

2 fresh thyme sprigs

2 small smoked ham hocks (6 ounces each)

1 tablespoon kosher salt

1 Sort through the beans, place them in a bowl, and cover with 6 inches of cold water. Soak overnight.

2 Drain the beans, place them in a large saucepan, and cover with 2 inches of cold water. Add the carrot, celery, onion, parsley, bay leaf, thyme, and hocks. Bring to a boil and reduce the heat to a simmer. Cook until the beans and hocks are tender, 45 to 60 minutes. Remove from the heat and add the salt. Let the beans rest for 15 minutes to absorb the salt.

3 Drain the cooked beans. Discard the cooked vegetables and herbs. Pull the meat from the cooled bones, adding it to the beans. Discard the bones, skin, and fat. Set the beans aside.

For the soup

2 tablespoons olive oil

1 small red onion, thinly sliced

2 garlic cloves, minced

3 cups rich chicken stock

2 tablespoons minced fresh thyme leaves

4 tablespoons ($1/2$ stick) unsalted butter, softened

Salt and freshly cracked black pepper

1 cup coarsely chopped fresh flat-leaf parsley

1 recipe Wilted Field Greens with Country Ham and Hickory Nuts

1 recipe Corn Bread

1 For the soup, heat the oil in a large skillet over medium heat, add the onion, and cook until translucent and slightly browned, about 5 minutes. Stir in the garlic and add the beans and meat; stir gently.

2 Pour in the chicken stock, bring to a boil, reduce the heat, and simmer for 15 minutes. Stir in the thyme and butter. Season with salt and pepper.

✣ Ladle the soup beans into warm bowls and sprinkle with chopped parsley. Serve with Wilted Field Greens with Country Ham and Hickory Nuts and Corn Bread.

she used for the eyes, so I'd flick them off and watch them melt there on the snowy cement.

GG was always baking. One day she'd fix baking-powder buttermilk biscuits. The next it would be refrigerator rolls or Parker House rolls (a favorite, because I'd get to climb up on her tall kitchen stool with the red seat and take the sharp scissors to cut crosses in the top of each piece of dough).

But it's her soup beans and corn bread that I've been eating for as long as I can remember eating anything. It was her staple. Though my mother was a fancy cook— we subscribed to *Gourmet* (and this was the sixties!)—GG was the cook in our family. She lived with her daughter, my grandmother, in a wonderful white house, across from City Park in Kokomo, Indiana. This was an hour's drive away, and my mother and father and my sister and brother would visit every weekend.

GG always planted a big vegetable garden, but all I can recall are the eggplants she grew because they were so pretty, and lots of leaf lettuce, which, as a little kid, it was my job to pick.

Whenever I opened the oven at GG's, there would be a hot skillet inside. Always. If she was cooking a pot roast or chicken pot pie, that nine-inch cast-iron skillet would be there, because, as she said, "If you don't have a red-hot pan, you can't get a great crust. And crust is what makes great corn

WILTED FIELD GREENS WITH COUNTRY HAM AND HICKORY NUTS Serves 8

- -

1/4 cup fruity olive oil

1 cup thinly sliced red onion (1 medium)

3/4 cup hickory nuts or pecans

3 ounces country ham, slivered (3/4 cup)

2 tablespoons maple syrup

2 tablespoons red wine vinegar

10 cups loosely packed mixed
   salad greens

Kosher salt and freshly cracked
   black pepper

1 Heat the oil in a medium skillet over medium heat and add the onion. Stir regularly until the onion starts to brown, about 5 minutes.

2 Add the nuts and toss to toast lightly, about 2 minutes. Add the ham and heat thoroughly. Add the maple syrup and vinegar, stir to combine, and remove from the heat.

3 Place the washed and dried greens in a large salad bowl. Gently toss them with the warm dressing. Sprinkle with salt and pepper to taste.

CORN BREAD Serves 8

----

1 1/2 cups stone-ground yellow cornmeal

1/2 teaspoon kosher salt

3/4 teaspoon baking soda

2 large eggs

1 3/4 cups buttermilk

4 tablespoons (1/2 stick) unsalted butter

1 Preheat the oven to 425°F. Place a seasoned 9-inch cast-iron skillet in the oven to heat for 15 minutes.

2 Whisk together the cornmeal, salt, and baking soda in a mixing bowl.

3 In a second bowl, beat the eggs to combine, then whisk in the buttermilk.

4 Carefully remove the hot pan from the oven. Place the butter in the pan, allowing it to coat the bottom as well as the sides. Pour the melted butter into the egg and buttermilk mixture and quickly whisk together.

5 Pour the egg mixture into the dry ingredients and stir just to combine. Spoon the batter into the prepared hot pan.

6 Bake the corn bread for 20 to 25 minutes, until a toothpick poked in the middle comes out clean.

7 Place a plate on top of the skillet; carefully invert the skillet to release the corn bread onto the plate, then remove the skillet.

bread." I'd watch her slide the skillet from the oven and then flip out the whole piece of corn bread: the bottom would be dark brown. Then she'd flip the whole bread over again, and the top would be as bright yellow as the butter she'd brought out. She'd slice the whole skilletful horizontally, spread butter in between, and then cut the sandwiched layers into wedges, one for each soup bowl.

She'd ladle navy beans and broth over that. The beans would have simmered all day in a pot of water with onions and a ham hock from Mr. Puckett's grocery. The big onion chunks would have turned perfectly clear. Until I learned differently much later, I honestly used to think that onions were clear. And that comprised the soup. No other seasoning except for salt, maybe.

Right before we'd all gather to eat, she'd cook some bacon and then stir sugar, cider vinegar, and water into the rendered fat to make a dressing for the lettuces I'd picked. So we'd have this smoky, tart salad along with the incredibly plain beans and corn bread.

At home, Mom cooked soup beans and corn bread, too—often this was for Thursday night supper—even though she loved to do fancy things from the magazines. It didn't occur to me until a few years ago that Dad got paid on Friday and that Thursday dinner probably meant stretching the last of the previous week's paycheck.

When I turned nine, my mother started working, so I had three hours before anyone came home from work, and that's when I started cooking.

My mother, grandmother, and GG have all passed away. Now, when I make this family staple, it's more of a meat dish. I like pork shoulder rather than a bare ham hock. I use chicken stock with lots of thyme. I substitute shallots for the harsher white onions. And though I can't do this at home, at the restaurant there are always hot skillets in the oven.

Susan Goss, a native of Indianapolis, Indiana, began her culinary career in 1983 with Something Different, Carryout Cuisine. Twenty years later she continues to create culinary news in Chicago, first at the much-lauded Zinfandel, which featured ethnic American cuisine, and currently at West Town Tavern, which serves contemporary comfort food in a cozy, historic building. Always active in hunger relief, Susan is an organizer for Share Our Strength's Taste of the Nation events and a teacher in its Operation Frontline classes, teaching nutrition classes to children and adults at risk of hunger in the Chicago community.

Mary Sue Milliken
CHICKEN MEATBALL SOUP

I've always been a voracious traveler. I don't mean to imply that I had to get out of East Lansing, but I did love the experience of other places. And I've always loved food. I started cooking in fifth grade. Coffee cake was one of my first culinary triumphs. (I didn't drink coffee, but I was thrilled when I saw all the tiny layers of dough rise into a beautiful golden cake.)

I can't remember a year that I haven't enjoyed some major travel adventure. Sweden, France, England, Mexico, Bali, Ethiopia, Japan, Belize, Cuba, Chile, Greece, Spain, Germany, China: in every country, I always try to cook with a family. It's only half satisfying to discover a country's food through restaurants. It's so much more vivid and gratifying to experience food in a family's home.

The first big trip I took without my parents began in a pickup truck with my aunt Helen. I was sixteen. We drove cross-country from Michigan to Washington, staying the night with friends of friends and people my aunt barely knew. To show our appreciation, we'd always cook a meal for our hosts. We'd found a recipe for Greek meatballs with mint and rice, and we served them with an egg-lemon

CHICKEN MEATBALL SOUP

Serves 6

----

3 garlic cloves, minced

1 bunch fresh cilantro, leaves chopped, stems discarded

1 tablespoon salt

1½ teaspoons freshly cracked black pepper

1 pound ground chicken, preferably dark meat

1 large egg, beaten

⅔ cup fresh bread crumbs

⅓ cup vegetable oil

1 large onion, diced

4 medium carrots, diced

¼ head green cabbage, cored and thinly sliced

1 to 2 jalapeño peppers, stemmed, seeded, and julienned

3 medium plum tomatoes, cored, seeded, and diced

10 cups chicken stock

1½ cups cooked rice or small pasta such as orzo, optional

3 tablespoons white vinegar

1 Combine the garlic, cilantro, 1 teaspoon each salt and pepper, chicken, and egg in a mixing bowl. Stir in the bread crumbs.

2 Roll the meat mixture between your palms into walnut-size balls. Place them on a tray, cover with plastic wrap, and refrigerate for at least 30 minutes.

3 Heat 2 tablespoons of the vegetable oil in a large stockpot over high heat. Add the onion, carrots, the 2 teaspoons of salt, and the ½ teaspoon of pepper. Sauté for 3 minutes. Add the cabbage, jalapeños, and tomatoes and cook, stirring frequently, until the vegetables are soft, about 3 minutes. Pour in the chicken stock and bring to a boil, reduce the heat, and simmer, uncovered, for 15 minutes.

4 Heat the remaining oil in a medium skillet over medium heat until nearly smoking. Add the chilled meatballs in batches, shaking the pan to prevent sticking. Brown the meatballs on all sides and transfer them with a slotted spoon to paper towels to drain.

5 Add the cooked meatballs to the simmering soup and cook for an additional 5 to 10 minutes. For a heartier variation, add the rice or pasta if desired. Stir in the vinegar.

sauce. We also had a version that was more Italian-style with tomato sauce. Ground meat and rice didn't break our tiny budget.

Our meatball dish got better and better at every home we visited. Just the experience of cooking together made it better. But

HIDDEN KISSES Makes 16

Lately I've found an even easier "gift" to make on my travels. I tuck a five-pound slab of great chocolate in my suitcase, enough for several batches of Hidden Kisses. This is a shortbread dough wrapped around a big chunk of chocolate that can be made in no time at all. Wherever I am, I can always pick up sugar, butter, and flour if they're not in the house. And it's a small enough indulgence that no one can resist, even after another dessert. Store the recipe on your Palm Pilot (I don't trust my memory for anything), pack some great chocolate, and you'll always be ready to offer up this little treat.

$^1/_4$ cup sugar

8 tablespoons (1 stick) unsalted butter, softened

Pinch of salt

1$^1/_4$ cups all-purpose flour

One 3-ounce bar fine-quality chocolate (a favorite is Scharffen Berger 70%)

1 Preheat the oven to 350°F.

2 Cream together the sugar and butter in an electric mixer until light and fluffy. Add the salt and flour and mix until just moistened.

3 Chop the chocolate into bits the size of hazelnuts. Divide the dough into 16 pieces. Pat each piece into a disk in the palm of your hand. Place a piece of chocolate in the center of the dough. Wrap the dough around the chocolate.

4 Place the cookies on uncoated cookie sheets and bake until the bottoms begin to turn golden, 10 to 12 minutes. Transfer the cookies to a cooling rack.

beyond that I came to feel a special closeness with my aunt on our journey. My aunt and I separated at Bainbridge Island, Washington, where I began a two-thousand-mile bike ride down the Olympia Trail with a group of ten sixteen-year-olds. Strangers who are about to spend the next six weeks together sort out who's good at what very quickly. For most of the trek the kitchen equipment resided on my bicycle. Those

meatballs helped cement my new friendships.

Years later, on my own travels, I took to making meatballs in the homes of families I'd visit. Food is my way to connect with people. It's certainly part of the joy of being a chef. There hasn't been a country I've visited where you can't buy a little ground meat and flour. And meatballs are a perfect offering: they're small enough to join in with other dishes, they're versatile, and they can accommodate all kinds of flavors and sauces. I've made them with turkey, chicken, lamb; I've used bread crumbs or even noodles instead of rice. In Thailand, I learned to prepare meatballs with rice noodles and pork and float them in a broth. I've reinvented them with whatever local ingredients call out to me. The meatball recipe I'm including here was based on that tasty Thai soup but reinvented on a trip to Mexico, where I was inspired to add crunchy fresh cabbage and some spicy jalapeños.

A few years ago, Aunt Helen was in the late stages of cancer and I needed to visit. It's a major trek from southern California, and my son, who came with me, was just four months old. A couple of planes and then a couple of hours in a rental car later, I stopped and picked up ground beef on the edge of town. I hadn't planned to cook for my aunt, but the idea just came to me as I was driving.

I cooked up the meatballs Greek style this last time. When I started frying them in my aunt's small pan in her compact kitchen, the smell of mint and sizzling meat just reconnected us. It's hard saying farewell, and I've had blessedly little experience. But there we were, Aunt Helen on the couch and me tending the sauce and the salad in the kitchen, and it was a way for us to reminisce without using the words for good-bye.

Mary Sue Milliken and her business partner of twenty years, Susan Feniger, are two of America's most beloved chefs. They are the chef-owners of the critically acclaimed Border Grill restaurants in Santa Monica, Pasadena, and Las Vegas, as well as Ciudad in downtown Los Angeles. Natural teachers, the partners have created 396 episodes of *Too Hot Tamales* and *Tamales World Tour* series with the Food Network, authored five cookbooks, hosted the "Hot Dish" radio feature on station KFWB, and launched a line of prepared foods, "Border Girls" brand at Whole Foods Markets.

Michael Chiarello
OLD HEN PASTINA BRODO

This dish tells less of a story than it suggests a way of living: a way of living out of your backyard, from your garden, in tune with your family's roots. It's about living in the country, about chicken coops and eggs, about vegetable patches and rows of herbs. It's about a cuisine, about the stories your family shares, year after year.

OLD HEN PASTINA BRODO

Serves 4

One 4- to 5-pound chicken, rinsed and
  drained

1 onion, halved

1 carrot

2 celery ribs

2 tomatoes, peeled, seeded, and diced

1 bay leaf

$^3/_4$ pound acini de pepe

Gray salt (or coarse sea salt) and freshly
  ground black pepper

3 cups packed chopped mustard greens

Freshly grated Parmesan cheese

Hot sauce, optional

1 Preheat the oven to 300°F. Place the
chicken in a deep ovenproof roasting pan
with the onion, carrot, celery, tomatoes, and
bay leaf. Add cold water to cover two-thirds
of the bird. Bring to a simmer on the stove
over medium-high heat. Cover and place in
the oven, braising for $1^1/_2$ hours or until the
bird is completely cooked. Remove from the
oven. Turn the bird over in the broth and
cool.

2 Remove the cooled chicken from the
broth and shred the meat. (Discard the
bones and skin.) Strain the broth and allow it
to settle for 20 minutes, then remove and
discard the fat.

3 Bring a medium pot of salted water to a
boil. Cook the acini de pepe until al dente,
10 to 12 minutes. Drain the pasta.

4 Pour the reserved broth into a large pot.
Bring to a simmer over high heat and season
with salt and pepper. Add the cooked
pasta, shredded chicken, and mustard
greens. Allow the greens to wilt.

✢ Ladle the soup into warmed bowls and
sprinkle with Parmesan cheese, black pepper, and the hot sauce if desired.

Everyone's family develops a sense of
how foods ought to taste. These "family flavors" determine what you think of as especially satisfying. It's your home palate: how
you like your tomatoes, what tenderness you
expect in a pasta, how much saltiness you
want in a broth.

My parents and grandparents, who are
from Calabria, found they could maintain
much of their lifestyle when they came to
Turlock, in California's Central Valley.
Immigrant families with an agricultural past
could take their Old World ways and reinvent them in a new community.

And so while this dish is simple, it helps me
tell certain stories with my kids: the need to

be self-sufficient, the need to preserve things from our family's heritage. These may be basic, obvious concepts, but they're vitally important because the growth in our region is so fast and convenience is such a temptation. The huge shopping center that's sprung up nearby can provide everything—theoretically. My parents' generation sought out these easier solutions; they came to rely on convenience centers. But my grandparents knew that whatever you can make at home provides a grounding, a solidity in light of so much else that goes by quickly and carelessly. And I think my generation has begun to look back toward our grandparents' generation and their earlier appreciation of self-reliance and more homemade goods.

So each component of this brodo is a local family taste. First, the old hen. Italians have an expression: *Conosco miei polli,* "I know my chickens." It's an idiom, which means something like "I know my business just as the farmer knows his chickens": which one lays the most eggs, which one is getting older, and so on. The only way to cook a bird with this much soul and heritage is to stew its tougher meat slowly in liquid. It's like mutton that way. So, if you don't have a barnyard of birds or a neighbor who does, you'll want to find the most natural, range-fed bird you can.

The mustard greens grow wild in the val-ley, and they're also cultivated here to put nitrogen back into the soil. In March you can look over the vineyards, and though the vines are bare, the fields are yellow from the wild mustard leaves. They're pretty pungent, so often my daughters and I will collect a mix of greens: mustard and dandelion and then Swiss chard or black cabbages.

As for the pasta, I like acini de pepe, "the peppercorn," in this soup since it adds an extra little texture in the mouth, a slight al dente bite.

The only additional thing we need is a little hot sauce with this. We make our own "brand" that's just jalapeños, red bell peppers, and tomatoes, chopped up and cooked down, which we put up in old seven-ounce Coke bottles. It, too, is a family taste, part of the story I'm hoping my daughters will be telling their children one day when there's an old hen in the yard and mustard greens in the valley to pick.

Michael Chiarello, known for Tra Vigne Restaurant, the Napa Valley icon, is host of three PBS shows, the author of six books, and the creator of NapaStyle specialty foods and hand-crafted products (www.napastyle.com). His show, *Michael Chiarello's Napa,* airs every week on over 170 public television stations nationally. He also serves as a frequent lifestyle contributor to CBS's *The Early Show.* His latest book, *Michael Chiarello's: Casual Cooking,* accompanies a new PBS series. Michael is also a winegrower; his acclaimed Chiarello Family Vineyards wines are grown from his eighty-five-year-old vineyards in Napa Valley.

Hiro Sone NIKU-JAGA

I grew up in a small village 330 miles north of Tokyo. Most everything we ate came from the vegetable fields behind our house. My mother, very curious about Western foods, planted things our village had never grown before: cauliflower, green cabbage, asparagus, *watermelons!* She planted strawberries, and my brother and I would fight over the berries, eating them even before they had ripened just so the other brother didn't get them first.

Our family farmed Japanese rice, as did most everyone in the village. It was exhausting, nearly full-time work. We'd start the rice kernels in a hothouse we'd build each year. Each family had one. And when the sprouts had grown about five inches tall, we'd plant them in the wet soil of the paddies. We had to water the fields, which were fed by a creek with gates for each family's paddies. All summer we'd weed the paddies. But har-

vesting took the most time, and our neighbors would help us, and then we'd go help the neighbors with their paddies.

This is a simple stew that I began to cook by myself when I was eight or nine, serving lunch to my family and neighbors who'd come to help us work in the rice fields.

Someone—usually my mother or grandmother—would come in for lunch an hour earlier than the rest of us to prepare the meal. We'd have had tea and something sweet around ten o'clock, so everyone was famished by lunchtime from the morning's labor.

Lunch would be several kinds of pickles—those, at least, were ready—some simply prepared fish or chicken, and often a broth with noodles, a salad or steamed vegetables, and always steamed rice.

But the most vivid memory I have is cooking niku-jaga, this stew of potato and mushrooms stewed with meat, to ladle over the rice. We used a traditional rice pot, made of very thick iron. Very heavy for a little kid to lift! It would sit inside one of two holes in a huge table, under which a wood fire would be burning. The pot had a heavy lid that sealed in the steam. All the food from that kitchen had a slight smokiness from the wood stove.

In the remote part of Japan where we lived, beef was almost never an option, so

NIKU-JAGA Serves 4

1 medium onion, quartered

3 pounds beef short ribs, bones removed, sliced against the grain into $1/4$-inch pieces

$1/2$ cup soy sauce

$1/3$ cup mirin (available at Asian markets)

$1/4$ cup sugar

2 large Russet potatoes, peeled and cut into $1 1/2$-inch cubes

4 large shiitake mushrooms, stemmed and halved

$1/4$ cup chopped scallions, both white and light green parts

Shichimi (Japanese pepper mix, available at Asian markets) for garnish

Steamed Japanese rice, as an accompaniment

1 Place the onion and beef in a medium saucepan and add enough cold water to cover. Bring to a boil over medium-high heat. Skim off the impurities that rise to the surface. Add the soy sauce, mirin, and sugar. Bring back to a boil, reduce the heat, and simmer, covered, until the meat is tender, 30 to 35 minutes.

2 Add the prepared potatoes and simmer until the potatoes are tender, about 20 minutes.

3 Add the mushrooms and simmer for another 5 minutes.

✣ Spoon the beef and vegetables into individual warm bowls, sprinkle with scallions, and add a dash (or more) of the shichimi. Ladle the broth over all and serve with a side of steamed Japanese rice.

we usually added chicken to this dish—we raised our own birds. But things have changed in twenty years. Now beef is available most everywhere in Japan, and I like to make this stew with beef short ribs. And rice planting has changed, too. There's a co-op in each village where the rice is sprouted. And planting is done by a machine with something like twenty "hands" that set the sprouts in the ground.

Sometimes, here in St. Helena, I make this

dish for the staff at our restaurant, an experience that isn't all that different from those childhood lunches in my Japanese village: a bunch of us field hands gathering together to share something delicious before heading back out to work.

Hiro Sone is chef at Terra, a restaurant steeped in tradition and housed in a century-old fieldstone building in St. Helena, in Napa Valley's wine country. His

Claud Mann
POSOLE DE PERLITA

Posole soup is a one-dish Mexican supper my wife Perla's family has shared every Christmas as long as anyone can remember. Simultaneously comfort and celebration, the hominy and pork (or even free-range turkey) soup is passed around the table, and each person garnishes a huge bowl of the broth, hominy, and shredded meat in a different way: chopped lettuce, avocado, shredded cabbage, fresh chiles, radishes, cilantro, onions, chile sauce—it's like creating a beautiful garden in the center of the table, and conversation plays as big a part in the dish as the edible ingredients.

This recipe began with Perla's grandmother. I suppose anything that comes from a grandmother's hands is comforting. On our very first date, Perla's mother and grandmother were making posole soup at her sister's. It was my first visit there. Her mother is Austrian-Hungarian, but she grew up in Argentina and learned to cook from Perla's father, who was from Acapulco. Every single Christmas, Perla's mother would buy a pig's head from Grand Central Market, the only place that supplied Mexican foods and produce. Back then the reason to cook the head was economical: use every part of the animal. Today it's more expensive to buy the head than the rest of the pig's body.

Now when I make the soup I use a pork shoulder, which is called the butt. (The derrière is actually the ham.) And I use pig's feet, to replace the flavoring the cartilage from the head would have provided. Unlike other stocks, there's no mirepoix. Just garlic, bay leaf, and black peppercorns—Perla's mom wouldn't add more than water and salt. Still, this version has met with her approval. The key to a great stock is to keep the water just this side of simmering so the meat doesn't dry out and the fat isn't incorporated into the stock. At the family gatherings someone is always famished and goes over to the stove to turn the heat up to a boil and speed things along, but you can't do that. It's a long simmer, but as soon as you can pull the bone free, the soup is ready. You pick off the fat, shred the meat from the bone, and serve it in a separate bowl.

I've been tempted to use fresh hominy,

POSOLE DE PERLITA

Serves 10 to 12

For the soup

3 pounds bone-in pork shoulder butt, cut into 4 pieces

3 pounds pig's feet, neck bones, or shanks, cut into 2-inch-thick pieces (have the butcher cut these for you)

2 large white onions, quartered

2 whole heads garlic, halved across the middle

1 bay leaf

2 tablespoons sea salt

4 cups fully cooked Mexican hominy (see Note)

1 recipe Ancho Chile Sauce

For garnish, optional

Coarsely ground dried red chile

Dried Mexican oregano

Finely chopped white onion

Halved lemons and limes

Finely chopped red cabbage

Thinly sliced radishes

Diced avocado

1 recipe Ancho Chile Sauce

1 Rinse the meat and bones, place in a large stockpot, and cover with 5 quarts cold water. Add the onions, garlic, bay leaf, and salt. Bring to a full boil over high heat. Reduce the heat to low and simmer, uncovered, for $2^1/2$ hours. Occasionally skim off any foam that rises to the surface. The meat is finished when it falls easily from the bones. Remove the pot from the heat and cool.

2 Remove the meat from the broth, shred into large chunks, and set aside. Discard the bones, skin, fat, and knuckles.

3 Skim the fat from the broth and discard. Add the hominy to the broth and bring to a boil over high heat. Reduce the heat to a low simmer and cook until the hominy softens and expands, about 30 minutes. Return the meat to the broth. Taste and reseason if necessary. Cover and keep warm.

✣ Arrange any or all of the garnishes in serving bowls. Ladle the soup with meat into large heated serving bowls. Pass the garnishes and Ancho Chile Sauce at the table.

✣ Transfer any leftover soup into smaller, shallow containers so they will cool quickly before refrigerating.

but Perla's convinced that the real dish needs Mexican white hominy: large, rough kernels straight from the can.

It's the condiments that reflect the regional aspects of Mexico. Perla insists on the purity of a white broth, while I'm of the red school, so I make a red-chile puree and leave it on the side as another condiment, which I swirl into the clear stock. We always add Mexican oregano, crushing the leaves between our hands so that the smell is everything. And then tons of lemons—each person squeezes half a lemon into the soup, which turns the broth cloudy. And then we pass around the various condiments. We know some families who offer red cabbage as well. And some who put green apples in the soup. And the only other side dish we serve is fresh tortillas.

For fifteen years I've cooked posole soup for our family at Christmas. So it's a complete meal. And it's so filling! Partly because you end up eating at least three bowls . . . until you need a nap. Which is a good thing,

because by *that* time someone's started an argument, so it's a good time to retreat to the couch.

Note: Mexican-style hominy is found in Latin American groceries. Try to purchase half-cooked hominy from a tortilla factory and finish cooking it at home. Alternatively purchase pozole from a health food or gourmet store and cook according to the directions, 3 to 5 hours. Fully cooked canned or frozen hominy is available at most grocery stores.

ANCHO CHILE SAUCE
Makes 2$\frac{1}{2}$ cups

----

6 to 8 dried ancho chiles, stems and
  seeds removed, coarsely torn

1 teaspoon sea salt

1 teaspoon sugar

2 tablespoons white vinegar

Combine the chiles, 2$\frac{1}{2}$ cups water, salt, sugar, and vinegar in a small nonreactive saucepan over high heat. Cook for 5 minutes. Cool slightly and puree in small batches. Strain and pour into a serving bowl.

Chef de cuisine for *Dinner & a Movie*, Claud Mann graduated from the California Culinary Academy and cooked his way up and down the West Coast, including stints as executive chef at the five-star Palmilla Hotel in Cabo San Lucas and Nicola restaurant in Los Angeles. His nonprofit endeavors include Project Open Hand and his own guerrilla catering company, Eat the Rich, which simply never made a penny. Claud also co-runs Mechuda Music, an independent record label, with his wife, vocalist Perla Batalla. They live in Ojai, California, with their daughter, Eva, and are breaking ground on a home-style organic restaurant.

PASTA AND RICE

Lidia Bastianich
RICOTTA GNOCCHI WITH CONTESSA SAUCE

Mark Militello
SEMOLINA CRÊPES STUFFED WITH HOMEMADE RICOTTA
AND PROSCIUTTO

Roberto Donna
RAVIOLI DI VITELLO ALLA PIEMONTESE (VEAL RAVIOLI
WITH A RED WINE REDUCTION)

Emeril Lagasse
PENNE WITH BOLOGNESE SAUCE

Jeffrey Buben
GUMBO-STYLE RISOTTO

Jennifer Jasinski
SWEET PEA RISOTTO

Martin Yan
HOME-STYLE CLAY POT

Takashi Yagihashi
ROASTED AMISH CHICKEN AND SHRIMP
WITH ASIAN NOODLE SALAD

Lidia Bastianich RICOTTA GNOCCHI WITH CONTESSA SAUCE

I grew up close to Trieste on the peninsula of Istria, which is now part of Croatia. My brother Franco and I, together with our cousins, would often visit my grandmother in the country on Sundays, and we would always make either gnocchi (potato dumplings) or fresh pasta (either fuzi or garganelli). It was a tradition for the children to help with these dishes. For the fuzi we would simply take the diamond-shaped pieces of dough and roll them around our index fingers to make the fuzi shape. For the gnocchi dough my grandmother would mix it and roll it into small balls. Then the children would roll each gnocco ball down the fork so that each dumpling had little ridges, perfect for holding sauce. We made so many gnocco balls—but it didn't take so long since we all chipped in. For just one dinner we would make maybe three hundred gnocchi.

Along with the gnocchi or the pastas, my grandmother would prepare a sauce made from one of the ducks, chickens, or rabbits that lived in her courtyard. It was a long stewing process, so the smell of rosemary, caramelized onions, cloves, and bay leaves would fill the kitchen as we helped with the dough.

There were also goats in our courtyard, and in the spring my grandmother would make ricotta from the fresh milk for special gnocchi. The cheese makes the dough lighter; it puffs up when it's boiled. We ate these gnocchi with nothing more than butter, sage, and cheese. I love this method: you sauté fresh sage leaves in butter, and they release a lot of aroma. Then, with just a little of the cooking water from the boiling gnocchi, you have a light sauce. You fish out the gnocchi as soon as they rise to the top of the pot, rolling them in the saucepan's buttery sage and

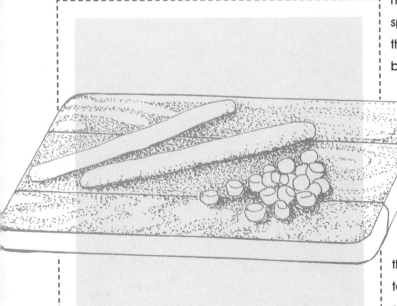

RICOTTA GNOCCHI WITH CONTESSA SAUCE Serves 6

For the gnocchi

1 1/2 pounds fresh ricotta cheese or 3 cups packaged whole-milk ricotta cheese

1 3/4 teaspoons salt, plus more for the cooking water

2 large eggs

1/2 cup freshly grated Parmigiano-Reggiano cheese

1/2 teaspoon freshly ground white pepper

1/4 teaspoon freshly grated nutmeg

2 cups all-purpose flour or as needed, plus more for forming the gnocchi

For the sauce

8 tablespoons (1 stick) unsalted butter

4 thin slices (1 ounce) prosciutto, sliced into 1/4-inch strips

10 fresh basil leaves, torn into quarters

1/4 cup pine nuts

1 1/2 cups heavy cream

1 cup freshly grated Parmigiano-Reggiano cheese

1 Fit a colander inside a large bowl. Line the colander with a double thickness of cheesecloth or a basket-type coffee filter and spoon in the ricotta cheese. Cover the bowl with plastic wrap and allow the cheese to drain in the refrigerator overnight or for up to 24 hours. Discard the liquid in the bottom of the bowl.

2 Bring 6 quarts of salted water to a boil.

3 In a medium bowl, beat the eggs and 1 teaspoon salt until foamy. Add the grated cheese, pepper, and nutmeg, then mix in the ricotta until thoroughly blended. Gradually add as much flour as necessary to form a soft and sticky dough. (This is a sticky dough: do not work in all of the flour to make a firm or smooth dough—that will create tough, heavy gnocchi.)

4 Divide the dough into 6 equal pieces. Flour your hands and the work surface lightly to prevent the dough from sticking. Roll each piece into a rope about 1/2 inch wide and about 18 inches long. Cut the roll crosswise into 1/4-inch lengths. Dust the gnocchi lightly with flour. Transfer the cut gnocchi to a tray. Repeat the process with the remaining rolls.

5 To prepare the sauce, melt the butter in a skillet large enough to hold all of the gnocchi over medium heat. Add the prosciutto, basil, and pine nuts. Cook, stirring, until the pine nuts are lightly golden in color and aromatic, 4 to 5 minutes. Pour in 1 cup heavy cream, bring to a boil, and continue to boil for 3 minutes or until the sauce is lightly thickened. Set aside.

6 Add the gnocchi, a few at a time, to the boiling water; when all have been added,

return the water to a boil and stir frequently. Cook with the pot half-covered, stirring occasionally, until the gnocchi float to the surface and are tender, about 5 minutes.

7 Dip a slotted spoon or skimmer into the water and transfer the gnocchi into the skillet with the cream sauce. Bring all to a boil, gently tossing the gnocchi with the sauce. Whip the remaining $1/2$ cup cream. Remove the gnocchi from the heat and fold in the whipped cream and grated cheese. Taste, adjust the seasonings, and serve.

sprinkling it all with Parmigiano-Reggiano. It's a perfect dish.

Just like my grandmother taught me about food, I try to do the same today with my four grandchildren—Olivia, Lorenzo, Miles, and Ethan. When they were small, just one or two months old, I would crush herbs from my garden under their noses—sage, basil, rosemary, and bay leaves. I would then repeat the herbs' names to them, sometimes in English, sometimes in Italian. Their noses would twitch with these new and powerful sensations. At that age the brain is such a sponge, and our olfactory powers are so underutilized. Smells can provide such deep memories: they can bring you right back to a place faster than any stories.

I make gnocchi with my grandchildren just as my grandmother made them with me. "Nonni, are we going to make gnocchi today?" Now I have a box in the kitchen so even the littlest one can reach the table and help me shape the gnocchi balls with a fork. I can't even imagine how many gnocchi I have made since first rolling them with my grandmother . . . and now with my grandchildren.

Lidia Bastianich is the star of public television's *Lidia's Italian American Kitchen* and *Lidia's Italian Table*, which air nationwide and in Japan, Australia, and Canada. Lidia is the author of the series' companion cookbooks as well as *La Cucina di Lidia*. She is the co-owner of Felidia, Becco, and Esca restaurants in New York and Lidia's in Kansas City and Pittsburgh. She runs a travel company, Esperienze Italiane, with her daughter Tanya. In addition, she has two sauce lines, Lidia's Flavors of Italy and Williams Sonoma's Lidia's Regional Italian Flavors.

Mark Militello SEMOLINA CRÊPES STUFFED WITH HOMEMADE RICOTTA AND PROSCIUTTO

My Sicilian relatives immigrated to America, along with many Italians, to work on the Niagara Falls Water Authority Project. They settled around Buffalo, New York, which has a history of pride in its glorified local foods. The most famous are Buffalo wings, of course, but there's beef on weck, an amazing sandwich on a special roll (in a four-day visit I'll have eight of them), Salen's famous charbroiled hot dogs, Weber's great relish, and Texas sauce.

When my relatives came together for family dinners—usually a Wednesday or a Sunday—we were typically twenty people, and up to forty on special holidays. My grandmother and all her sisters would take over the kitchen. I can still see them rolling out pasta with broom handles on our kitchen table.

Dinner began with an antipasto course—not meats and cheese, but simple and classic Italian dishes like oranges with sliced fennel bulbs. Then we'd have a pasta course—manicotti, hearty rigatoni, ravioli, or an amazing version of chicken and rice that was like a brothy risotto—and then a meat course, though after the pasta course we weren't all that hungry.

These crêpes are based on my grandmother's manicotti. Real Italian manicotti is not a tube pasta but a rolled pancake that's stuffed and then baked. I make my batter with semolina flour, which is used in some pasta, of course, and I fold it rather than roll it. My filling is traditional, too, but I like fresh ricotta, which I don't recall my grandmother making. When you make the cheese yourself, you can control the moisture, which is key.

It's a cold-weather dish, perfect for the town of Buffalo, where for six months you're basically cooped up inside. The winter is long and severe since the city sits right on the lake, and the snow drifts are so large that one morning I looked out my bedroom window, and our dog, a big collie-mix, was looking in. This was the second floor. The dog had just walked up the icy drift. And the city was often imposing curfews, so we were supposed to stay home and be safe. And eat.

These baked crêpes, with the creamy ricotta and tangy sauce, make for perfect comfort food, even now. We dine at home a lot (since I spend more than enough time in my restaurants), and Sunday, in particular, is when I'm likely to serve up a platter of these crêpes for my family and my kids' friends. I may remember my grandmother's manicotti

SEMOLINA CRÊPES STUFFED WITH HOMEMADE RICOTTA AND PROSCIUTTO Serves 6

For the crêpe filling

5 ounces fresh spinach (about 6 cups loosely packed)

1 recipe Homemade Ricotta

1/2 cup grated mozzarella cheese

2 large egg yolks

Pinch of freshly grated nutmeg

Salt and freshly ground black pepper

For the crepes

3/4 cup all-purpose flour

1/4 cup semolina flour

4 large eggs

1 1/2 cups whole milk

1/4 cup beer

Salt

4 tablespoons (1/2 stick) butter, clarified

10 very thin prosciutto slices, cut in half widthwise

1 recipe Tomato Sauce

2 tablespoons freshly grated Parmesan or Romano cheese

1 To make the crêpe filling, blanch the spinach in boiling water until wilted, about 1 minute. Drain and cool in a bath of ice water. Drain and squeeze the moisture from the spinach in a towel. Finely chop the dried spinach.

2 Combine the ricotta, spinach, and mozzarella. Stir in the egg yolks and nutmeg, then season with salt and pepper to taste. Cover and refrigerate. This step can be done several hours in advance.

3 To make the crêpes, place the flour and semolina in a large bowl. Make a well in the center. In another bowl, mix together the eggs, milk, beer, and a pinch of salt and pour into the well in the flour. Using a whisk, slowly pull the flours into the liquid. Continue to mix until the batter is smooth. Do not over-mix. If the batter is lumpy, pass it through a strainer. Cover and allow to rest at room temperature for 45 minutes.

4 Heat an 8-inch nonstick pan over medium heat. Lightly coat the pan with 2 teaspoons of the clarified butter. Add a small ladle of batter to the hot pan and allow the batter to coat the entire surface. Cook until the edges of the crêpe are golden brown, about 2 minutes, and then flip over with a rubber spatula. Cook the other side until light brown. Slide the crêpe out of the pan to cool. Continue to form crêpes until the batter is gone, making about 20 crêpes. They can be made ahead of time and stacked between sheets of wax or parchment paper and refrigerated in an airtight container. Bring to room temperature before filling.

5 Preheat the oven to 325°F.

6 Place 5 to 6 crêpes on a work surface.

Place a slice of prosciutto on top of each crêpe. Place 1^1/$_2$ tablespoons of the ricotta-spinach filling in one quarter of each crêpe. Fold each crêpe in half to cover the filling; fold again, covering the filled side with the unfilled side of the crêpe. The end result is a pie-shaped wedge that is a quarter of the original crêpe. Repeat the process with the remaining crêpes.

7 Ladle 4 cups of the tomato sauce into the bottom of a large nonreactive casserole pan. Place the filled crêpes on top of the sauce and then cover with the remaining sauce. Bake for 35 minutes.

✤ To serve, place 2 or 3 crêpes on each plate and cover with spoonfuls of tomato sauce. Sprinkle with grated cheese.

HOMEMADE RICOTTA Makes 2 cups
----

6 cups whole milk
1 cup heavy cream
^{1}/$_4$ cup fresh lemon juice (1 to 2 lemons)

1 Combine the milk and cream in a heavy nonreactive saucepan. Bring to a boil and reduce the heat. Gently stir in the lemon juice with a wooden spoon. Watch for the milk curds to separate from the whey. Do not overstir. Remove the pan from the heat and set aside to rest for 3 minutes.

2 Pour the mixture through a fine-mesh strainer. Allow the curds to drain for 5 min-

utes. Discard the liquid in the bottom of the bowl (the whey) and place the solids (the curds) in a bowl. Cover and refrigerate for 3 to 4 hours or until the cheese becomes firm.

The mixture will tighten up once it has cooled. This can be prepared 2 days in advance and refrigerated in an airtight container.

TOMATO SAUCE Makes 2 quarts
----

^{1}/$_4$ cup extra virgin olive oil
10 garlic cloves, smashed
^{3}/$_4$ cup chopped onion (1 medium)
One 28-ounce can peeled plum tomatoes
10 fresh plum tomatoes (1^1/$_2$ pounds), cored and halved
Salt and freshly cracked black pepper

1 Heat the oil in a nonreactive pan over high heat. Add the garlic and stir until lightly toasted, not burned, about 1 minute. Reduce the heat, add the onion, and cook until translucent but not brown, about 4 minutes. Add the tomatoes and 2 cups water and bring to a boil. Reduce the heat to a simmer, season with salt and pepper to taste, and cook for 1 hour and 15 minutes.

2 Pass the sauce through a food mill and adjust the salt and pepper if necessary. The sauce can be stored in an airtight container in the refrigerator for several days.

as a cold-weather dish, but they're just as nourishing and delicious here in south Florida.

Before starting the crêpes, prepare the ricotta and the tomato sauce according to the directions given. Both may be done well in advance and kept refrigerated.

Since the late 1980s south Florida chef Mark Militello has been creating innovative contemporary American cuisine. Highly acclaimed, he received the Beard Foundation Award as the best regional chef in the Southeast, two Golden Dish awards from *GQ* magazine, a Best Restaurant Award from *Food & Wine* magazine, and was recently profiled in the prestigious eight-week series "The Chef" in the *New York Times*. Militello is chef and co-owner of Mark's Las Olas and three namesake restaurants, in South Beach, Boca Raton, and West Palm Beach.

Roberto Donna RAVIOLI DI VITELLO ALLA PIEMONTESE (VEAL RAVIOLI WITH A RED WINE REDUCTION)

This dish is one of the first I ever made. When I was four and a half, my family moved into a double house: on one side we ran a grocery store, and we lived in back of that; on the other side Antonio Guerra ran a restaurant, with an upstairs party room where they could host weddings for 400 or even 500 people. (Italian weddings are never little affairs!)

I lived in that kitchen. It was the center of everything. Most mornings I would wake at 5:30 and run down to the kitchen. You see, it had a big coal stove that had to be started up early in the morning, and then by nightfall it could die down. Around midnight, as his last duty, the chef would slide in a huge tray of *budino de crema caramela*—a crème caramel made with the milk from the cows next door. The oven would cool all night and cook the custards perfectly. First thing in the morning, I'd grab one of the crèmes for breakfast. Then, at 6:30, the bread would come in warm from the bakery, and I'd take a small bread, tuck some prosciutto inside, and that would be the rest of my breakfast. (The days I didn't wake up at 5:30, the smell of the warm bread lifted up to my bedroom window and had me jumping from bed.)

Antonio and his father let me help with peeling potatoes and washing the greens, but what I wanted to do was make the ravioli with them—except I couldn't reach the worktable to fill the ravioli mold! So much

RAVIOLI DI VITELLO ALLA PIEMONTESE (VEAL RAVIOLI WITH A RED WINE REDUCTION) Serves 10 to 12

For the filling

1^1/2 pounds boneless veal shoulder, cubed

^{1}/2 pound mortadella, cut into 2-inch pieces

1 fresh rosemary sprig, leaves only

1 fresh sage sprig, leaves only

3 garlic cloves

1 medium onion, chopped

1 carrot, chopped

1 celery rib, chopped

^{1}/4 cup olive oil

Salt and freshly ground black pepper

2 large eggs

^{1}/2 pound Parmesan cheese, grated (2 cups)

2 tablespoons ricotta cheese

Pinch of freshly grated nutmeg

Pinch of freshly grated lemon zest

To assemble the ravioli and finish the dish

1 recipe Fresh Homemade Pasta

2 large egg whites

2 tablespoons salt

12 tablespoons (1^1/2 sticks) unsalted butter

3 fresh sage leaves

1 recipe Red Wine Reduction

1 Preheat the oven to 375°F. Combine the veal, mortadella, rosemary, sage, garlic, onion, carrot, celery, olive oil, and salt and pepper to taste in a large ovenproof nonstick skillet. Roast for 1 hour, basting and stirring every 15 minutes. Do not let the meat or vegetables brown. Cool.

2 Grind the cooked meat and vegetables together in small batches; use the meat grinder attachment for an electric mixer or a hand grinder. Add the eggs, 3 ounces (^{3}/4 cup) of the Parmesan cheese, the ricotta, nutmeg, and lemon zest and mix well to incorporate. This can be done a day in advance.

3 Cut the pasta dough into 4 pieces and roll out each piece using a pasta machine. Keep the dough covered with a cotton tea towel until ready to roll out. Moving from the machine's widest position to its thinnest, pass

time was spent at that table preparing ravioli—for a big wedding, they'd have to make ten or fifteen pieces for every person, and that's five or ten thousand ravioli, not including what they'd need for the dinners downstairs in the dining room.

Finally, when I was about six years old, I could just see the top of the worktable—its each piece of dough through the machine 6 or 7 times. Lightly dust the dough with flour whenever necessary to keep it from sticking.

4 In a small bowl, mix together the egg whites and 2 tablespoons water. Lay 1 sheet of pasta on a work surface. Cut the dough in half and cover half with a towel. Brush the entire surface of the exposed pasta sheet with the egg wash. Make two rows of ravioli by placing teaspoons of filling $1/2$ inch apart from one another in 2 rows centered equidistant from the edges of the pasta. Sandwich the filling with the second, covered half of the pasta, pressing gently in the spaces between the mounds of filling to release trapped air. With a pasta cutter, slice among the rows, creating squares of equal size. Transfer the ravioli to a tray covered with a tea towel that has been dusted lightly with flour. Repeat with the remaining pasta and filling.

5 Bring a large pot of water to a boil and add the salt. Add the ravioli to the boiling water and cook for 4 minutes.

6 Melt the butter in a large skillet and add the sage leaves. Sauté the leaves for 1 to 2 minutes. Add the cooked ravioli and gently coat with butter.

✤ To serve, transfer everything to a platter and sprinkle with the remaining Parmesan cheese. Drizzle with the warmed Red Wine Reduction.

FRESH HOMEMADE PASTA

$3^3/4$ cups all-purpose flour, plus extra
   for rolling
1 tablespoon salt
2 tablespoons olive oil
5 large egg yolks

1 **To prepare the dough, combine $3^1/2$ cups of the flour, the salt, olive oil, and yolks in the bowl of an electric mixer and, using the dough hook attachment, mix on low speed for 3 minutes. If the dough is too stiff, add water a teaspoon at a time and mix briefly until the dough is smooth and elastic.**

2 **Place the dough on a floured surface and knead in the remaining $1/4$ cup flour. Work the dough for 1 minute or until well blended. Seal the pasta in plastic wrap and refrigerate for 2 hours.**

edge came up to my nose—and Antonio let me fill the ravioli mold. On tiptoes, I could see the pockets in the dough, and I'd roll the meat filling into a short rope between my hands and then pinch off a piece and then go down the line, pinch, pinch, pinch, popping a small ball into each of the squares. It's one large ravioli mold, about two feet square, made of steel, I guess, with ninety square holes, like a grid.

Then Antonio would brush the filled pasta with a little egg wash, place the other sheet of pasta on top, and then tamp it down with his hand to press out all the air. And then he'd invert the whole filled mold and cut out the individual ravioli by hand with the little wavy wheel that rolls along and crimps the edges. Eventually I got to make them all by myself.

By the time I was eight, I was working every Friday, Saturday, and Sunday night.

My pay was Popsicles, but soon enough I was earning a little real money, too.

As for this sauce, it is the venerable sauce that was always cooking in a huge pot on the stove. Into that the chefs tossed all the bones, the extra sausages, bottles of wine, whatever was left over, and it simmered and reduced (you could hear it bubbling, *tick, tick, tick,* in the background), and from that, once a week, they made this marvelous brown sauce, straining it and seasoning it perfectly. The version I share with you here is a little different, you understand, but it captures the flavors of that kitchen.

RED WINE REDUCTION

Makes $1/2$ cup

----

1 tablespoon pancetta

1 small onion, chopped

1 celery rib, chopped

1 small red bell pepper, peeled with a
   vegetable peeler and chopped

6 garlic cloves, chopped

2 small tomatoes, chopped

2 small green apples, peeled, cored,
   and chopped

$1/2$ cup balsamic vinegar

2 tablespoons port

1 bottle Cabernet Sauvignon

1 Heat a medium skillet over medium-high heat and add the pancetta to render some of the fat. Lower the heat and add the onion, celery, bell pepper, and garlic; cook until the vegetables are limp and soft, about 5 minutes. Add the tomatoes, apples, vinegar, and port and cook until the liquid is just a glaze on the vegetables, 10 to 15 minutes. Add the wine and slowly reduce by half, skimming off any fat residue.

2 Strain the liquid through a strainer lined with a double layer of cheesecloth. Pour the liquid back into the cleaned pan and reduce the liquid to $1/2$ cup. This step can be done several days in advance and the reduction refrigerated in an airtight container. Warm before serving.

If you come to my restaurant in Washington, D.C., I can make you the ravioli with Antonio's very mold. He gave it to me when I opened my restaurant. It's more than sixty years old—I don't think they're even made anymore—and it's what I use every day to make my own pasta.

Roberto Donna is a Beard Award–winning chef and restaurateur in Washington, D.C., committed to featuring the authentic flavors of Italy's Piedmont region in his seven restaurants. Galileo was named one of the twenty finest Italian restaurants in the world by the president of Italy. A broad sampling of his recipes is featured in his book, *Cooking in Piedmont with Roberto Donna.*

Emeril Lagasse PENNE WITH BOLOGNESE SAUCE

When I asked my family, my in-laws, my daughters which recipe might be our family dish, they all agreed it should be this Bolognese sauce. And it's my wife's favorite dish. I don't make anything as often as I do this sauce.

Now, it probably surprises no one that I didn't grow up Italian. My mom's Portuguese, and my dad's French-Canadian, but ever since I was a little boy I've had vivid memories of food; this Italian sauce is inspired by my frequent visits to Bologna and that region of Italy. It's also true that while I was trained in American schools—my culinary background is classical French, the grandfather cuisine with its passion and deep roots—I've come to love Italian cooking, which is like the grandmother cuisine with its simplicity and restraint.

So when I get up on Sunday morning, I make my coffee and start cutting vegetables to get this Bolognese sauce started. What makes it so special is the slow simmering throughout the day. It gives me time to do a salad course or to start a loaf of fresh bread. And in my household this pot of sauce is a magnet. Nine out of ten times that I make it—during football season, especially—I don't know how many people I'm going to be feeding. Could be my parents, my in-laws, some intimate friends . . . this sauce is my Sunday way of catching up with everyone.

I might also have a pot of gumbo cooking on the stove. A side of sausage and peppers. Maybe meatballs in their own gravy. But this Bolognese sauce is the highlight of these great get-togethers.

PENNE WITH BOLOGNESE
SAUCE Serves 12 with leftovers

----

2 tablespoons olive oil

$1/2$ pound ground white veal

$1/2$ pound ground pork butt

$1/2$ pound ground beef round

**$1 1/2$ teaspoons salt, plus extra for cooking
the pasta**

1 teaspoon freshly cracked black pepper

1 cup chopped onion

$1/2$ cup chopped carrot

$1/2$ cup chopped celery

1 teaspoon chopped garlic

1 teaspoon dried basil

1 teaspoon dried oregano

1 bay leaf

**Two 28-ounce cans whole peeled toma-
toes, drained, coarsely chopped**

Two 15-ounce cans tomato sauce

3 tablespoons tomato paste

1 teaspoon sugar

$1/2$ cup whole milk

2 pounds dried penne

Freshly grated Parmesan cheese

1 Heat the oil in a large heavy saucepan over medium heat. Add the ground meats and season with $3/4$ teaspoon salt and $1/2$ teaspoon pepper. Cook until the meat has browned, about 5 minutes. Stir to break it up into small bits.

2 Add the onion, carrot, celery, garlic, basil, oregano, bay leaf, and the remaining $3/4$ teaspoon salt and $1/2$ teaspoon pepper. Cook the vegetables until soft, about 5 minutes.

3 Add the tomatoes, tomato sauce, tomato paste, sugar, and 2 cups water to the pan. Bring to a simmer over medium-high heat. Lower the heat to medium-low and simmer, uncovered, for 1 hour, stirring occasionally. When ready to serve, add the milk to the sauce and cook for 1 minute. Keep warm.

4 Bring a large pot of salted water to a boil and add the penne. Stir to keep the pasta from sticking together. Cook until al dente, 10 to 12 minutes. Drain the pasta.

✛ Transfer the penne to a large serving bowl, gently toss with the sauce, and serve with Parmesan cheese.

The sauce is a combination of veal, pork, and beef, but I've also done this recipe with only ground turkey, which my kids sometimes prefer. It's the clarity of ingredients and the cooking method that's the central thing. It belongs with the same memories of cooking as the vegetable soup I made as a little kid with my mother, who was the first person who inspired me, taking the time to teach me how to cook. We would make a vegetable soup together, and we would make it over and over and over. This Bolognese sauce has the same preparing of several vegetables, the same long and aromatic simmering, and the same need to make it week after week.

Now, there are always leftovers. I count on it, and what I do is, I'll leave out the last addition of the milk. I serve up however much of the sauce we need, and then I add ice cubes to the rest of the pot. It brings down the temperature quickly so I can refrigerate the sauce. And then, the next day, I can slowly bring the sauce up to a simmer and reduce it a bit so the water evaporates—and I add the milk then, which brings a whole new flavor to the sauce. (The ice cubes are the best way to cool soups, sauces, beans, or gumbos at home, too.)

Every family should have a dish for catching up with friends after a busy week, a pot of something wonderful to fill the house, and everyone in it, with marvelous memories.

Emeril Lagasse is currently the chef-proprietor of eight restaurants: three in New Orleans, two in Las Vegas, two in Orlando, and one in Atlanta. Emeril became a national TV personality with the Food Network's production of *The Essence of Emeril* and *Emeril Live*, which reaches more than seventy million homes daily. A food correspondent for ABC's *Good Morning America*, he has authored seven books, including *Emeril's New New Orleans Cooking, Prime Time Emeril,* and the kids' cookbook *Emeril's There's a Chef in My Soup!* His website is www.emerils.com.

Jeffrey Buben GUMBO-STYLE RISOTTO

When two strangers meet and start cooking together, there are going to be certain dishes worth fighting over, dishes that require compromise. Chicken and dumplings is one that my wife and I are still negotiating. We each grew up loving our own family's recipe.

This gumbo-style risotto is an example of a compromise, a middle ground that we've established between two rather distinct meal "cultures": one from my own upbringing and one from my wife Sallie's. In her family a great deal of effort was made so that everyone could sit down together for dinner each night. She came from a southern tradition, and dinners were central to each day. Gumbo was a favorite, with its filé powder and fantastic mix of shellfish.

GUMBO-STYLE RISOTTO

Serves 6 to 8

1/4 cup olive oil

1/4 cup chopped celery

1/4 cup chopped onion

1 small red bell pepper, roasted, peeled,
seeded, and chopped (1/4 cup)

2 tomatoes, peeled, seeded, and
chopped (1 cup)

3 garlic cloves, chopped

Salt and freshly cracked black pepper

1 cup chopped fresh okra

6 ounces tasso ham, diced (1 cup)

1 fresh bay leaf

2 teaspoons Worcestershire sauce

Pinch of cayenne pepper or to taste

6 cups Shrimp Stock

2 cups Carnaroli or Arborio rice

12 medium shrimp, peeled, deveined,
and diced, shells reserved for stock

24 crawfish tails, peeled and deveined,
shells reserved for stock

1/2 pound jumbo lump crabmeat, picked
over and cleaned

2 teaspoons gumbo filé powder

2 tablespoons plus 2 teaspoons unsalted
butter

2 tablespoons chopped fresh cilantro
for garnish

1 Heat 2 tablespoons of the olive oil in a medium saucepan over medium-high heat. Add the celery, onion, roasted pepper, tomatoes, and garlic. Season with salt and pepper to taste and cook until the onion is translucent, 3 to 5 minutes. Add the okra, ham, bay leaf, Worcestershire, cayenne, and stock. Simmer for 6 minutes. Set aside, covering to keep hot.

2 Heat the remaining 2 tablespoons olive oil in a large heavy saucepan. Add the rice and stir well to coat the grains. Add the hot gumbo sauce 1 to 2 cups at a time, stirring the entire time; allow each addition to be incorporated before adding the next. Continue adding sauce until it all has been incorporated into the rice, about 20 minutes. Add the seafood and gumbo filé to the rice during the last few minutes of cooking. When done, the rice should be creamy but also slightly al dente.

3 Fold in the butter and check for seasoning.
❖ To serve, spoon the risotto into warm bowls and sprinkle with chopped cilantro.

But when I was growing up, both of my parents worked—and they had different schedules. Basically, my mother fed everyone à la carte (I had three siblings, and we rarely converged at the table), so she was the last one to sit down and have dinner. Part of my early "training" as a chef had to come from my volunteering to start dinner. Someone had to!

Early in our marriage this particular difference was a point of contention, especially since we're in this restaurant business that doesn't really allow for meals together. Yet this dish, something we cooked up together, is just the right food to share with friends and family since everyone can join in. (While it's not a difficult dish to prepare, there are enough elements that it possesses what I call the Tom Sawyer effect, which I appreciate: everyone loves to jump in and help . . . not even realizing that the chef himself didn't do much at all.)

SHRIMP STOCK Makes 6 cups

----

1 1/2 tablespoons vegetable oil

1 pound fish bones, rinsed well and cut into 3-inch segments

2 pounds shrimp and crawfish shells, rinsed (see Note)

1 large onion, chopped

2 leeks, white parts only, chopped

2 celery ribs, chopped

1 1/2 cups (21 ounces) crushed tomatoes

1 1/2 tablespoons tomato paste

3/4 cup dry white wine

3 sprigs each fresh thyme, tarragon, and flat-leaf parsley

2 small bay leaves

2 whole peppercorns

1 Heat the oil in a large saucepan or stockpot over medium heat. Add the fish bones and shells, onion, leeks, and celery. Stir until all parts are evenly distributed in the pan and coated with oil. Stir in the tomatoes and tomato paste and cover. Cook for 5 minutes without disturbing the pan.

2 Uncover the pan and pour in the wine. Bring to a simmer and reduce the wine by half. Add 2 quarts cold water and the herbs and peppercorns. Bring the broth to a simmer and continue to simmer over low heat for 25 minutes.

3 Strain the stock through a strainer placed over a large bowl. Discard all the solids. The stock can be refrigerated for 2 days or frozen for 1 month.

Note: Use the reserved shells from both the shrimp and the crayfish. Additional shrimp shells will be needed. Ask your fishmonger to save these for you or freeze shells from other recipes. Approximately 10 pounds of unpeeled shrimp will yield 2 pounds of shells.

But there are other enduring qualities that Sallie and I love about risotto. We first learned to cook it in Gattinara, at the home of the winemaker we were visiting. In that region of Italy risotto is a staple, an almost daily ritual. It's as comfortable as chili or mashed potatoes is in America. Sallie came to so love risotto that each time we sat down for a meal in Italy I'd ask her, "What do you feel like eating?" and invariably the answer was risotto.

Now, wherever we travel, risotto is like our suitcase dish: something we can cook for our hosts or travel companions. It's adaptable to whatever a region or a season has to offer. If we're near a coast, we look for local shellfish. In the fall we love a combination of squashes such as butternut, delicata, and kabocha, and shift the spices to nutmeg, cinnamon, and mace. In winter we love wild mushrooms and thyme. Of course, spring is when we add in those young vegetables with some tarragon or spring peas. And in summer the risotto contains okra, corn, or tomatoes.

Another virtue of this dish: leftovers. There's nothing more versatile than extra risotto. I like to stuff quail or turkey or chicken with it. Or I spread risotto on baking sheets, cover it with wax paper, and refrigerate it overnight. Then I cut it into squares, dredge the squares in flour, and panfry them for a great lunch entrée: crisped risotto squares with a spicy arugula salad.

Sallie and I still don't share as many meals together as we might like, but this gumbo-risotto has become so familiar it's like our home plate.

Winner of a Beard Award for Best Chef/Mid-Atlantic, Jeffrey Buben is chef and owner of two acclaimed Washington, D.C., restaurants: Vidalia, provincial American cooking delivered with southern hospitality, and Bistro Bis, creative contemporary French bistro cooking. Jeffrey is a 1978 graduate of the Culinary Institute of America and currently serves on the school's alumni board of directors. With over twenty years in the industry, he has worked in such notable establishments as the Sign of the Dove, Le Cygne, and Le Chantilly in New York and at distinguished hotels including the Four Seasons, the Mayflower, and the Hotel Pierre.

Jennifer Jasinski
SWEET PEA RISOTTO

My mom met her friend Stan when I was in elementary school. Eventually they bought a house together, and Stan took half the backyard and put in gardens:

SWEET PEA RISOTTO Serves 6

----

2 quarts chicken stock

4 tablespoons (^{1}/2 stick) unsalted butter

^{1}/2 cup minced onion

2 cups Carnaroli or Arborio rice

^{1}/3 cup white wine

2 cups shelled fresh English peas,
   blanched (frozen may be substituted;
   no blanching necessary)

1 cup Pea Mousse

^{3}/4 cup freshly grated Parmigiano-
   Reggiano or Grana Padano cheese

Salt and freshly ground white pepper

1 teaspoon white truffle oil

1 Pour the stock into a medium saucepan and bring to a boil over high heat. Reduce the heat and keep the liquid at a simmer while making the risotto.

2 Melt 3 tablespoons of the butter in a wide heavy pot. Add the onion and cook over medium heat until translucent, 3 to 5 minutes. Add the rice and stir to coat the grains with the butter. Pour in the wine and stir vigorously until the liquid has nearly evaporated, about 3 minutes.

3 Add 1 cup of the simmering stock to the rice, stirring constantly, until the rice absorbs it. Continue the process, adding the stock in ^{1}/2-cup increments until all of the stock is used and the risotto is cooked, 20 to 23 minutes. Taste the rice for doneness: it should be al dente.

4 Add the peas and warm thoroughly. Remove from the heat and stir in the Pea Mousse, the remaining 1 tablespoon butter, and cheese. Season with salt and pepper to taste and drizzle with the truffle oil.

✧ Spoon the risotto into warmed bowls.

six-foot-by-eight-foot planter boxes. We'd never grown anything before, even though this was Santa Barbara, which is not so much a city as a big orchard. Suddenly we were growing peas, corn, zucchini, carrots, rhubarb, tomatoes, lettuces—Stan rotated the crops every year. And he had a giant composter, a big chicken-wire barrel that he'd made (I didn't even know what com-

post was). We even grew avocado trees, which gave us more fruit than we could possibly consume. We'd take lemons and salt out into the yard and just eat the avocados right there in the yard.

Stan grew up on a farm in Kentucky, and he couldn't imagine not having a garden. Aside from vegetables, we grew raspberries and blackberries along the fences, and since my mother loved strawberries, Stan planted those in his beds, too, and she made summer jam.

Stan took complete care of the garden. My sister Jill would never eat a single thing from it, my brother was always off somewhere being too cool, and me, I'd come home from school, let out the dogs, our beagle-mutt Suzie (really a loaf of bread on legs) and our Irish setter Targa, and go sit out in the dirt among the garden's rows and eat all the berries and all the peas—the pods, too. Somehow, Mom and Stan never managed to harvest enough peas—even saving them up!—to serve a nice bowl of them for a real dinner.

Soon enough, I decided that all fruits and veggies tasted better right off the vine . . .

PEA MOUSSE Makes 2 cups

- 1 tablespoon plus 1 teaspoon salt
- 1 pound fresh shelled English peas (frozen can be substituted)
- 1 tablespoon unsalted butter
- 2 tablespoons chopped shallots
- 1 teaspoon sugar
- 1/4 teaspoon freshly ground white pepper
- 1/3 cup freshly grated Parmigiano-Reggiano or Grana Padano cheese
- 1/2 teaspoon chopped fresh mint leaves
- 1 teaspoon chopped fresh thyme leaves
- 1 tablespoon minced fresh flat-leaf parsley
- 1/2 cup mascarpone cheese
- 1 teaspoon white truffle oil

1 Bring a large pot of water to a boil. Add 1 tablespoon of the salt and the peas. Cook until barely tender, 10 to 12 minutes. Drain and immediately plunge the peas into ice water. (This not only cools the peas but helps to retain the bright color.) Drain the cooled peas and set aside. (If using frozen peas, simply defrost and skip step 1.)

2 Melt the butter in a small skillet. Add the shallots and cook over low heat until translucent, 3 to 5 minutes. Remove from the heat; scrape the shallots into a small bowl and place in the freezer to chill quickly.

3 Place the blanched peas in a food processor fitted with the steel blade and process until very smooth. Add the cooled shallots, the remaining teaspoon of salt, the sugar, pepper, grated cheese, mint, thyme, and parsley and continue to process. Pour the smooth puree through a fine-mesh strainer over a bowl. Gently whisk the mascarpone into the puree, then stir in the truffle oil. This mixture can be made 1 day in advance and refrigerated in an airtight container.

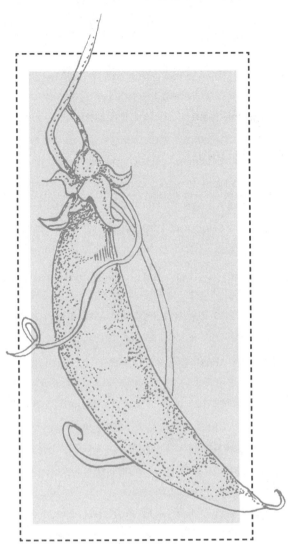

cooking more than my one night. I had lots of cookbooks, including my very important *Winnie the Pooh Cookbook,* and one with a big dragon on the cover with make-your-own-Shake'n'Bake chicken. As much as Stan loved cooking himself, he loved that I enjoyed it so much.

I have never lost my love of those sweet, precious peas. I include peas in my recipes all the time: for halibut, I make a white nage with blended peas and mint. I make a wonderful compote with cipolline onions, morels, and peas, to accompany quail. But the most fabulous may be this risotto with peas and mascarpone. It manages to have that fresh, snuck-from-the-garden taste.

Jennifer Jasinski, executive chef at Panzano, creates innovative northern Italian cuisine in her popular Denver, Colorado, restaurant. Her broad culinary experience began with education at the Culinary Institute of America and training at the Rainbow Room in New York City and includes several restaurants under the mentorship of Wolfgang Puck: Eureka in Los Angeles, Postrio in San Francisco, Spago in Las Vegas, and Granita in Malibu. She also worked as corporate chef at Wolfgang Puck Food Company.

but the English peas, shelling peas with that juicy little fruit inside, those I utterly loved.

My mom worked full-time, and she was going back to school in microbiology, which required a pretty long commute. So Stan and we kids did the cooking. My mother made a week's schedule, assigning us each a night to cook. But pretty soon I started

Martin Yan
HOME-STYLE CLAY POT

Each time I use a clay pot I see time passing and how much my world has changed. I was born in Kwang Zhou, once called Canton, and lived there until I was thirteen. It was the harshest of economic times, right before the Cultural Revolution, and most people had very little; everything from meat to cooking oil was rationed.

My mother cooked all our meals on a little wood burner with two cast-iron woks and a couple of clay pots. And it's the clay pots that hold so many emotions and memories—it's as if memories were held inside the clay pots just the way they would retain heat all through the meal. (In the winter we'd even warm our hands around the clay pots on the table; there's no central heating in China—even now.) The pots were dark and blackened from use on the outside, but the insides were shiny with glaze.

There's so much clay in southern China, just as in Mexico, so earthenware is used in every kitchen. There are stores that sell nothing but clay pots in dozens of sizes, shapes, and designs. There's always a bucket of water at the front of the store. To inspect a pot, you knock on the clay to make sure it rings with an even, solid feel, then you dunk the pot in the water to check for possible cracks.

My grandmother and my aunts and uncles often shared our meals, and my mother could make a number of dishes with just a few pieces of cookware. She used the smaller clay pot for casseroles or other simple dishes. She had a bigger, taller clay pot for soups. And then she had a couple with handles for making rice, to which she'd often add Chinese sausage, preserved side pork, or duck. The dishes could then be served in the pots (which meant fewer pots to clean up!), and the contents would stay warm inside much longer.

The clay pot is perfect for slow- or long-cooked dishes because above the fire the earthenware heats evenly and slowly. And when rice cooks in the pot, the rice starch at the bottom caramelizes and that wonderful aroma permeates the entire pot of rice. (You

HOME-STYLE CLAY POT

Serves 6

----

2 tablespoons vegetable oil

2 teaspoons minced fresh ginger

1/4 pound Chinese preserved duck, cut
   into 1-inch slices (see Note), or boneless
   skinless chicken thighs, cut into 2-inch
   pieces

2 cups long-grain rice

3 cups chicken stock

1/4 pound Chinese roast pork (char siu;
   see Note), diced into 1/4-inch pieces

2 Chinese sausages, cut diagonally into
   1/4-inch slices (see Note)

1 tablespoon soy sauce or oyster sauce

2 teaspoons toasted sesame oil

2 baby bok choy, thinly sliced

2 teaspoons chopped fresh cilantro

1 Heat a 2-quart clay pot or heavy saucepan over high heat until hot. Add the oil and swirl it around the bottom of the pot. Stir in the ginger and cook for 10 seconds. (If using the chicken meat rather than the duck breast, add the chicken now and stir-fry for 2 minutes.) Add the rice and stock and bring to a boil.

2 Lay the preserved duck, roast pork, and sausage pieces on top of the rice. Reduce the heat to medium-high and cook, uncovered, for 8 to 10 minutes or until the surface of the rice develops small craters or holes. Reduce the heat to low and cook, covered, for an additional 10 minutes. Turn off the heat and steam the rice, covered, for 10 minutes.

3 Add the soy sauce, sesame oil, bok choy, and cilantro; mix well and replace the cover. Steam for 5 minutes.

✛ Present the clay pot in the middle of the table, allowing each person to take portions of the meats as well as the rice.

Note: Chinese preserved duck, Chinese sausages (usually frozen), and roast pork can be found at Asian markets.

can't get that effect with an electric rice cooker!)

One more wonderful quality of the clay pot is when you've almost emptied it, there's the crispiest rice baked onto the bottom surface. (It's how the rice for sizzling rice soup was first made.) After most of the rice had been removed, my mom would pour leftover tea or broth into the pot, then stir it around, and that not only helped to dislodge the rice crust from the pot but also made a very tasty rice soup.

So now that all this time has passed and nearly everything is available to me in terms of modern cookware (anodized, nonstick, cast aluminum . . .), there are still times when nothing appeals to me, from an emotional or a culinary perspective, like an old blackened clay pot.

Martin Yan, celebrated host of more than eighteen hundred cooking shows, including the popular *Yan Can Cook*, is a teacher, author, respected food and restaurant consultant, and certified Master Chef. His twenty-five cookbooks include *Martin Yan's Asian Favorites* and the award-winning *Chinese Cooking for Dummies*. Martin is a recipient of many national and international recognitions, ranging from an Emmy Award to a Beard Foundation Award for Best TV Food Journalism. He is a 2001 inductee of the Beard Foundation's D'Artagnan Cervena Who's Who of Food & Beverage in America.

Takashi Yagihashi
ROASTED AMISH CHICKEN AND SHRIMP WITH ASIAN NOODLE SALAD

On the same block where my family lived in Mito (a midsize city, ten miles from the Pacific Ocean and a hundred miles from Tokyo), there was a great noodle shop owned by one of my father's friends. Noodle shops are a way of life in Japan, and they're everywhere. Most people eat fast, inexpensive lunches there, and the variety of noodle dishes they offer is amazing: different broths (with shoyu or miso or chicken stocks) and different noodles (thin rice noodles, thicker egg noodles, soba wheat noodles), and then dozens of garnishes you can add. Some noodle shops even let you customize your own dishes.

I would walk there and have lunch by myself, or sometimes my mother and father would join me at the counter. There were maybe ten seats, and the noodle maker would cook and serve everyone while talking with us about his family or the local news. Sometimes I'd start with *gyoza* (filled dumplings) or the steamed *shu mai* dumplings, but then it was always one of two favorite noodle dishes. My year-round choice was a kind of Thai noodle dish: a clear broth with rice noodles and braised beef and tripe, Thai basil, cilantro, bean sprouts, and a lime to squeeze on top—very light but still sustaining.

But all year long I waited for summer, when the best dish of all was available: cold noodles (no one offers cold noodles in cold weather) that's almost a salad with all the

ROASTED AMISH CHICKEN AND SHRIMP WITH ASIAN NOODLE SALAD Serves 4

as a main course, 6 to 8 as an appetizer

One $\frac{1}{2}$-pound boneless chicken breast, skin on (preferably Amish or free-range)

Salt and freshly ground black pepper

12 to 16 cooked jumbo shrimp, shelled and deveined

1 recipe Citrus Vinaigrette

1 pound dried Asian egg noodles, cooked according to package directions and tossed with 2 teaspoons vegetable oil

1 cup pea pods, blanched and julienned

1 cup thinly sliced red onion

1 cup fresh bean sprouts

1 medium carrot, julienned

2 cups coarsely shredded iceberg lettuce

1 seedless cucumber, sliced into thin disks

2 teaspoons chile oil

$\frac{1}{2}$ cup sesame seeds

1 Preheat the oven to 450°F.

2 Season the chicken with salt and pepper. Heat an ovenproof skillet over medium heat and set the chicken inside, skin side down.

Cook until golden brown, 3 to 4 minutes. Turn the breast over and cook 2 more minutes. Transfer the pan to the oven and roast for 5 minutes or until the meat is cooked through but moist. Transfer the chicken to a plate, cool completely, then cut into thin slices.

3 Butterfly the cooked shrimp: with a paring knife, starting at the inside curve of the shrimp, cut three-quarters of the way through the flesh. Gently open the "halves," keeping the shrimp in one piece. Five minutes before serving, toss the shrimp with $\frac{1}{4}$ cup Citrus Vinaigrette.

4 Combine the noodles, pea pods, onion, sprouts, carrot, and lettuce in a bowl. Toss with 1 cup Citrus Vinaigrette.

✤ To serve the salad, divide and arrange the strips of chicken among the plates. Form a 4- to 5-inch circle of cucumber disks on top of the chicken. Mound a large spoonful of the noodle mixture on top of the cucumbers. Place 2 or more shrimp on each plate. Toss the remaining $\frac{3}{4}$ cup vinaigrette with the chile oil and drizzle it around the plate, outside the cucumber circle. Scatter sesame seeds on top.

fresh garnishes that go on it. Every noodle shop does it a little differently, but typically they all have the chilled noodles, shrimp and chicken, cucumbers, and maybe roasted pork, pickled ginger, bean sprouts, or boiled eggs. Some noodle shops even put ice right on the noodles, as if to tell customers to eat quickly before the ice melts and you lose the great flavors. My mother would make a version of this dish at home as well. It's casual, homey food, but it's full of bright, contrasting flavors gathered together in the summer.

When I make these noodles today, I often use yuzu juice, though that fruit can be hard to find here in the States. Sometimes I can find bottled fresh yuzu juice from Japan at great Asian markets. It has an extra tartness and fragrance that's unique. If you can find it, replace the orange juice in this recipe with an equal amount of yuzu juice, but add a bit more sugar.

Takashi Yagihashi is executive chef of Tribute, in Farmington Hills, Michigan, which serves "contemporary French cuisine with an eclectic Asian twist." Takashi was born in an oceanside town northeast of Tokyo, studied interior design in Japan, and moved to the United States to experience the freedom offered by American kitchens. A Beard Foundation nominee for Best Chef/Midwest, and one of *Food & Wine*'s Ten Best New Chefs of 2000, Takashi often lends his culinary expertise to help raise money for those in need, most recently Chefs Across America, aiding families of the September 11th attacks.

CITRUS VINAIGRETTE Makes 2 cups

$3/4$ cup fresh lemon juice (5 lemons)

2 cups fresh orange juice (5 oranges)

$1/3$ cup sugar

$1 1/2$ teaspoons *togarashi* (ground red chile mixture, available at Asian markets)

$1 1/2$ teaspoons Dijon mustard

2 tablespoons soy sauce

2 tablespoons toasted sesame oil

$3/4$ cup canola oil

1 Combine the juices in a small nonreactive saucepan over high heat and reduce the liquid to 1 cup. Let cool.

2 Combine the sugar, *togarashi*, and mustard in a bowl. Whisk in the soy sauce and the oils. Gently whisk in the reduced juice. The dressing can be prepared 1 day ahead of time and stored in an airtight container.

SEAFOOD

Todd Gray
WEEZIE'S SOFT-SHELL CRABS WITH NEW BAY SEASONING

Robert Kinkead
FRIED IPSWICH CLAMS WITH FRIED LEMONS

Michael Lomonaco
SARDE A BECCAFICO (ROASTED STUFFED FRESH SARDINES)

Traci Des Jardins
GRANDPA DES JARDINS' SHRIMP CREOLE

Sara Moulton
GREEK-STYLE GRILLED FISH, WITH GRILLED EGGPLANT, TOMATO, AND FETA STACKS

Lisa Schroeder
MOROCCAN POACHED HALIBUT

Floyd Cardoz
GOAN PAN-ROASTED COD WITH KANJI AND PICKLED MANGO

Tom Condron
ROASTED WILD SCOTTISH SALMON WITH CRUSHED ENGLISH PEAS, WILD SPRING ONIONS, AND MOREL VINAIGRETTE

Paul Kahan
SEARED WALLEYE WITH VERJUICE AND WALNUT OIL

Frank Bonanno
MUSTARD-CRUSTED FLOUNDER WITH A LEMON CAPER SAUCE

Joanne Bondy
MARINATED TROUT WITH BLUE CHEESE GRITS AND MUSHROOMS

Todd Gray WEEZIE'S SOFT-SHELL CRABS WITH NEW BAY SEASONING

The Chesapeake Bay was where we spent our weekends as a family. We have a grand wooden racing boat, a Hinckley named *Allegro,* and when we weren't fishing or crabbing, we'd be sailing.

I particularly loved soft-shelling with my father on the James River, on the lower part of the bay. The walk down to the river's edge was steep and rocky (half the fun was trying to carry all the gear!). The only sounds that broke the stillness were the faint horns of distant tugboats and fishing vessels. The spectacular and huge osprey and the lanky blue herons were so abundant. And this was truly locals territory: no tourists in sight. Just well-manicured lawns with neighborhood kids racing back and forth. But in *my* world there was only me, my brother, my dad, and a river full of crabs.

Soft-shells are Maryland blue crabs in the process of molting: they shed their hard shells and generate a new one. But for those two weeks before the new shell hardens, the whole crab is edible, and there's no need to spend hours picking meat out of the hard shells.

(Don't get me wrong: we loved hard-shells, too, but they came with a whole different set of rituals. You pile the steamed whole crabs on a table with a newspaper "tablecloth." There's hammering. There's twisting the legs free. There's jimmying with a knife. There's prying up the thinner shell on the belly to "unlatch" the carapace—the male crabs have the Washington Monument formed in the shell; the females have the Capitol. There's a heap of shells growing on the table. You swat at the flies—an inevitable part of the experience. And, in this region, there's a time-honored sense of pride regarding the speed and the quantity of meat you can pick.)

My brother, my dad, and I would fashion chicken-wire baskets, attach a line to each, and scoop the soft-shells right off the river floor. In those early years of the 1970s, crabs were abundant: we would get as many as thirty or forty in an hour. Today we'd be lucky to find two dozen in the same hour.

We would haul the crabs back to the house in cardboard boxes lined with wet newspaper. My mom, Weezie (short for Louise), would clean them, toss each one in a bag of flour, salt, pepper, and Old Bay Seasoning, and then shake the bag so they'd be well coated. Then she'd melt butter in her skillet and brown the crabs. When she wanted an upscale presentation, she'd

WEEZIE'S SOFT-SHELL CRABS WITH NEW BAY SEASONING

Serves 6

----

4 cups all-purpose flour

1 tablespoon salt

³/₄ teaspoon freshly cracked white pepper

2 teaspoons New Bay Seasoning

12 soft-shell crabs (ask your fishmonger to clean them)

¹/₂ pound (2 sticks) unsalted butter, clarified, plus 4 tablespoons (¹/₂ stick)

Juice of 2 lemons

2 tablespoons chopped fresh parsley

1 tablespoon extra virgin olive oil

3 ears fresh corn, kernels scraped from the cob (3 cups)

6 to 8 ounces fresh pea shoots (available at Asian markets or specialty greengrocers)

1 Preheat the oven to 200°F.

2 Place the flour and seasonings in a large paper bag, seal, and shake to combine. Add the crabs 2 at a time and shake carefully. Place the coated crabs on a tray.

3 Heat the clarified butter in a large heavy skillet. Sauté the crabs, in 2 or 3 batches, for 3 minutes on each side. Transfer them to a tray and keep warm in the oven.

4 Wipe the grease from the pan and add the 4 tablespoons butter, lemon juice, and parsley, whisking all together. Transfer to a bowl and keep warm.

5 Heat the olive oil in a small skillet over medium-high heat and sauté the corn and pea shoots together until the shoots wilt, 3 to 4 minutes.

✣ Place a small amount of corn and pea shoots in the center of 6 plates. Top with 2 crabs. Spoon the lemon-parsley butter over all.

NEW BAY SEASONING

Makes ¹/₂ cup

----

¹/₄ cup fine sea salt

2 rounded tablespoons celery seeds

1 rounded teaspoon mustard seeds

Rounded ¹/₂ teaspoon fennel seeds

¹/₈ teaspoon freshly ground white pepper

¹/₈ teaspoon cayenne pepper

¹/₄ teaspoon ground allspice

1 tablespoon paprika

3 bay leaves

1 teaspoon grated fresh ginger

¹/₄ teaspoon ground cinnamon

Combine all the ingredients in a spice grinder or food processor and grind to a fine powder. Store in an airtight container for up to 3 months. New Bay Seasoning can be ordered from www.equinoxrestaurant.com.

add lemon wedges and parsley. But she made her own cocktail sauce, her own tartar sauce, and an unbeatable potato salad with sweet onions and mustard. There's nothing more Lower Bay than summer softies and potato salad.

Other nights, we'd run in to Newport News for supplies and to check out what the local fishermen had caught: oysters, clams, rockfish, croaker, and spot. As the sun went down and our sunburns set in, the air would thicken with the smell of salt and fresh fish.

Back on the porch for Weezie's "happy hour," Mom and Dad had their whiskey sours and shrimp cocktails, or maybe oysters on the half-shell, and we kids had clam dip with chips while we played Twister and Monopoly until the sun set and dinner was served.

Today my wife, Ellen, and I take our son crabbing, and this recipe is how I cook the soft-shells, updating the Old Bay Seasoning. The flavors in my blend are much fresher and brighter; you can taste each component in the finished crab. I grind all the spices, and I even cook up my own celery salt—and that really boosts the flavor. But we also sell our New Bay Seasoning from the restaurant for anyone who'd rather be enjoying a sunset on the Chesapeake than grinding spices indoors.

Todd Gray attended the University of Richmond as well as the Culinary institute of America. After spending seven years at the famed Galileo, he opened Equinox, two blocks from the White House, with his wife, Ellen. Reviving and reinventing the classic cuisine of the Chesapeake Bay, Equinox has earned both local and national accolades and awards, including a Beard Best Chef nomination.

Robert Kinkead FRIED IPSWICH CLAMS WITH FRIED LEMONS

From the age of eight I spent my summers on Cape Cod, where my grandfather had a house that he'd bought years and years earlier. When I was older, I worked summer jobs on the cape. I even married a woman from the cape. Late summer through early fall is peak time for great foods in that area. Farm markets are crammed with bushels of produce. We'd cook fresh succotash with shell beans and corn and make fantastic tomato salads. We'd have fresh corn on the cob, pies and cobblers with all the plums, peaches, apples, and pears, and the seafood, of course, was unbeatable, from the lobsters to the local fish.

FRIED IPSWICH CLAMS WITH FRIED LEMONS Serves 6

For the lemons

3 lemons, cut into $1/8$-inch slices

1 tablespoon salt

1 tablespoon sugar

For the clams

48 Ipswich or other soft-shell clams
   (also known as steamers)

Peanut oil for frying

2 cups all-purpose flour

1 teaspoon salt

$1/2$ teaspoon freshly ground black pepper

$1/4$ teaspoon cayenne pepper or to taste

2 cups buttermilk

1 recipe Tartar Sauce

1 Shuck the clams if you have purchased them in the shell. Slide an oyster knife into the unhinged side of each clam, carefully prying open the shells. Slice the knife around the margin of the clam meat, scraping the bottom shell to loosen the clam in one piece. Discard the shells. Slip off and discard the black sheath surrounding the siphon (the small "neck"). Rinse the shucked clams in running cold water.

2 Place the lemon slices on a tray and sprinkle both sides with salt and sugar. Transfer the slices to a rack and place in a dry area for 3 hours so the lemons can dehydrate. Rinse well in cold water and pat dry. Set aside.

3 Heat the peanut oil to 350°F in a deep pot. Stir together the flour, salt, and peppers in a mixing bowl. Pour the buttermilk into a second, shallow bowl.

4 Fry the lemon slices first: dip each slice into the buttermilk and then into the seasoned flour. Fry the slices in small batches until they just turn golden brown, 1 to 2 minutes. Transfer to a tray lined with paper towels. The lemons can be fried 1 hour in advance and kept in a warm oven.

5 Remove any of the cooked lemon particles from the oil using a small metal strainer or a long-handled slotted spoon.

6 Dip each clam into the buttermilk and then into the seasoned flour. Place them in the hot oil individually (they tend to clump together). Cook until crispy and brown, 3 to 4 minutes. Remove from the oil and transfer to a tray lined with paper towels. Sprinkle with salt and pepper to taste.

✤ Arrange the clams on a warm tray with a bowl of Tartar Sauce and the fried lemons.

TARTAR SAUCE Makes 2 cups

---

1 large egg yolk

1 small egg

1/2 tablespoon fresh lemon juice

1 tablespoon red wine vinegar

1/2 tablespoon Dijon mustard

1/2 teaspoon sugar

Salt and freshly ground black pepper

1 cup peanut oil

6 cornichons, finely diced

1 tablespoon drained capers, finely diced

1/2 small onion, minced (1/4 cup)

1/2 tablespoon chopped fresh chives

Combine the yolk, egg, lemon juice, vinegar, mustard, sugar, and salt and pepper to taste in the bowl of a food processor. Process for 30 seconds. With the machine on, add a thin, steady stream of oil until the mayonnaise is emulsified (smooth, thick, and creamy). Fold in the remaining ingredients, taste, and adjust the seasonings.

More than ten years ago, when I opened Kinkead's in Washington, D.C., I knew that I wanted to feature some of the New England dishes that I'd grown up loving. I could only hope that they'd catch on here. I tried baked stuffed clams—called "stuffies" on the cape—which are chopped-up clams with chorizo and peppers that are breaded and baked. They didn't go over real well. I tried clam cakes, which are more like clam fritters. Not those, either. And folks didn't really take to steamers. But the lobster roll and the fried clams were instant successes. They are both the kinds of food that make anyone who's ever lived near a beach just light up the moment they're spotted on a menu.

Now, I know Ipswich clams from Cape Ann aren't always available, and there's simply no good alternative; you can use fried clam strips in this recipe, but you'll have to picture me cringing over your shoulder. You simply need freshly shucked soft-shell clams.

As for the lemons here, which are hardly traditional cape fare, I was inspired by Moroccan salted lemons and pickled lemons, and since lemons are traditionally squeezed on the clams, I wanted to do some variation with dried and fried lemons. When I first served this dish, I remember a woman came up to me and exclaimed,

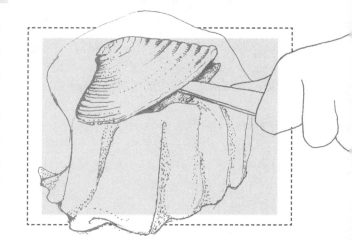

"Those are the best clams I've ever eaten—and the potatoes are *unbelievable!* They have the most intense lemon flavor! Where did you get them?" I told her they were very special ones that grew on trees.

Note: If you're in a creative, Moroccan mood, try frying oranges with the same technique; they're perfect with a lamb dish. Or you might try fried limes with conch fritters.

Winner of a Beard Award for Best Chef/Mid-Atlantic, Robert Kinkead is chef and owner of the four-star restaurant Kinkead's in Washington, D.C. Bob adapts unique dishes from around the world to American ingredients and tastes, resulting in light, yet intensely flavored, dishes. In September 2001 he opened Colvin Run Tavern in Fairfax, Virginia. Bob serves on the board of directors at Sullivan College's National Center for Hospitality Studies and as president of the Council of Independent Restaurant Owners. His successes include Twenty-One Federal, the D.C. restaurant that launched him into national prominence.

Michael Lomonaco
SARDE A BECCAFICO (ROASTED STUFFED FRESH SARDINES)

My mother was a good home cook. In Brooklyn, where I grew up, she prepared the Italian specialties of her hometown, an isolated hill town near Mount Etna. Historically the *mezzogiorno* part of Italy—that crescent south of Rome that runs from the shin to the toe of Italy's boot—is where most of the Italians in this country emigrated from at the turn of the twentieth century.

People from that part of Italy have been known for their cooking for more than three thousand years, when the Greeks took Sicilians back to their country to serve as cooks. Sicilians have a great respect for food, founded somewhat on the scarcity of ingredients. Much of their cooking took . . . well, *courage!* Can you imagine being the first to cook an artichoke, cardoons, sea urchins?

I was served these roasted sardines by my wife Diane's grandmother, Josephine Spadaro, who, at ninety-eight years of age, is a superb chef, and I mean that literally, even though she's been a home cook all her life. Josephine's marinated eggplant is perfect. Her hand in seasoning is flawless.

SARDE A BECCAFICO (ROASTED STUFFED FRESH SARDINES) Serves 6 to 8

----

3 pounds (15 to 18) fresh sardines

$^1/_4$ cup plus 2 tablespoons extra virgin olive oil

1 medium onion, diced (1 cup)

1 cup fresh Italian bread crumbs

$^1/_4$ cup grated pecorino cheese

$^1/_4$ cup finely chopped fresh flat-leaf parsley

$^1/_4$ cup dried currants, plumped in hot water to cover for 15 minutes

$^1/_4$ cup pine nuts

1 tablespoon each freshly grated lemon zest and freshly grated orange zest

15 to 20 fresh bay leaves

Salt and freshly cracked black pepper

6 to 8 lemon wedges

1 Clean and gut the sardines (or ask the fishmonger to do this). Split open each fish like a book, flattening it slightly. Rinse under cold water for 5 minutes. Pat dry.

2 Preheat the oven to 375°F.

3 Heat 2 tablespoons of the olive oil in a medium skillet over medium heat. Add the onion, reduce the heat to low, and sauté until the pieces are translucent, 7 to 8 minutes. Add the bread crumbs and cook until the crumbs turn golden, an additional 2 to 3 minutes. Remove from the heat and mix in the cheese, parsley, currants, pine nuts, and zests. Set aside.

4 Place the opened fillets in a large nonreactive baking pan (or 2 smaller ones), skin side down (the fillets should be snug but not overlapping). Cover each cavity with a spoonful of filling. Insert bay leaves like partitions between the fish. Season lightly with salt and pepper and drizzle with the remaining $^1/_4$ cup olive oil.

5 Place the baking dish(es) in the oven and bake for 15 to 20 minutes or until the fish have cooked completely.

✛ To serve, place 2 or 3 sardine fillets on each plate and garnish with lemon wedges.

She has utter surety making sausages. Over thirty years I've eaten so many meals she's cooked: pasta with cauliflower and saffron, spaghetti with escarole . . . she's an encyclopedia when it comes to Sicilian foods.

Josephine taught me so much about authentic cooking, and this recipe is a family heirloom—from the bigger family of the

Sicilians in my life—and it's one of the joys of the table. It takes an odd little fish, with just enough oil under the skin to make it succulent, and with the brininess still on its skin, and combines it with the sweet and sour elements the Sicilians gathered from the Arabic and Spanish cultures that dominated their history. So it's tiny raisins, lemon juice, a frugal use of bread crumbs, the bay leaf plucked from the bush in your backyard, and the fresh sardines. As for the name, the *beccafico* (Italian for "fig pecker") is a small songbird like a blackcap or warbler, and it's said that when you clean and stuff this unattractive little fish in this special manner, you transform it into a beautiful songbird, the *beccafico*. Italians love to romanticize.

When my wife, Diane, and I vacationed in Sicily in 1996, it was the first chance either of us had to meet family members we'd known only from the stories we'd each heard growing up. Of course the trip ended up being not just a discovery of who these people were but also a discovery of who we were as Americans of Sicilian ancestry. The moment we arrived, we both felt as if we'd come to a place that felt like home: the people, the language, the cooking was so familiar but brought to life in a culture where this wasn't marginal or unique—it was dominant.

So the first time I ordered the *sarde a beccafico,* I wasn't enjoying it simply as an American chef of Sicilian heritage—no, it came with the richness of a culture being rediscovered. I was devouring an authentic flavor in the very setting where it is most prized, in a culture that so values people savoring food together. It was a once-in-a-lifetime moment, being welcomed by family you never really knew in a home and a homeland you never really understood was yours.

Michael Lomonaco was executive chef/director of Windows on the World. His inspired revitalization of New York's "21," coupled with his popularity as the charismatic host of Discovery Channel's *Epicurious* and the Food Network's *Michael's Place,* has made Michael one of America's most popular culinary stars. He is coauthor of the best-selling *The "21" Cookbook,* as well as a new book that takes the mystery out of creative home cooking. Michael has devoted much energy to Share Our Strength, City Harvest, and health-related charities. He is cofounder of Windows of Hope, the fund that aids families of food-service workers lost in the September 11th attacks.

Traci Des Jardins
GRANDPA DES JARDINS' SHRIMP CREOLE

Food has always been the center of my family's gatherings. My mom is Mexican, so my maternal grandparents shared dishes like chile verde, fresh tortillas, menudo, and Spanish rice. My paternal grandmother, of Nordic descent, was a terrific baker: fresh dinner rolls, delicious rhubarb pie, and all kinds of cookies. My paternal grandfather's passion for food came from his Louisiana upbringing. He left the bayous when he was a teenager to come west to California's Central Valley and started farming: cotton, sugar beets, and a Japanese-style short-grain rice. Yet he never lost his passion for fresh seafood. His only options were to beg one of his children traveling from the coast to pick some up for him or to drive the two hours to and from the coast. He did both with great frequency.

Every September we'd have some big family gathering around harvest time, and Grandpa would organize all of the cousins to go crawdad catching. We'd arm ourselves with rubber boots, small buckets, big buckets, and nets, and we'd set forth to capture the little creatures. My grandfather always told me I was the best at it (I am quite sure he told us all the same thing), and I was determined to fill my buckets faster than anyone else. I'd creep into the shallows barefoot, trying not to muddy the water, and then grab the unsuspecting crawdad right behind the pincers. We suffered many pinched fingers and toes, but at the end of the day we'd have a huge sense of accomplishment. Then, later, there'd be even more to accomplish: after the crawdad boil, there was peeling. And more peeling.

Thanksgiving was our biggest gathering, and it still is. The holiday always began Wednesday night with Grandpa Dick's shrimp Creole. We all pitched in to peel the shrimp—or *not* (there was always discussion over whether it's best to cook them in the shells or peel them first).

The kitchen filled with the aroma of frying pork, onions, and peppers; bubbling tomato sauce; and, of course, the wonderful scent of shrimp simmering away. And there was rice, always rice, usually in lieu of bread.

The following days were spent hunting duck and pheasant. We cooked the turkeys on the grills, along with lambs from the local Basque sheep herders, and suckling pigs twirling on the rotisserie. Thanksgiving was five full days of eating, drinking, and enjoying each other's company. But of all that we ate the favorite dish—even after three generations of preparing foods—had to be shrimp Creole.

GRANDPA DES JARDINS' SHRIMP CREOLE Serves 8 to 10

1 pound coarsely ground pork shoulder

1/2 teaspoon dried thyme

1/2 teaspoon dried basil

1/2 teaspoon dried oregano

1/2 teaspoon cayenne pepper

6 celery ribs, diced

2 medium onions, diced

2 green bell peppers, seeded and diced

2 garlic cloves, minced

1 cup red wine

1 1/2 pounds fresh or one 10-ounce can whole plum tomatoes, slightly chopped or crushed

3 tablespoons tomato paste

2 cups Shellfish Stock

5 pounds jumbo (15-to-16 count) shrimp, peeled and cleaned, shells and heads reserved

1 bunch scallions, chopped

8 cups steamed short-grain white rice

3 tablespoons chopped fresh flat-leaf parsley

1 Brown the pork in a large heavy skillet. Pour off the excess fat. Add the dried herbs and spices, celery, onions, and green peppers. Cook over medium-high heat until the vegetables are translucent, about 10 minutes. Add the garlic and cook for 5 more minutes. 2 Stir in the wine, tomatoes, and tomato paste, stirring to incorporate. Cook for 10 minutes. Pour in the stock and simmer, covered, for 45 minutes.

3 Add the cleaned shrimp and scallions to the sauce and simmer until the shrimp are just cooked, 5 to 8 minutes.

✣ Place a generous spoonful of hot rice in warmed bowls and cover with the Shrimp Creole. Sprinkle with chopped parsley.

SHELLFISH STOCK Makes 2 cups

Reserved shells and heads from the cleaned shrimp

1/2 onion, coarsely chopped

2 celery ribs, coarsely chopped

1 leek, coarsely chopped

1 carrot

2 garlic cloves

3 cups chicken stock

Place the shrimp shells and heads in a large saucepan. Add the remaining ingredients and simmer for 1 hour. Strain, pressing the shells and vegetables to release all of the cooking liquid.

Sara Moulton GREEK-STYLE GRILLED FISH, WITH GRILLED EGGPLANT, TOMATO, AND FETA STACKS

I was fifteen when I visited Greece for the first time—just the right age to be absolutely stunned by the country. My older sister and I were on spring break with my mom, the walking encyclopedia, who was on a mission to improve our minds with a tour of the ruins. Moved though I was by all the awesome history, I was really knocked out by the country's eternal, natural charms. I had never seen a place so beautiful—the contrast of the blue Mediterranean with the white houses was startling. And the food! I already lived to eat, but this was a revelation—how could food so simple be so intensely flavorful?

Our most memorable meal was lunch at a dockside restaurant near Piraeus. My mom had taken the trouble to assemble an eclectic bunch of about a dozen guests. These included a Greek movie director, an American painter, and a pair of well-connected Athenian ladies accompanied by a little white poodle named Frou Frou. My favorite guest was introduced to us as an Australian scholar. He was maybe twenty-eight and devastatingly handsome. It turned out he wrote pornography on the side.

The group of us spent four hours eating lunch. We sat outside on the dock at a big, long table. I'm sure they served us many appetizers, the usual dips, and the crusty bread I had already come to love. We washed it all down with retsina, the resin-flavored Greek wine with an aftertaste like rocket fuel. It is bone dry and perfect with Greek food. It cuts right through all the olive oil.

When it came time to order our entrées,

GREEK-STYLE GRILLED FISH

Serves 4

1/4 cup extra virgin olive oil, plus
   additional for brushing and drizzling
2 tablespoons fresh lemon juice plus
   1 lemon, cut into wedges, for garnish
2 tablespoons finely chopped fresh
   oregano leaves
Salt and freshly ground black pepper
Four 6-ounce striped bass fillets with skin,
   boned and rinsed
1 recipe Grilled Eggplant, Tomato, and
   Feta Stacks

1 Whisk together the 1/4 cup olive oil, the lemon juice, oregano, and salt and pepper to taste. Pour the marinade into a large resealable plastic bag and add the fish.

Seal the bag and turn it several times to coat the fish. Refrigerate the bag for 30 minutes, turning it once after 15 minutes.

2 Prepare a grill so that one side is hot (you should be able to hold your hand about 5 inches above the grill for no more than 2 seconds).

3 Drain the fish and pat dry with paper towels. Place the fish on a tray, lightly brush with olive oil, and season with salt and pepper.

4 Place the fillets, skin side down, on the hot part of the grill and cook for 3 minutes. Turn the fish over and grill for 2 to 3 more minutes or until just cooked through.

✢ Place the fillets on warm plates. Drizzle with olive oil and garnish with lemon wedges. Accompany with the Grilled Eggplant, Tomato, and Feta Stacks.

---

each of us went into the restaurant and chose a fish from a tankful that had been caught that morning and were still swimming around. Simply grilled, the fish was served up perfectly fresh and sweet. It was a real eye-opener for someone who was sure up until that moment that she didn't even like fish.

Meanwhile, the retsina was kicking in and everyone was getting very relaxed, me

included. This was the first liquor ever to pass my lips. Our Australian "scholar" turned my way and declared that I looked like Alice in Wonderland. What a wonderful compliment! I thought. At the other end of the table my mother was engrossed in a conversation of her own. During dessert our scholar held up an apple and wondered if I knew which was its sweetest part. I did not. I had never heard of such a thing. It is the *bottom* of the

GRILLED EGGPLANT, TOMATO, AND FETA STACKS Serves 4

----

3 tablespoons red wine vinegar

2 teaspoons minced fresh rosemary

Salt and freshly ground black pepper

$1/4$ cup plus 2 tablespoons extra virgin olive oil

1 medium eggplant (1 pound)

2 medium tomatoes ($3/4$ pound)

$1/4$ pound feta cheese, crumbled

1 Prepare the grill so that the temperature on one side is hot and the other is just medium-low (you should be able to hold your hand 5 inches above the grill for about 5 seconds).

2 Whisk together the vinegar, rosemary, and salt and pepper to taste. Slowly whisk in the olive oil.

3 Peel the eggplant and cut crosswise into $1/3$-inch slices (12 slices total). Cut the tomatoes crosswise into $1/3$-inch slices (8 slices total). Place the vegetables on a tray and brush generously with the dressing.

4 On the grill's hot side, grill the eggplant until just cooked through, 2 to 3 minutes per side, brushing with more of the dressing. Grill the tomato slices for 1 minute per side. (The vegetables should retain their shape.) Transfer the vegetables to a tray as they finish grilling.

5 Arrange 4 stacks of vegetables on the cooler side of the grill: start with the eggplant, add a slice of tomato, then add some crumbled cheese. Repeat. Top each stack with a third slice of eggplant. Cover the grill and cook the stacks for 3 to 5 more minutes or until the feta melts. Serve immediately.

apple, he sagely informed me. I was smitten. I wasn't sure why he was telling me this little nugget, but I was delighted that he bothered to talk to me at all.

After dessert my sister and I walked to the end of the dock to look out at the Mediterranean. The sky seemed to be coming down. The sea rose up to meet it. Then it occurred to me that I'd drunk a little too much retsina. But I was very happy. —SM

A graduate of the Culinary Institute of America, Sara Moulton worked at the Harvest Restaurant in Cambridge, La Tulipe in Manhattan, and Cybele's in Boston, where she worked on the acclaimed PBS series *Julia Child and More Company*. In 1982 she cofounded the New York Women's Culinary Alliance. She joined *Gourmet* as a food editor in 1984 and now works as its executive chef. Sara worked in various capacities for ABC-TV's

---

Lisa Schroeder
MOROCCAN POACHED HALIBUT

I was brought up to be a Zionist, and in 1975, at seventeen, I moved from Philadelphia to Israel to attend Hebrew University and to help "settle the Jewish homeland." After a single month there I met my future husband, a Moroccan Jew raised in Paris. His father and mother were amazing cooks and together took great pains to prepare traditional Jewish-Moroccan dishes whenever they came to visit. I was often their faithful assistant, learning to cook all their specialties so I could impress their son after they returned to Paris.

Fridays were spent preparing the Sabbath meals—Friday dinner and Saturday lunch—when observant Jews set all work aside, which includes cooking. The day would begin with a thorough housecleaning, followed by a trip to *Machane Yehuda,* the open-air market. We'd purchase the most beautiful tomatoes and peppers for the traditional salads; chicken and meats for the main course; and tilapia that would be pulled from a tank of water, batted on the head, then cleaned and sliced into fillets right on the spot. Then it would be home with our heavy bags, dreading the painful climb up four flights of steps.

All the meals needed to be prepared before sundown, beginning with the poached fish, which could rest at room temperature until dinner. We'd make zucchini stuffed with ground beef, chicken stewed with peas, chicken braised with mushrooms, or everyone's favorite, couscous—not just the grain, but the complete stew with lamb, *merguez* (a lamb sausage), cabbage, zucchini, and leeks ladled atop the steamed semolina.

Finally, we would start the dafina, the Sabbath stew: chickpeas, peeled potatoes, short ribs, garlic, saffron, and eggs—still in their shells—which we'd cover with water and simmer on the lowest heat from Friday evening until Saturday afternoon. The dafina's aromas filled the house: the fragrance of saffron and the maturing richness of garlic and browning beef bones cooking for twenty hours—you could see how the flavors intensified by noting how brown the white eggs had turned from the juices. I'll never forget how that smell was like our

MOROCCAN POACHED HALIBUT Serves 4

For the fish

Four 6-ounce fillets halibut or salmon

1 bunch fresh cilantro

1 bunch fresh flat-leaf parsley

Salt and freshly ground black pepper

10 whole garlic cloves

1 lemon, sliced

4 whole serrano chiles

For the cooking liquid

1 cup vegetable oil

¼ teaspoon freshly ground black pepper

1½ teaspoons paprika

⅛ teaspoon cayenne pepper or to taste

½ teaspoon salt

French bread, as an accompaniment

1 Rinse the fish well. Spread the cilantro and parsley (stems and leaves) in the bottom of a large sauté pan. Season the fish lightly with salt and pepper and lay the fish on the bed of herbs. Place the garlic cloves, lemon slices, and chiles around the fish.

2 Combine 1 cup water with all of the ingredients for the cooking liquid and pour this over the fish.

3 Cook over high heat until the liquid boils. Lower the heat to a simmer and cover the pan with a lid. Cook for 5 to 7 minutes, until the fish is almost done. Remove the lid and continue to cook until most of the water has evaporated (if the fish looks like it is going to overcook, turn the heat up to high so the water evaporates quickly, but take care not to scorch the fish).

✛ To serve, transfer the fish from the pan with a large spatula and place on a warm platter or individual serving plates. Arrange the garlic cloves, lemon slices, and peppers around as a garnish and pour the sauce (the seasoned cooking oil minus the cilantro and parsley) on and around the fish. The fish can be served immediately or at room temperature. Offer French bread for dipping into the sauce.

anticipation all Saturday morning as we waited to sit down at lunch. (Nor will I forget how we'd all have to take a nap afterward.)

I'd never been much of a fish eater until I ate this fish with my Moroccan ex-in-laws. The cilantro and parsley, combined with the lemon, garlic, and spices, create an aromatic oil you just have to soak up with a little bread. We always ate the fish at room temperature, and to this day that is how I prefer to eat it. (Where did we get this idea that food should be excruciatingly hot all the time? There are times when a cooler temperature just reveals more flavor.)

Just to finish the story of my *aliyah* (which in Hebrew literally means "going up," but it's used to mean "immigrating to Israel"): When I became pregnant with my daughter Stephanie, I clearly realized that a child needs more than just parents around her—she needs grandparents, cousins, aunts, and uncles. So I made *urida* (which literally means "going down") and left Israel to be near my family. This is key to why I started Mother's Bistro & Bar: it's a celebration of families and the mothers who typically keep those family traditions alive. Each month we feature a menu built around one mother and the foods of her background, whether Greek or Cambodian or French. We cook what I call "mother foods": foods that tell children where they come from, who they are, and how they are loved in this world that's always going up and going down.

Lisa Schroeder is chef-owner of Mother's Bistro & Bar in Portland, Oregon, a restaurant featuring the slow-cooked dishes and authentic recipes of mothers—her own and those in her community. With over twenty years of culinary experience, including apprenticeships in France with Roger Vergé and careers at both Lespinasse and Le Cirque, Lisa is an active community member, teaching in the Operation Frontline nutrition education program and working for both Chef's Collaborative 2001 and the Slow Food Movement.

Floyd Cardoz GOAN PAN-ROASTED COD WITH KANJI AND PICKLED MANGO

My family comes from Goa, on the west coast of India, but my father moved to Bombay to go to school. Growing up in a big city like Bombay, we always looked forward to our yearly vacation at my grandmother's on the Goan shore. It was the city kids' summer vacation in the country.

Nine of us would pack into the car (no air-conditioner) to drive for eighteen hours, some three hundred miles. Usually we'd start early in the morning. We were always hungry, so my mum would have packed cold roast chicken, boiled eggs, spiced pot roast sandwiches: food was one thing we could look forward to on the hot drive. The "highways" were two lanes; the driver had to practically swerve off the road to pass someone.

By our city standards, my grandmother's house was primitive. Goa had no running water (she drew water from a well) and no electricity (oil lamps were lit at dusk). She had a wood-burning stove and cooked over a wood fire (which also meant kids were banned from the kitchen).

Mango, cashew, and coconut trees surrounded her house, and her yard was filled with mangoes that had bloomed in the spring and were just ripening. We'd pluck them from the trees (the fallen mangoes were fed to the pigs) and slice them open to eat right there in the yard.

Our month was a typical vacation: sleeping, playing in the yard, swimming at the beach twice a day—and eating. There was fruit and toast and eggs when we awakened. Then at 11:00 we'd have a midday snack. We'd eat lunch at 1:30. Then tea was served with more foods—Mum's almond cake and *bhajias,* her vegetable fritters—at 4:00. And later we'd all gather for a big dinner. We Goans love to eat and drink.

Every morning at exactly 11:00, we had to sit down with Nana and eat kanji: traditional boiled-rice slurry. We *had* to eat it because, as she said, Dad ate it when *he* was young. The rice came from her own rice paddies, a typical Goan rice that's reddish in color with a fairly strong aroma—more like a nourishing brown rice—that we didn't find all that appealing. The rice would have been sown during the monsoon season (which began shortly after we'd have returned to Bombay), harvested in November, and then parboiled and sun-dried on mats. We'd be eating rice from the previous year's crop.

Even though my father's family was well to do, my grandmother always served this simple, nourishing rice gruel and accompanied

PICKLED MANGO Makes 2 cups

1 green mango, peeled and sliced
   1 inch thick
One 2-inch piece fresh ginger, peeled
   and sliced
1 serrano chile, halved
2 tablespoons sea salt
1/4 cup white vinegar
1 tablespoon sugar

Combine all the ingredients with 1 cup water. Cover and let stand overnight at room temperature. Remove only the mango slices and mince. Return the bits to the pickling liquid and refrigerate. You will have more pickled mango than necessary for the fish recipe. The extra, which will keep for 2 weeks in an airtight jar in the refrigerator, can be used in a vinaigrette or as a garnish for a martini.

GOAN PAN-ROASTED COD WITH KANJI AND PICKLED MANGO Serves 4

For the rice

2 tablespoons vegetable oil

2 whole cloves

1 bay leaf

1 large shallot, minced
 (about 2 tablespoons)

One 1-inch piece fresh ginger, peeled
 and minced

One 2-inch fresh rosemary sprig

1 1/2 cups white basmati rice, picked over,
 washed, soaked for 20 minutes,
 and drained

1/4 cup dry white wine

1 quart chicken stock

2 ounces salt cod (bacalao), thinly sliced

8 pieces kokum, plumped and julienned
 (a dried sour plum available at Indian
 markets)

2 cups unsweetened coconut milk

Salt and freshly cracked black pepper

1/4 cup chopped fresh chives

2 fresh cilantro sprigs, chopped

1 cup cooked fresh or frozen peas,
 optional

1/2 cup cooked mung beans, optional

For the fish

Four 6-ounce pieces cod (2 inches thick,
 skin left on)

Salt and freshly ground black pepper

5 tablespoons vegetable oil

6 tablespoons Pickled Mango

it with a toasted, salted fish (very close to bacalao) or with her own mango pickle, made from her trees' unripe fruits.

This was not a dish I relished eating, and yet it still reminds me of home and takes me to a place of comfort. Whatever I cook comes from the heart, from a place of comfort; I can't make food any other way. But I also couldn't prepare my grandmother's version of kanji.

Now, instead of using water as the stock,

I prepare a fresh clam broth. I substitute basmati rice in place of the Goan rice. I use the salted, dried cod as a flavor enhancer, and I simply pan-roast a piece of cod to go with it. Then I finish the dish with a couple things: a little coconut milk for the rice and a homemade mango pickle that's quite salty, minced on the top of the fish.

Even with these changes, my recipe for kanji reminds me of my dad, that house, that smell of wood fire, that husky rice, the

1 For the rice, heat the oil in a heavy pot over medium heat. Add the cloves, bay leaf, shallot, and ginger. Sauté for 4 to 5 minutes. Add the rosemary, rice, wine, and 3 cups of the stock. Bring to a boil and simmer until the rice is tender, about 20 minutes. Not all of the liquid will be absorbed at this point.

2 Remove and discard the cloves, bay leaf, and rosemary.

3 Heat a small heavy skillet over medium heat and add the sliced salt cod. Cook until the fish gets toasty and dry on both sides, 3 to 5 minutes. (The pan will smoke.) Break the cooked fish into small pieces. Set aside.

4 To finish the rice, plump the kokum in 1 cup warm water for 15 or 20 minutes. Remove from the water and julienne. Heat the remaining 1 cup chicken stock and the coconut milk to a high simmer, then add the cooked rice, toasted salt cod, and kokum. Taste and season the rice with salt and pepper (additional salt may not be necessary). Turn off the heat, cover, and keep warm.

5 Cook the cod next. Season it with salt and pepper to taste. Heat the oil in a heavy skillet over medium-high heat. Pan-sear the cod, skin side down first, then turn the fish and sear the other side. Three minutes per side should create a crispy exterior on the fish fillet.

✤ To assemble the dish, toss the rice with the chives, cilantro, and the peas and mung beans if desired. Place a spoonful of rice in a warmed soup plate. Top the rice with the cooked fish and garnish each with $1^1/2$ tablespoons Pickled Mango.

perfume of mangoes, and all of us kids gathered at the dining room table, poking at our bowls of rice beside my grandmother.

Floyd Cardoz is executive chef at Tabla and Bread Bar, part of the Union Square Hospitality Group. A native of Goa, Floyd was raised in Bombay. In his cooking, Floyd looks to tap the great and unexplored potential of the vast cuisines of India while utilizing Western culinary traditions. Trained in Bombay and Switzerland, he worked for six years under Gray Kunz at New York's venerable Lespinasse. He lives with his wife, Barkha, and sons, Peter and Justin.

Tom Condron ROASTED WILD SCOTTISH SALMON WITH CRUSHED ENGLISH PEAS, WILD SPRING ONIONS, AND MOREL VINAIGRETTE

I grew up with eight older brothers. There's sixteen years between me and my oldest brother. My father was brigadier general in the Royal Marines, and most of my brothers attended one or another military academy, so our whole family didn't get to spend much time together. (My father did have two bodyguards who often lived with us, and *they* were more like brothers to me.)

As a break from his travels and military work, my father took us fishing, usually in Yorkshire, England's big farm belt, or near my mom's family home in Cheshire. (There was nothing to catch—or worth eating—in the nearby Thames.) Usually we hooked striped bass and trout, and we'd always eat them. Those evenings my father was home, he loved nothing more than sipping port, eating a little Stilton cheese, and tying flies.

Our family always came together for a spring fly-fishing trip in the Shetland Islands, the northernmost part of Scotland. We'd fly to Dundee and then drive eight hours to the north. The islands are as far north as Alaska, and at five in the morning, when we'd set off to fish, the sky would be as brilliant as you'd expect at noon.

If we were lucky, we'd catch eight or ten fish. We really weren't that good. Plus we younger kids were throwing stones and being noisy, the older kids were visiting with one another, and Dad was asking each of his sons about boarding school. But my dad took such pleasure in having his sons fishing together that he didn't mind those days when we'd end up having steak-and-kidney pie or lamb for dinner instead of salmon. Still any fish we did catch was a good

ROASTED WILD SCOTTISH SALMON WITH CRUSHED ENGLISH PEAS, WILD SPRING ONIONS, AND MOREL VINAIGRETTE Serves 4

----

¹/₄ cup olive oil

Four 8-ounce fillets Scottish salmon or wild Pacific Northwest or Maine salmon

Sea salt and freshly cracked black pepper

Leaves from 1 fresh thyme sprig, stem discarded

6 tablespoons unsalted butter

1 recipe Crushed English Peas

1 recipe Morel Vinaigrette

8 ramps (small wild spring onions), grilled, for garnish

Heat the olive oil in a sauté pan over high heat. Season the salmon with salt and pepper to taste. Cook the fillets skin side down for 4 minutes, then turn them over and add the thyme leaves and butter. Baste the fish with the butter and thyme for 3 minutes or until the salmon is medium-rare (cook longer for medium-well). Transfer the fish to a tray.

✥ To serve, place a generous spoonful of the Crushed English Peas in the center of warm dinner plates. Place a salmon fillet on top and ladle ¹/₄ cup or more of the Morel Vinaigrette over the fish. Garnish with the grilled ramps.

CRUSHED ENGLISH PEAS
Makes 3¹/₂ cups

----

2 tablespoons olive oil

1 tablespoon finely chopped shallots

1 tablespoon minced garlic

2 pounds freshly shelled or frozen English peas

1 cup chicken or vegetable stock

Minced leaves from 1 fresh thyme sprig

Minced leaves from 1 fresh tarragon sprig

Juice of 1 lemon

Sea salt and freshly cracked black pepper

1 Heat the olive oil in a medium saucepan over medium heat and add the shallots and garlic. Cook until translucent, about 4 minutes. (The garlic should not color.) Add the peas and cook for 4 minutes. Add the stock and cook until the peas are tender, 10 to 12 more minutes. (If using frozen peas, add the stock and frozen peas at the same time; cook only until the peas are tender, 4 to 8 minutes total.)

2 Remove from the heat and add the herbs, lemon juice, and salt and pepper to taste. Mash the peas with a fork while still hot. Keep warm until ready to serve.

MOREL VINAIGRETTE Makes 2 cups

----

1 1/4 cups extra virgin olive oil

2 tablespoons finely chopped shallots

1 tablespoon minced garlic

1/4 cup finely diced carrot

1/4 cup finely diced celery

1/4 cup finely diced onion

1 cup sherry vinegar

3 cups rich chicken stock

2 tablespoons porcini oil or white truffle oil

Sea salt and freshly ground black pepper

1/2 pound fresh morels

1/4 cup freshly shelled English peas,
   cooked (or frozen)

1 Heat 2 tablespoons of the olive oil in a medium saucepan over medium heat and add the shallots, garlic, carrot, celery, and onion. Cook the vegetables until translucent and soft, stirring occasionally, 7 to 8 minutes. (The garlic should not color.)

2 Add the vinegar and reduce by a third. Add the stock and reduce the liquid again by half. Remove from the heat and whisk in the porcini oil and 1 cup of the remaining olive oil. Season with salt and pepper to taste, then set aside. (This can be prepared several hours in advance or stored in an airtight container and refrigerated for 3 days.)

3 To finish the dressing, heat the remaining 2 tablespoons olive oil in a medium skillet over medium-high heat. Add the morels and pan-roast them for 3 minutes. Add the vinaigrette and heat until warm. Finally, add the peas and keep warm until ready to serve.

twenty or more pounds since they were just arriving at the streams to spawn after almost a year of feeding at sea.

Lucky for us, morels and spring onions (we call them *ramps* here in the States) were also abundant, and we younger kids would forage for them. Since I tended to pick up everything and put it in my pockets, I was a natural at morel hunting. I suppose I knew my calling from a very young age.

Now that my father's deceased, all my brothers and their wives and my twenty-seven nieces and nephews still get together when the Scottish salmon are running. We're a big crowd, almost fifty people, so the adults stay in local hotels and all the kids bunk in my brothers' RVs and tell ghost stories until they fall asleep.

Since I'm the official chef, my father's job at the fire has fallen to me. There's nothing like preparing a fish that's going to be on someone's plate less than an hour after it was pulled from the stream. One of our iron skillets is more than two hundred years old, and it probably weighs about as many pounds. It's thirty-two inches across, and it has a stand and legs so it can straddle a fire. It's always been in our family. My older brother Daniel stores it at his home in Edinburgh, and it takes three of us to maneuver the skillet into place. Each time I slide a salmon fillet into that pan, and hear the sizzling and smell the searing skin, I can't help thinking about all these generations who've returned here year after year to sustain themselves with these great fish . . . and all the generations of fish who have returned here, too.

The son of a British Royal Marines general, Tom Condron was born in Pennsylvania but raised abroad, spending time in more than fifty countries. At fourteen he joined the kitchen at England's famed Dorchester Hotel. Later he completed a five-year apprenticeship under Anton Mossiman, one of eight Michelin three-star chefs Tom has worked with throughout his career. He earned degrees in economics from the University of Florida and in culinary arts from Johnson and Wales College. Tom joined Mimosa Grill in Charlotte, North Carolina, in 1997, where he merges extraordinary international experience with southern cuisine.

Paul Kahan
SEARED WALLEYE WITH WALNUT OIL AND VERJUICE

When I was a boy, my father and I would try our luck fishing every now and then. We'd drive from Chicago to Port Washington to pick up chub that the local fishermen would have caught. He liked to brine the fish and then smoke them. He owned a deli, Fan's Fisheries, and these chubs were a staple item there. So while we were at the lake, we'd fish for perch, I think. (We caught so few fish, I can't remember what kind they were!)

Dad's deli had a huge refrigerator, of course, and a guy named Billy kept it running. His family had a cabin way up on a lake in central Wisconsin. One year, when I was about seven, he invited us up for the weekend. I think he had six kids—pretty much country brutes, at least compared to the city kid I was.

As soon as we got there, one of his older sons—he was probably sixteen—waded into the lake to some shallow area and just stood there. A few moments passed. Then suddenly he plunged his arms into the water and just grabbed this huge walleye with his hands and yanked it from the splashing

SEARED WALLEYE WITH WALNUT OIL AND VERJUICE

Serves 4

Four 5-ounce walleye fillets

Salt and freshly ground black pepper

3 tablespoons olive oil

4 tablespoons ($^1/2$ stick) unsalted butter

2 teaspoons each chopped fresh chervil,
   tarragon, and chives

1 recipe Verjuice Sauce

$^1/2$ cup seedless red grapes, thinly sliced

1 recipe Walnut Oil Vinaigrette

Roasted beets (gold, chioggia,
   or a mixture), as an accompaniment

Haricot verts, quickly blanched, as an
   accompaniment

1 Preheat the oven to 450°F. Season the fillets with salt and pepper to taste.

2 Heat the oil in two large ovenproof sauté pans over high heat until the oil begins to smoke. Add the fish and sear until the edges of the fish are golden brown, 3 to 4 minutes.

3 Transfer the pans to the oven and roast until the fillets are almost cooked through (cooking time will depend on the thickness) and are a deep golden brown. Add half of the butter and herbs to each pan. Baste the fillets with the melted butter for 1 minute.

✤ Spoon the warm Verjuice Sauce on each warmed dinner plate and place a fillet on top. Sprinkle each fillet with sliced red grapes and drizzle the Walnut Oil Vinaigrette over all.

water. Grabbing the fish by the gills, he walked into the house with the fish still alive and wiggling. It had to be a seven- or eight-pound fish. He had no bait, no pole, no net: Was this how we were all going to be fishing over the weekend?

(Later I came to understand that walleye like to come in to the shallower, warmer water and just sun there. So if you stand still enough, they won't notice you. Not that I've tried this method myself.)

That night Billy cooked up that walleye for us, and I tasted the best piece of fish I've ever had in my life. He filleted it, cut it into perfectly square pieces, dredged each square in bread crumbs, and simply pan-fried them. I've been in love with the sweetness of walleye since that moment.

I don't get to fish enough these days. I do one ice-fishing trip each winter, and occasionally I try for walleye on the Canadian border.

In early summer, when walleye's available, I love to cook those big fillets: they're so meaty, and I use the rest of the fish to make a marvelous fumet; walleye contributes a

VERJUICE SAUCE Makes 2 cups

----

2 cups white verjuice (see Note)

$^1/_2$ pound seedless red grapes, washed and stemmed (about 1$^1/_4$ cups)

4 tablespoons ($^1/_2$ stick) unsalted butter, cold, cut into bits

2 tablespoons extra virgin olive oil

Salt and freshly ground black pepper

1 or 2 drops honey or champagne vinegar, optional

1 teaspoon each chopped fresh chervil, tarragon, and chives

1 Combine the verjuice and grapes in a small saucepan and cook over medium heat until the liquid has reduced by half, about 20 minutes. The grapes should be soft and plump. Remove from the heat and allow to cool slightly.

2 Puree the verjuice and grapes in a blender or food processor. Continue to run the machine and add the butter, 1 piece at a time, until it is all incorporated and the sauce is smooth. Add the olive oil. Taste and adjust the seasoning. Add the honey or champagne vinegar if desired to adjust the sweetness or acidity.

✢ To serve, gently heat the sauce, taking care not to boil it. Stir in the herbs.

WALNUT OIL VINAIGRETTE
Makes $^1/_2$ cup

----

2 tablespoons sherry vinegar

1 small shallot, finely minced

1 tablespoon whole-grain mustard

1 teaspoon honey

Salt and freshly ground black pepper

5 tablespoons walnut oil

1 teaspoon minced fresh thyme

Combine the vinegar, shallot, mustard, honey, and salt and pepper to taste and allow to sit for 10 minutes. Slowly whisk in the walnut oil. Add the thyme. Taste and adjust the seasonings. This can be prepared 1 or 2 days in advance and refrigerated in an airtight container. Bring the dressing to room temperature and shake well before using.

great sweet flavor without adding the oiliness that some fish contribute.

At the same time, our local grapes are just coming on, and verjuice, the tart pressing of unripened grapes, can add a perfect acidity to the fish, with more depth of flavor than vinegar and without the harsher tartness of a lemon. Finally, try serving this dish with a variety of roasted beets and quickly blanched haricot verts, and you have a complete, sensational meal.

Of course, nothing can substitute for the utter pleasure of eating a fish you just saw snatched from the water, but the recipe should still make any piece of walleye an early-summer treat.

Note: Verjuice is not that expensive, though it can be hard to find. It's called *acresta* in Italy, *verjus* in France, and *hosrum* in the Middle East, so you can find it under those names as well at specialty markets. I use Fusion's Napa Valley Verjus, which comes in both white and red. Fusion, P.O. Box 542, Rutherford, CA 94573; www.verjus.com.

In 1999 *Food & Wine* placed Paul Kahan on its Best New Chefs list. His restaurant, Blackbird, has rapidly joined the ranks of Chicago's most esteemed restaurants, landing on *Gourmet*'s list of Chicago's top five restaurants. A Beard Foundation nominee for Best Chef/Midwest, Paul continues to extol the virtues of local organic ingredients in his cuisine.

Frank Bonanno MUSTARD-CRUSTED FLOUNDER WITH A LEMON CAPER SAUCE

My earliest culinary memories are of the summers spent at the New Jersey shore. My father is a compulsive fisherman. He'd be happy if he could fish every day. (As it is, he manages about three days a week.)

At a very early age he taught his kids how to fish and how to clean fish properly. We cleaned each fish the moment it left the water; we had a cutting board that popped right into a rod holder on the back of the boat. Even at eight years old, I'd be gutting and filleting the fish myself. The head and bones we took home to make bouillabaisse or some other fish soup, so nothing went to waste.

When I was about seven years old, I remember my dad and my three brothers all went out fishing for flounder. Other days we'd catch tuna, bluefish—pretty much anything that part of the Atlantic Ocean offered. We left at the crack of dawn. I was in charge of making the sandwiches for the trip. With a little help from my father and a great Italian deli nearby, I made hero sandwiches: some great bread, sopressata, fresh mozzarella, olive oil, vinegar, lettuce, and Parmesan shaved paper-thin. (This sandwich certainly helped me understand that you don't need a lot of fancy flavors to make delicious food.)

So that day we had great luck. We took off on Dad's thirty-five-foot Bertram, found a great spot, and tossed our lines. The lures bounced along the bottom, and the flounders kept biting. We caught a lot of fish, and I, *I* caught the biggest flounder and had the proud opportunity to rub it in with my brothers.

MUSTARD-CRUSTED FLOUNDER WITH A LEMON CAPER SAUCE Serves 4

For the fish

Four 6- to 8-ounce flounder fillets

4 tablespoons ($^1/_2$ stick) unsalted butter, softened

Salt and freshly ground white pepper

$^1/_4$ cup Dijon mustard

$^1/_2$ cup dry Italian bread crumbs

For the sauce

$^1/_4$ cup olive oil

2 garlic cloves, chopped

$^1/_4$ cup drained capers

1 cup dry white wine

4 tablespoons ($^1/_2$ stick) unsalted butter, softened

$^1/_4$ cup chopped fresh tarragon

$^1/_4$ cup chopped fresh flat-leaf parsley

Salt and freshly ground black pepper

Juice of 1 lemon

Wilted spinach, as an accompaniment

New potatoes, boiled and tossed in butter and parsley, as an accompaniment

1 Preheat the broiler. Oil a baking sheet with vegetable spray. Place the fish on the pan. Gently spread 1 tablespoon of the butter on each fillet and season with salt and pepper. Coat each fillet with 1 tablespoon of the mustard. Sprinkle the bread crumbs evenly over the top of the fillets. Set aside.

2 To make the sauce, heat the olive oil in a large sauté pan. Add the garlic and cook over low heat until tender but not brown, 2 to 3 minutes. Add the capers and cook for 1 minute. Add the white wine and reduce the liquid by half. Gently mix in the butter, a tablespoon at a time. Add the herbs, taste, and adjust the seasonings. Remove the sauce from the heat; keep warm.

3 Place the fish under the broiler for 6 to 8 minutes or until the fish is moist but cooked through. The bread crumbs should be golden and crispy.

✤ Transfer the fillets to individual plates, squeeze lemon juice over each fillet, and spoon the sauce all around. Accompany the fish with wilted spinach and boiled new potatoes tossed in butter and parsley.

I was glowing on the entire ride back to the dock.

At home my mom assessed the day's catch, decided what else she needed to round out the perfect flounder dinner, and off we went to the market. We picked spinach, Red Bliss potatoes, some nice lettuces for a salad (we ate salad for dessert in our family, with wonderful cheeses like young pecorino and various blue cheeses). And, of course, we stopped by Hoffman's Ice Cream Shop so I could order a quart of mint chocolate chip, my favorite.

My brothers and I, with more than a little help from Mom, cooked dinner that night. The centerpiece was the broiled flounder with a Dijon mustard crust and a white wine caper sauce with fresh tarragon and parsley and a squeeze of lemon. We were eating the very fish we'd caught that day, and it had to reflect how fantastic our day at sea had been. And do I need to say that I served myself the biggest fillet from the very fish I'd caught?

My family gets together to fish as often as we can. My father has a smaller boat now, and he lives in Florida, so we've been catching different fish, like tarpon. But of all the fish I've learned to cook in all kinds of sauces and with any number of cooking techniques, few give me as much pleasure as this mustard-crusted flounder.

Frank Bonnano is chef and owner of Mizuna, which features his French-Asian cuisine, and the newly opened Luca di Italia, which features the authentic, rustic cuisine inspired by his three grandparents from Palermo. Before opening his restaurants in Denver, Frank received his degree in finance from the University of Denver, attended the Culinary Institute of America, and interned at the French Laundry, Gramercy Tavern, Restaurant Daniel, and in Alba, Italy. For several years, Frank worked as chef at Mel's Bar and Grill in Denver as well. Much of his philanthropic efforts benefit children's welfare in Denver.

Joanne Bondy
MARINATED TROUT WITH BLUE CHEESE GRITS AND MUSHROOMS

To this day my fantasy getaway is to return to western North Carolina and the Blue Ridge Mountains. My dad would drive the four of us there in his green Impala every summer from our home in central Florida. It was an eight-hour ride, but the entire trip was filled with anticipation that elevated with every stop at a fruit and vegetable stand in Georgia and South Carolina.

We always stayed in the same cabin, down the gravel road that ran beside a beautiful, cold stream. The forest surrounding the cabin was so thick it was hard to tell what time of day it was once we ventured through.

With no TV, radio, or telephone, we found

MARINATED TROUT WITH BLUE CHEESE GRITS AND MUSHROOMS Serves 4

----

³/₄ cup light olive oil

¹/₂ cup apple cider or juice

1 tablespoon chopped fresh tarragon

1 tablespoon fresh lemon juice

1 teaspoon salt

¹/₂ teaspoon freshly ground black pepper

8 trout fillets

1 recipe Blue Cheese Grits with Oven-Roasted Mushrooms

1 Combine the olive oil, cider, tarragon, lemon juice, salt, and pepper. Place the fillets in a shallow dish and cover with the marinade. Turn each fillet to ensure even coverage. Marinate for 1 hour.

2 Prepare a medium-hot grill. Place the fish on the rack, flesh side down, and cook for 5 minutes, basting the entire time with the marinade. Carefully turn the fish and continue basting the second side for 5 minutes. Transfer the cooked fish to a tray.

3 Place the remaining marinade in a small saucepan over high heat and quickly bring to a boil, reducing it for 1 or 2 minutes.

✛ Place 2 fillets on each warmed plate with a generous spoonful of Blue Cheese Grits, topped with a spoonful of Oven-Roasted Mushrooms. Drizzle the reduced marinade over all.

ways to entertain ourselves. My brother and I searched for crawdaddies in the stream and built rock forts in the icy water to capture them. We'd take our bamboo cane poles and a can of corn for bait and head down to the stream's soft currents to "trout fish." (Or we'd walk down to the trout pond if we hadn't caught anything.) A good day of trout would be about eight fish. We knew a man who would clean our trout on his tree stump of a cutting board.

Wandering along the serpentine trails would lead us to all kinds of wild mushrooms. We'd line wooden peach baskets with damp moss and begin our hunt. Near the oak and hickory trees beside the trickling streams we'd find gypsy and chicken mushrooms. Past the apple orchards, in the meadows, we found Caesars. The pine trees that were decaying gave us a real gift: orange chanterelles.

Back at the cabin I spread the mushrooms out on the wooden picnic table. I took out my *National Geographic* book on mushrooms and also looked at the shapes of the mushrooms' spores with my little microscope

BLUE CHEESE GRITS WITH OVEN-ROASTED MUSHROOMS

Serves 4

For the grits

1/4 teaspoon salt

1 cup stone-ground white corn grits

1/2 cup heavy cream

2 large eggs

1/4 pound Saga or other favorite blue cheese

1 Preheat the oven to 350°F. Lightly oil a 9-inch square baking dish with vegetable spray.

2 Combine the salt and 3 cups water in a saucepan and bring to a boil over high heat. Add the grits and stir constantly until the mixture bubbles, about 5 minutes. Reduce the heat to low and stir for an additional 5 minutes. Remove from the heat.

3 In a small bowl, combine the cream and eggs, quickly stirring this into the grits. Add the cheese and stir until incorporated. Pour into the prepared pan and bake for 45 minutes or until the top has browned lightly. This can be done ahead of time and reheated. The cold grits can also be cut into shapes and reheated.

For the mushrooms

2 tablespoons unsalted butter, softened

2 tablespoons dry white wine

Pinch of fresh thyme leaves

1 tablespoon chopped fresh flat-leaf parsley

Salt and freshly ground black pepper

1 pound favorite wild mushrooms, cut into bite-size pieces

4 Combine all the mushroom ingredients in a baking dish and toss. Bake at 350°F for 15 minutes or until tender. Keep warm for serving.

and staining kit. The ones that I concluded weren't poisonous we ate—unless they had too many worms. One of the older, local men who helped maintain the campgrounds often came by to offer an opinion on the mushrooms I wasn't sure about.

Some days we'd walk to the orchard to pick apples and buy cider. Or we'd go to the grist mill, a big old brown, boxy building, with a gigantic water mill right on the stream. Another short, whiskery guy would pour some cornmeal that he'd just ground into a cotton sack for us.

Eventually we grew older, and the trips we took as a whole family grew fewer. Our evenings of grilled trout, grist-mill grits, wild mushrooms, and local apple cider became memories. But it is my memories and these simple treasures of local ingredients that inspired this meal.

Joanne Bondy is executive chef of, and partner in, Ciudad, an award-winning restaurant in Dallas, Texas, recently named by *Esquire* as one of the 20 Best New Restaurants in America. Ciudad features Spanish, Aztec, Mayan, and French cuisine in a singular culinary experience. Joanne's previous experiences as a chef include the opening of Mariel Hemingway's Sam's Café, banquet chef at the Fairmont Hotel in Dallas, and chef de cuisine at the Arizona Biltmore.

POULTRY

Gordon Hamersley
SLOW-ROASTED ORANGE DUCK WITH A SPICY BARLEY SALAD

Karen and Ben Barker
DUCK WITH GREEN CURRY

Stephan Pyles
HONEY-FRIED CHICKEN WITH MINTED CREAM SAUCE AND SPICY SWEET POTATO PUREE

Suzanne Goin
THE DEVIL'S CHICKEN WITH POTATOES, LEEKS, AND MUSTARD BREAD CRUMBS

Susan Feniger
BOMBAY CHICKEN WITH CURRIED TOMATOES

Patrick O'Connell
BLUEBERRY VINEGAR–MARINATED SQUAB ON CREAMY POLENTA

Gordon Hamersley SLOW-ROASTED ORANGE DUCK WITH A SPICY BARLEY SALAD

I cooked a duck for my own wedding in 1982. I had been working at Ma Maison in Los Angeles, and I'd come back, as I did every year, for a big get-together on the East Coast, where my family's from originally. This tradition started when I became a chef; everyone loved the idea of gathering together so I could cook up a grand meal. That year I traveled with Fiona, who was to be my wife—a surprise to everyone but my mother.

The seven guests arrived—my brothers, my sister, a couple of cousins, and one stranger to the family whom we introduced over cocktails just before we all went to the table for dinner: he was a justice of the peace that my cousin Herb knew. We were getting married before dinner was served.

You can imagine the shock. Though everyone knew that Fiona and I were quite intent on getting married, no one expected the surprise, save my mother, who was very sick at the time—she died later that year. This had to be a secret wedding so

that we could change things at the last minute if necessary.

We'd thought about having a large wedding . . . for about ten seconds. At the time my family was on the East Coast, our friends were on the West Coast, and Fiona's entire family lived in England. The key thing for us was finding a way to have my mother present.

So we had the ceremony—which took all of two minutes as we exchanged vows— and then I dashed into the kitchen to take the duck out of the oven.

I'd made a first course of tiny bay scallops. The main course was the slow-roasted duck. Its meat was utterly tender, and the orange glaze, which had caramelized in the process, made the skin crispy and the turnips beneath rich and aromatic. There was a sweet-and-sour sherry-vinegar sauce to pass around. Duck is one of my favorite things to cook, and though we think

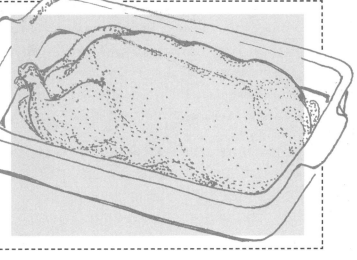

SLOW-ROASTED ORANGE DUCK WITH A SPICY BARLEY SALAD Serves 4

----

³/4 cup fresh orange juice (2 oranges)

¹/4 cup fresh lime juice (2 limes)

¹/4 cup balsamic vinegar

¹/4 cup soy sauce

¹/4 cup Thai-style chile paste

1 teaspoon dried tarragon

1 teaspoon salt

Pinch of freshly ground black pepper

1 Long Island duck, trimmed of fat, liver and giblets removed, rinsed well, and dried

8 fresh tarragon sprigs

4 garlic cloves, smashed

1 small onion, sliced

2 tablespoons vegetable oil

1 recipe Spicy Barley Salad

1 Combine the juices, vinegar, soy sauce, chile paste, dried tarragon, salt, and pepper in a bowl. Place the duck in a large non-reactive container and apply 1 cup of the marinade to the duck, both inside and outside. Cover and refrigerate for 2 to 3 hours, turning the bird several times. Reserve the remaining marinade for the barley salad.

2 Preheat the oven to 325°F.

3 Remove the duck from the marinade and stuff its cavity with the tarragon sprigs, garlic cloves, and onion slices. Place the bird on a rack fitted into a roasting pan and add 2 cups water to the pan.

4 Roast the bird for 3 hours or until the temperature at the thickest part of the thigh reads 165°F and the leg joint moves easily. Begin to check the temperature after 2¹/2 hours. Add water while roasting if necessary to keep some liquid in the pan. The skin of the duck will become a dark mahogany color as it cooks.

5 Remove the duck from the pan and allow it to rest for 10 to 15 minutes. Cut the breast meat off the bone and remove the legs. Allow the meat to cool completely.

6 Heat the oil in a large sauté pan over medium heat. Place the duck pieces, skin side down, in the hot oil. Reduce the heat to low and cook for 8 to 10 minutes. The fat will render from the skin, making it very crispy. Carefully remove the pieces from the pan, taking care not to tear the skin.

✤ Arrange a mound of the Spicy Barley Salad on plates and top with a piece of the duck.

SPICY BARLEY SALAD

Makes 4 1/2 cups

----

1 cup pearl barley

2 teaspoons salt

2 tablespoons vegetable oil

2 red bell peppers, julienned

1 garlic clove, minced

1 jalapeño pepper, minced

3 scallions, sliced

2 oranges, peeled and cut into segments

1 lime, peeled and cut into segments

15 fresh tarragon leaves, torn in half

15 fresh mint leaves, torn into bits

1/2 cup marinade reserved from the duck

1 In a large pot, bring 2 quarts water to a boil. Add the barley and salt, lower the heat to a simmer, and cook until the barley is tender, about 30 minutes. Drain in a colander and allow the barley to sit for several minutes. Stir with a fork to separate the grains. Pour the barley onto a sheet pan lined with plastic wrap so it can cool quickly. Place it in a salad bowl.

2 Heat the oil in a large sauté pan over high heat. Just as it begins smoking, add the red peppers, garlic, and jalapeño. Cook for 2 to 3 minutes, stirring, until the peppers are just tender. Toss the contents of the pan into the salad bowl, along with the remaining ingredients, gradually adding the reserved marinade (start with 1/4 cup and taste; add more as desired). Reseason with salt if necessary.

of duck as a celebratory dish, it really shouldn't be: it has incredible flavor, and it's so easy to prepare.

There was a tarte tatin for dessert as well as a number of toasts by various guests—welcoming Fiona into the family, wishing everyone happiness—but they couldn't go on forever, because the World Series was starting.

The dinner party retired to the basement, which was full of St. Louis Cardinals fans, and we all watched the ball game.

I try to cook that duck on our anniversary each year. It was Willie McGee's first year in the major leagues, and he is the only player Fiona ever remembers to this day.

Gordon Hamersley is a respected cooking teacher at Boston University and the chef and co-owner, with his wife, Fiona, of Hamersley's Bistro in Boston, Massachusetts, voted "Best of Boston" by *Boston* magazine from 1988 through 1996, and retired to its "Best of Boston Hall of Fame." He received the Beard Best Chef/

Northeast Award in 1995, as well as five prior consecutive nominations. His new book *Bistro Cooking at Home* is published by Broadway Books. Gordon serves on the board of the New England Culinary Institute and several environmental groups pledged to protecting the area's vast natural resources.

Karen and Ben Barker
DUCK WITH GREEN CURRY

Karen and I met on our first day at the CIA. We sat next to each other in Sanitation Class. (Talk about romantic.) We were married and out of school for several years, on the verge of opening a restaurant in North Carolina, when we took a food excursion to northern California.

But for all our culinary training, our knowledge of Asian cuisine was a one-week class in school: a few lessons in Cantonese and Hunanese wok cooking primarily. So when we arrived in San Francisco in 1986, we'd never eaten Thai food before. We decided to have dinner at Khan Toke Thai House, acknowledged to be one of the Bay Area's best. We removed our shoes. The hostess ushered us through a dark dining room to a low table with pillows for chairs. Most of the patrons looked Thai. We were in for something different.

We settled in, ordered, and began to feel as if we'd been invited into someone's home—that is, until a loud gong sounded, and out into the dining room paraded three musicians and a dancer. Much to our surprise, we had come on "entertainment night."

One player had a stringed instrument, and two others played cymbals

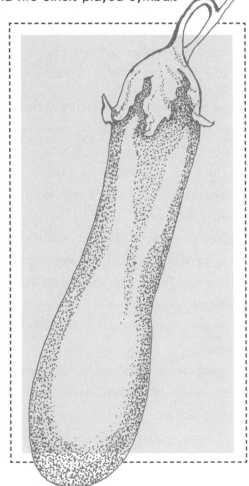

DUCK WITH GREEN CURRY

Serves 4

- -

1/2 cup thick coconut milk (see Note)

2 tablespoons fish sauce

1 recipe Green Curry Paste or
   a commercial brand, to taste

4 kaffir lime leaves (see Note) or
   1 tablespoon freshly grated lime zest

4 duck legs, skinned, boned, and cut into
   1-inch pieces

1 1/2 cups regular coconut milk

8 small Thai eggplants, halved, or 1 to 2
   small Japanese eggplants, cut into
   chunks, optional

2 red serrano chiles, sliced crosswise
   (seeds included)

1/4 cup chiffonade of fresh mint leaves

1/4 cup torn fresh basil leaves (1/2-inch
   pieces)

1/4 cup coarsely chopped fresh cilantro
   leaves (reserve stems and roots for
   the Green Curry Paste)

1/2 cup diagonally sliced scallions

4 cups cooked jasmine rice, as an
   accompaniment

1 Heat the thick coconut milk in a large wok or sauté pan over medium-high heat until it separates and the oil starts to bubble at the edges. Add 1 tablespoon of the fish sauce and the curry paste and fry for 2 to 3 minutes, until very aromatic. Add the lime leaves and duck legs, stirring to coat.

2 Add the regular coconut milk and bring to a simmer. Cook, uncovered, for 15 to 20 minutes or until the sauce has thickened and the duck is tender.

3 Add the eggplants if desired, the chiles, and the herbs and simmer for 5 minutes. Add the remaining tablespoon of fish sauce, taste, and add more lime, chile, or fish sauce to taste.

✤ Arrange the duck curry on a warm platter and sprinkle with scallions. Offer hot jasmine rice on the side.

Note: Use unsweetened coconut milk only. For the thick coconut milk, do not shake the can of milk prior to opening. Coconut milk separates in the can: the thick milk will be at the top. Spoon it out and measure according to the recipe. Fish sauce and kaffir lime leaves can be found at Asian markets.

and small drums. And then a woman dressed in what must have been more formal, royal garb, danced beside them, telling stories with her hands and body.

But the entertainment was not the only unexpected part of dinner. The entire meal was exotic, packed with new taste sensations. We shared a fantastic squid dish with

GREEN CURRY PASTE

Makes 1 1/2 cups

----

1 teaspoon coriander seeds

1 teaspoon caraway seeds

4 whole cloves

1/2 nutmeg, cracked into large bits

1/2 teaspoon black peppercorns

1/4 cup chopped fresh cilantro, washed roots and stems only (reserve leaves for another use)

3 shallots, peeled

5 garlic cloves

6 to 8 serrano chiles, sliced crosswise

2 inches galangal (see Note) or young ginger, thinly sliced

2 stalks lemongrass, tender white part only, sliced into thin rings

1 teaspoon Thai shrimp paste (see Note)

1/2 teaspoon salt

1 Combine the coriander seeds, caraway seeds, cloves, nutmeg, and peppercorns in a small dry sauté pan over low heat. Toast the spices for 2 to 3 minutes, shaking the pan frequently, until fragrant. Take care not to color or burn the spices. Cool and pour into a spice mill and grind to a fine powder. Set aside.

2 Combine the cilantro, shallots, garlic, chiles, galangal or ginger, and lemongrass in a food processor. Pulse to chop finely. Add the ground spices, salt, and shrimp paste and pulse to combine. Place in an airtight container and refrigerate. The paste may also be frozen for up to 1 month.

Note: Galangal is a rhizome similar to ginger, found at Asian markets; small, tender ginger can be substituted. Thai shrimp paste can also be found at Asian markets.

---

peanuts and cabbage and chiles. We ate summer rolls, with lettuce and rice papers wrapped around fresh noodles. What captured me in all the dishes was the forceful but balanced interplay of complex spices: fiery chiles and pronounced quantities of basil and cilantro. Karen and I were used to the refined and somewhat subtle foods of European cuisine, which rarely has the explosive *pow* of Thai flavors.

The duck curry that inspired this dish was vibrantly, resoundingly spicy but tempered by coconut milk and punched up with basil. Halfway through the dish I realized I was sweating *behind my ears!* I had eaten plenty of hot foods, living in the South (the capsicum-driven flavors of cayenne peppers), but this had never happened to me before. It was a pain-and-pleasure thing, which I now relish.

We hosted a Thai potluck dinner that fall; all of our cook-friends—none of them Thai—

researched and brought a dish. We had ten or eleven courses, all of them as authentic as possible.

Now we serve Thai-inspired dishes at Magnolia Grill in late summer, when fresh chiles are plentiful locally. We're tempted to sound a gong when someone orders one of these selections, but then we don't know any traditional Thai musicians and dancers here in Durham.

Ben and Karen Barker are the chef-owners of Magnolia Grill in Durham, North Carolina. The cookbook *Not Afraid of Flavor*, published by the University of North Carolina Press, features the grill's seasonally based, big-flavored food. They live in Chapel Hill with their son, Gabriel, who is also a chilehead.

Stephan Pyles HONEY-FRIED CHICKEN WITH MINTED CREAM SAUCE AND SPICY SWEET POTATO PUREE

Every Sunday, after church, we'd drive to my grandmother's house outside of Big Spring in west Texas. Maybe it's just my perspective as a chef today, but the whole weekend at her house was centered around food. Sunny-side-up eggs in bacon fat, sopped up with bread. Cottage potatoes. Freshly picked blackberries. Chocolate ice-box pies. Cobblers. And maybe most important, Sunday dinner's fried chicken. Even as a kid, I knew that my grandmother's tasted better than my mother's or the stuff at Kentucky Fried Chicken (particularly the batch of fried chicken that got me fired from my first job: I'd breaded a whole box of fried chicken in the gravy mix. "How come they keep turning black?" This should have been the end of my cooking career, but never mind.).

I assumed her fried chicken was so delicious because I was at my grandmother's house and I just generally loved being there. She let me help cook (to keep me busy; I had no visions of chefdom at six and seven). And she treated me like an adult: I'd have coffee, too—this much coffee and a whole glass of milk, and then I'd go play out where the chickens were running free. I thought her chickens were kind of scrawny. It was many years later that I understood that this huge difference in taste came from her having free-range birds.

Sunday morning, Grandmother would go out and catch a chicken. She'd wring its neck, cut off its head, and spend the rest of the morning plucking feathers. She didn't bat an eye at any of this. This was how things

HONEY-FRIED CHICKEN WITH MINTED CREAM SAUCE AND SPICY SWEET POTATO PUREE Serves 4 to 6

For the chicken

One 3-pound chicken, cut into 6 pieces

$\frac{1}{2}$ cup honey

1 tablespoon apple cider vinegar or champagne vinegar

1 tablespoon fresh orange juice

1 teaspoon fresh lemon juice

$\frac{1}{2}$ cup all-purpose flour

2 large eggs

$\frac{1}{4}$ cup buttermilk

Vegetable or corn oil for frying

Salt and freshly cracked black pepper

1 recipe Spicy Sweet Potatoes

For the sauce

$\frac{1}{2}$ cup dry white wine

$\frac{1}{2}$ cup chicken stock

$1\frac{1}{2}$ cups heavy cream

2 tablespoons chopped fresh mint

2 teaspoons freshly grated lemon zest

2 tablespoons reserved marinade

Salt and freshly cracked black pepper

1 Rinse the chicken well, pat it dry, and place in a shallow dish. Whisk together the honey, vinegar, and citrus juices and pour over the chicken. Turn the chicken once to cover with the marinade. Cover with plastic wrap and refrigerate for 4 to 24 hours, turning the chicken occasionally.

2 Sift the flour into a shallow bowl. In a second bowl, whisk the eggs and buttermilk together.

3 Preheat the oven to 200°F.

4 Heat the oil to 250°F in a large deep cast-iron or other heavy skillet. Cooking the chicken at this lower temperature prevents the honey from burning.

5 Remove the chicken from the marinade and pat dry. Strain the marinade and reserve 2 tablespoons for the sauce.

6 Dip the chicken in the egg wash and place on a tray. Sprinkle generously with salt and pepper, then dredge in the flour, coating the chicken thoroughly. Return the chicken to the tray.

7 Gently place the thighs and legs in the hot oil. Cook for 5 to 6 minutes on one side and then cook on the other side. Add the breast

pieces and continue to cook. Adjust the heat, if necessary, to cook the meat evenly. Turn the white meat after about 5 minutes. The dark meat will take 15 to 18 minutes total cooking time, while the white meat will take 10 to 12 minutes. Pierce the meat with a fork: juices will run clear, not pink, when completely cooked. Place the chicken on an ovenproof plate lined with paper towels and transfer to the warm oven.

8 To make the sauce, pour off the oil from the skillet, leaving only the solids at the bottom of the pan. Pour in the wine and stir to incorporate. Add the stock and reduce all by half. Add the cream, mint, zest, and reserved marinade. Bring to a boil and reduce the sauce until it is thick enough to coat the back of a spoon, 5 to 6 minutes. Strain the sauce and season with salt and pepper.

✛ On individual plates, place pieces of the chicken alongside a spoonful of warmed Spicy Sweet Potatoes. Ladle the sauce over both the chicken and the potatoes.

SPICY SWEET POTATOES
Makes 4 to 6 servings

- -

2 large sweet potatoes, peeled and diced

1 medium new potato, peeled and diced

6 tablespoons pure maple syrup

2 teaspoons salt

1 teaspoon cayenne pepper

1 tablespoon chili powder

4 tablespoons ($^1/2$ stick) butter, softened

1 Place the prepared potatoes in a medium pot and cover with cold water. Bring to a boil and reduce the heat. Simmer for 15 minutes or until the pieces are soft.

2 Drain the potatoes and transfer them to a food processor. Add the syrup and seasonings. Process for 1 minute, then add the butter, a tablespoon at a time, pulsing briefly after each addition.

were done. *So much work,* I thought. *Why doesn't she just go to the store to buy a chicken? A chicken already dead, plucked, cut up, and ready to fry?* Well, this was never a choice she considered.

My grandmother had strict rules about frying chicken: use a cast-iron skillet that you never wash—just wipe out the grease. Never deep-fry the pieces: use enough oil to come halfway up the chicken pieces so the half above the oil can steam.

In whatever I cook today, I try to hold on to that simpler time. It's looking for whole-some ingredients and chemical-free foods, sure, but there's something beyond that: I try to celebrate what's just in season, and I try for a simplicity of preparation. Southern cuisine is unadorned. And the food of the South—maybe because of the longer growing season—is probably the purest of any region: just pay attention to what's freshest right now.

Over the years this fried chicken is what I whip up to coddle a weary friend or to soothe my own harried soul. I serve it with spicy mashed sweet potatoes. My mother perfected this dish at the Truck Stop Café, the restaurant my family owned when I was young, by marinating the fresh chicken in honey and buttermilk. Over the years I've tinkered with the recipe, sneaking in a fruit vinegar or adding a creamy thyme sauce

with mint. But beyond all my innovations, what I most cherish about this dish is the crispiness of the chicken in the same bite as the soft, tangy potatoes: it's a sensation I want for my last meal on earth—although I hope I'll have many chances to enjoy it before that day arrives.

Stephan Pyles, considered the founding father of southwestern cuisine, is a four-time cookbook author and star of the twenty-six-part PBS series *New Tastes from Texas.* The creator of twelve restaurants, he has won awards including a Beard Foundation Best Chef Award, the Fine Dining Hall of Fame Award, and the American Academy of Achievement Award. He was Share Our Strength's Humanitarian of the Year for 1998.

Suzanne Goin THE DEVIL'S CHICKEN WITH POTATOES, LEEKS, AND MUSTARD BREAD CRUMBS

My mother comes from what you might consider a Puritan navy family from New England, and she grew up eating over-cooked pot roast, overcooked vegetables, and basically underwhelming food. She met my father, who's from Los Angeles, while they were in medical school. He had just taken on his surgery residency, and my mother, who intended to be a psychiatrist, was still doing her rotations; my dad ended up being her supervisor on her surgery stint. He waited patiently until the last day of her rotation to ask her out and, for the first date, took her to Fleur de Lys in San Francisco. Mom ordered some special house filet mignon, and it came covered with truffles, which my mother immediately scraped to the side of the plate, where they remained. My father managed to hide his horror and attempted to describe the glories of the truffle.

The first meal my mom cooked for him was Spam roast studded with cloves. Apparently my dad was fascinated. Still, he gave my mother Julia Child's *Mastering the Art of French Cooking,* which had just come out. As family legend has it, that book saved their marriage.

My mother took to cooking very quickly, even though she was working full-time as a doctor. Julia instructed her how *not* to overcook chicken (turns out it takes only five minutes, not forty-five minutes, to sauté a chicken breast!). One of her favorites, a simple dish, really, was *poulet grillé à la diable,* a grilled chicken with mustard and bread crumbs (the devil's contribution, I guess). She opted for broiled chicken thighs, which produced a bit of fat. When she pulled the roast-

ing pan from the oven and loosened the chicken from the rack, my sister Jessica and I would be standing right beside her. There would be these crispy, mustardy bread crumbs that had fallen off and browned in the grease. And we would snatch those crispy nibblets out of the burbling drippings, most of the time burning our fingers in the process.

Early on, I'd help my mother with weekday meals. She learned to make dishes like flank steak stuffed with ham and spinach, *boeuf haché* (my dad was a total Francophile), and leg of lamb with stuffed eggplant. And then my mom got the idea from one of her patients that to really enjoy a dinner party you should hire your kids to cook and serve. So I'd cook and my sister Jessica would serve, and that's how we would earn our allowances. At first Mom would decide the menu, but about the time I started middle school I took to leafing through her huge collection of magazines and cookbooks, picking out recipes to try. One of my big successes was a Roger Vergé recipe for a beef filet with black peppercorns, currants, and Armagnac. I also remember successes with gravlax and veal piccata and Dad's favorite dessert, floating islands. Oh, but there was the one Thanksgiving my mom and I did all the cooking and when we turned the turkey over it slipped out of the oven—and *out of its skin*—and fell to the

THE DEVIL'S CHICKEN WITH POTATOES, LEEKS, AND MUSTARD BREAD CRUMBS

Serves 6 to 8

For the chicken and the marinade

Two 3-pound chickens, butterflied (backbone split, breast- and backbones removed) and wings clipped

¹/₂ cup dry vermouth (Noilly Prat preferred)

2 medium onions, thinly sliced

1 tablespoon fresh thyme leaves (about 10 sprigs)

4 fresh hot chiles, seeded and minced

¹/₂ cup olive oil

For the sauce and cooking the chicken

3 tablespoons unsalted butter

1 cup fresh bread crumbs

2 tablespoons minced shallots

¹/₄ cup dry vermouth (Noilly Prat preferred)

¹/₄ cup Dijon mustard

1 teaspoon chopped fresh tarragon

¹/₂ teaspoon fresh thyme leaves

Salt and freshly cracked black pepper

¹/₄ cup olive oil

For the vegetables

4 small to medium onions, 2 red and 2 yellow, each cut into 8 wedges (leave root attached)

2 leeks, each cut lengthwise into 6 pieces

Salt and freshly cracked black pepper

2¹/₂ teaspoons fresh thyme leaves

2 Yukon Gold potatoes, steamed just until tender and cut into sixths

1 cup chicken stock

1 Rinse the chickens well, pat dry, and place in a nonreactive shallow dish. Whisk together the marinade ingredients in a mixing bowl. Pour over the chickens, turning once to cover evenly. Refrigerate overnight, covered with plastic wrap.

2 Brown 2 tablespoons of the butter in a small saucepan over low heat. Remove

floor . . . just as one of the guests walked in. We swore him to secrecy and carefully tucked the turkey back into its skin.

Today my sister, who's a writer, has joined me as the manager at Lucques. And I've continued to cook up something like our favorite devil's chicken, adding the leeks, the potatoes, and the variety of onions. My mother comes to eat here all the time, but she never orders the chicken. She says there are so many other things to try. Though I can't seem to convince her that she was the inspiration for one of the favorite dishes on our menu, I'm inspired nearly every day by the memories of those dishes we cooked together when I was younger.

from the heat and mix with the bread crumbs. Set aside.

3 Melt the remaining tablespoon of butter in a small skillet over low heat and add the shallots, cooking until translucent, 3 to 5 minutes. Add the vermouth and reduce the liquid by half. Stir in the mustard, tarragon, and $1/2$ teaspoon of the thyme leaves; set aside.

4 Preheat the oven to 400°F. Remove the chickens from the marinade, pat them dry, and season with salt and pepper to taste.

5 Heat a large heavy skillet or cast-iron pan over high heat. Add 2 tablespoons of the olive oil and sear 1 chicken at a time, skin side down. When the skin is brown and crispy, remove it, add the remaining 2 tablespoons oil, and repeat with the other chicken. Set aside both chickens.

6 Sauté the onions in the same skillet over medium heat until limp, about 5 minutes. Add the leeks and season with salt, pepper, and the remaining $2^{1}/2$ teaspoons thyme leaves. Remove the contents from the pan and set aside.

7 Sear the potatoes in the same skillet over medium-high heat until golden brown, 2 to 3 minutes on each side. Set aside.

8 Divide the vegetables between 2 large ceramic baking dishes and pour $1/2$ cup stock over each. Place the chickens over the vegetables, skin side up, and spread half of the mustard sauce over each chicken. Divide and sprinkle the bread crumbs over the top.

9 Bake the chickens for 25 to 30 minutes, until the chickens' juices run clear when the flesh is poked with a fork. The crumbs should be golden brown and the skin crispy.

✤ To serve, cut each chicken into serving portions and arrange on plates with the vegetables. Spoon the cooking juices over the vegetables.

Suzanne Goin began her culinary career as a high school intern in the pastry kitchen of the legendary Ma Maison. She spent two years at Alice Waters's Chez Panisse and a year of "stages" at three great restaurants in France. Upon her return to the States, Suzanne was hired by Todd English at Olives. She also worked as sous-chef and executive chef of Mark Peel and Nancy Silverton's celebrated Campanile before opening her own restaurant, Lucques, in 1998 with partner Caroline Styne in the former carriage house of silent-film actor Harold Lloyd.

Susan Feniger
BOMBAY CHICKEN WITH CURRIED TOMATOES

I've probably spent more than three months in India if you combine my visits. I go to see my friend who heads up the kitchen at the Meher Baba Center, a spiritual community and ashram. Each time I visit, I spend most of my time in the kitchen with him and his staff, preparing food nearly all day. It's twenty-one meals a week there and thousands of folks who arrive for the celebrations or weddings, and travelers who come just for one meal or for tea, and many others who arrive for a week or two of learning and spiritual enrichment. Tents cover the grounds of the ashram, and the kitchens are all outdoors, with deep holes in the dirt to use as ovens and woks set over embers. In addition to meals, we prepare snacks for the visitors such as potato or cabbage fritters in a chickpea batter with turmeric, cumin, ginger, and cayenne, served with cilantro-mint chutney.

My intention wasn't to embark on a culinary journey, but never having made Indian food before, I discovered a whole new awareness of what could be done without herbs, butter, cream, and so many other enrichments I'd always regarded as kitchen staples. I found an enormous assortment of flavors from such a narrow range of ingredients; basically, it was onions, okra, cauliflower, cilantro, yogurt, ghee, eggplant, potatoes, and rice. It was my first experience with variety that had nothing to do with abundance. Before coming to India, I didn't know one kind of dal, and suddenly I discovered ten kinds and an almost inexhaustible range of flavors they could incorporate. We'd create dals of curry with buttermilk, dals with slow-roasted garlic, dals enriched with yogurt and cucumbers. (Every morning a man from the market would arrive on his bicycle about 5:00, bringing us yogurt in screen-covered baskets; everything had to be used that day since we had no refrigeration.)

We'd be up at dawn drinking wonderful Indian tea around the fire pit outside. I'd sit on the back porch with the kitchen staff: the three men who prepared the main dishes and the eight women, ranging in age from twenty-five to sixty, who did the kitchen prep work. The women, all from the same village, dressed in brilliant, bold colors—turquoise or bright pink fabrics. Upward of thirty plastic or metal bangles lined their forearms. They sat on the ground grinding spices, preparing chutneys, peeling tamarinds, or making bread in the fireplace. One woman would

BOMBAY CHICKEN WITH CURRIED TOMATOES Serves 6

----

6 pounds chicken legs and thighs

Salt and freshly cracked black pepper

2 tablespoons olive oil

1 tablespoon fresh lime juice

2 tablespoons unsalted butter

5 shallots, diced

**1 bunch cilantro, a few sprigs set aside
  for garnish, the rest roughly chopped**

1 jalapeño pepper, chopped, with seeds

2 tablespoons ground cumin

2 cups chicken stock

3 large egg yolks

2 tablespoons brown sugar

1/4 cup red wine vinegar

**Cooked basmati rice, as an
  accompaniment**

**1 recipe Curried Tomatoes, refrigerated
  for 3 days**

1 Preheat the broiler or prepare a medium-hot grill.

2 Season the chicken pieces lightly with the salt and pepper.

3 Mix the oil and lime juice in a nonreactive bowl and brush the chicken with it.

4 Broil or grill the chicken over indirect heat for 15 minutes on each side or until the juice runs clear. Transfer the chicken to a platter and keep warm while you finish the sauce.

5 Melt the butter in a skillet over medium heat. Add the shallots and cook until soft and golden brown, about 10 minutes. Add the chopped cilantro, jalapeño, and cumin. Lower the heat and cook for 5 minutes. Add the chicken stock and increase the heat to high. Reduce the liquid by half.

6 Transfer the sauce to a blender and puree in small batches. Strain and return the sauce to the skillet over low heat.

7 Whisk together the egg yolks, sugar, and vinegar in a small mixing bowl. Ladle 1 cup of the hot puree into the egg mixture and whisk to combine. Return all to the remaining sauce. Stir constantly until the sauce is thick and the sugar has dissolved. (Do not allow the sauce to boil.) Adjust the seasonings to taste.

✤ Arrange the grilled chicken over basmati rice and spoon the sauce over the chicken. Garnish with the cilantro sprigs and Curried Tomatoes.

pat the dough into shape, and another woman would cook it on the fire, while a third would hold her baby next to her. The men cooked the dals, rices, sauces, and vegetables.

One evening we made what is honestly one of the most delicious dinners I have ever had anywhere in the world. It was basmati rice, a cumin-cilantro sauce, and pickled tomatoes. Preparing this dish in the States, I have added chicken to make a more substantial meal. (Even if chicken had been offered in that vegetarian community, I had no desire to eat the skinny chickens that were running madly around the streets.)

Along with a new culinary passion, I came back to the States with my own arms filled with bangles (I wore them for two years, until they began to break from the kitchen work) and chef's pants and jackets for me and my partner, Mary Sue, cut from the same wonderful cottons the village women wore. I had bought samples of my favorite fabrics, washed them so they didn't shrink or bleed, and hauled them out to the fields of the ashram to dry on these huge frames. In the

CURRIED TOMATOES Makes 3 cups

----

1 1/2 pounds firm plum tomatoes, quartered

3 serrano chiles, stemmed and sliced, with seeds

3/4 cup white vinegar

2 tablespoons sugar

1 tablespoon sea salt

1/3 cup olive oil

2 tablespoons freshly grated ginger

4 garlic cloves, minced

1 tablespoon yellow or brown mustard seeds

1 tablespoon cracked black peppercorns

1 teaspoon fennel seeds

1 teaspoon celery seeds

1 Combine the tomatoes and chiles in a large ovenproof nonreactive mixing bowl.

2 Boil the vinegar in a medium nonreactive saucepan. Add the sugar and salt. Cook until the sugar has dissolved, about 1 minute. Remove from the heat and set aside.

3 Heat the oil in a medium saucepan until it is smoking. Add the ginger, garlic, and the remaining spices. Stir constantly with a wooden spoon until aromas are released, about 2 minutes. Remove from the heat and stir in the vinegar.

4 Pour the mixture over the tomatoes and toss gently. Cover with plastic wrap and refrigerate for 3 days before serving.

distance I'd watch these billowing colors flap in the wind: pink, yellow-orange, vibrant purple, emerald green—the colors were as brilliant as the flavors I was learning to appreciate. A tailor in the village used the white chef uniforms I'd brought as patterns.

At Border Grill, for many years we were a spectrum of colors scurrying around the kitchen before the uniforms wore out and faded—unlike my memories of that place, its people, and those flavors.

Susan Feniger and her business partner of twenty years, Mary Sue Milliken, are two of America's most beloved chefs. They are the chef-owners of the critically acclaimed Border Grill restaurants in Santa Monica, Pasadena, and Las Vegas, as well as Ciudad in downtown Los Angeles. Natural teachers, the partners have created 396 episodes of *Too Hot Tamales* and *Tamales World Tour* series with the Food Network, authored five cookbooks, hosted the "Hot Dish" radio feature on station KFWB, and launched a line of prepared foods, "Border Girls" brand at Whole Foods Markets.

Patrick O'Connell
BLUEBERRY VINEGAR–MARINATED SQUAB ON CREAMY POLENTA

Many, many years ago, when the Inn at Little Washington was in its infancy, my kitchen staff was composed of people who had come to the back door looking for work. The building had been a gas station and we rented half of it for $200 a month, which was considered highway robbery in 1978. Our original kitchen was the grease pit. Our "courtyard garden" was the actual junkyard.

One of my employees was a tiny woman named Deb; she needed to stand on two wooden Coke crates just to reach the broiler. I thought I'd never be able to use her, but I discovered that she was perfect for helping me plate up the foods: literally, she could work in front of me, right under my arms, so it was as if I had four arms, like some Indian deity.

One day I was also taking the dinner reservations, and a garbled voice came on the phone. I tried and tried to understand what was being said. After many repetitions I realized the speaker had a nice chaw of tobacco in his cheek and blueberries to sell.

BLUEBERRY VINEGAR– MARINATED SQUAB ON CREAMY POLENTA Serves 6

For the blueberry vinegar marinade

2 cups fresh blueberries

$2/3$ cup red wine vinegar

$1/4$ cup olive oil

1 bay leaf

$1/4$ teaspoon dried thyme

1 teaspoon minced garlic

1 For the marinade, combine the blueberries and vinegar in a nonreactive saucepan and bring to a boil. Remove from the heat and cool to room temperature, about 1 hour.

2 Strain the vinegar (do not press the fruit, or it will cloud the liquid) and add it to the oil, bay leaf, thyme, and garlic. Mix together and set aside. The marinade can be prepared several days in advance and refrigerated in an airtight container.

For the blueberry sauce

2 tablespoons unsalted butter

2 cups fresh blueberries

$1/4$ cup chicken stock

Pinch of sugar, optional

3 For the sauce, melt the butter in a small saucepan, add 1 cup of the blueberries, and toss to coat well. Pour in the stock, bring to a boil, then lower the heat and simmer for 20 minutes or until the contents have reduced by almost half and the liquid coats the back of a spoon. Taste and add the sugar if necessary.

4 Strain and reserve the liquid. Keep it warm for serving. The sauce also may be cooled and refrigerated in an airtight container for up to 2 days.

For the squab

Six 10-ounce squabs, rinsed well

1 recipe Creamy Polenta

5 Lay each squab, breast side down, on a cutting board. With poultry shears, snip off the wing tip at the second joint. Remove each breast with the wing tip intact and remove the leg and thigh from the rest of the carcass in one piece. Save the remaining carcass for making stock.

6 Place the pieces in a shallow nonreactive pan or pans and cover with the marinade. Turn each piece to coat evenly. Let sit at room temperature for 2 hours or cover and refrigerate overnight.

7 Prepare a grill with medium-high heat and glowing embers. Lay the birds, skin side down, on the grill rack and cook for 2 minutes or until the skin is crisp but not burned. Turn the birds over with tongs and cook for 1$^1/_2$ minutes longer. Remove from the grill and place them on a baking tray. The squab can be prepared to this point up to 1 hour prior to serving.

8 To finish the dish, preheat the oven to 400°F. Add the remaining cup of blueberries to the sauce and heat until warm. Bake the birds for 2 to 3 minutes for medium-rare or longer for medium.

✤ Serve the meat on individual plates. Drizzle the sauce over each portion, accompanied by a spoonful of the Creamy Polenta.

CREAMY POLENTA Serves 6

----

1 tablespoon unsalted butter

1 tablespoon olive oil

1 teaspoon minced garlic

1$^1/_2$ cups heavy cream

1$^1/_2$ cups whole milk

$^1/_8$ teaspoon cayenne pepper

1 bay leaf

$^1/_2$ cup yellow cornmeal

$^1/_2$ cup grated Asiago or Parmesan cheese

1 Melt the butter in a heavy saucepan over medium heat. Add the oil and garlic. Cook for 2 minutes, stirring; do not let the garlic burn.

2 Add the cream, milk, and 1$^1/_2$ cups water to the pan and increase the heat to high. Add the cayenne and bay leaf. Let simmer for 5 minutes and then remove the bay leaf.

3 Whisking constantly, pour the cornmeal into the boiling liquid in a thin stream. Cook, stirring constantly with a wooden spoon, until the polenta is very thick, 10 to 15 minutes.

4 Remove the pan from the heat and stir in the cheese. Serve immediately or keep warm until ready to serve.

I couldn't make out anything else he said, but I said, "Sure, come on by. I can always use fresh blueberries." Local growers often called on us with great produce.

In no time at all a huge flatbed truck pulled up behind the kitchen door. Its wheels came up to my chin, its cab was even higher, and blueberries, in boxes, in crates—in every sort of container the driver could find—filled the truck bed. They were beautiful, huge berries. "Great, I'll take a couple flats," I told him. (I had no walk-in refrigerator at the time. In fact I hardly had much space in the entire kitchen.)

The man got very agitated. Again, I didn't understand what he was saying. But finally I pieced together some words: "But you said . . . you'd take *all* the blueberries. . . . My son's in the hospital . . . hit by a baseball bat. . . . " His expression was rather threatening, so after some fumbling, I just said, "OK, OK, I'll take them all." The cost was something like $128—more than half of our month's rent. But I paid him, and the staff began to haul the boxes inside.

We loaded our double-door refrigerators. We loaded a tiny Admiral refrigerator in our office, and then we loaded the blueberry flats on top of that, four or five layers, up to the ceiling.

Immediately I set to making blueberry sorbet and blueberry ice cream. At one point I asked Deb to bring in another flat of berries, and not two minutes later I heard this blood-curdling scream from the office. Just as I turned toward the door, a river of blueberries washed into the room. The refrigerator had fallen onto poor Deb. We were all ankle-deep in blueberries, and Deb was lying there amid the berries, a lovely deep purple but not really bruised since the berries had cushioned her fall.

After I ascertained that she was unharmed, my next concern was the berries. Even if we washed them well, I didn't feel comfortable serving them. And then it struck me that I might make a vinegar, a giant vat of blueberry vinegar. Gourmet shops had just begun featuring sherry and raspberry vinegars, so, I thought, why not blueberry? And the bottled blueberries would be sterile from the simmering and straining.

And that's how we created our "little blue chicken" dish, which has continued to evolve over these last two decades. Recently we've been using squabs with the blueberry vinegar, fanning the bright, rare meat over a little polenta and serving it with the pan juices and fresh blueberries. We also switch to blackberries when they're in season.

The finished vinegar is full of perfume and berry essence. You can bottle it to give as gifts or simply shelve the bottles in your pantry—you'll think of many ways to use it.

Patrick O'Connell, a native of Washington, D.C., is a self-taught chef who pioneered a refined regional American cuisine in the Virginia countryside. In 1978 Patrick and Reinhardt Lynch created the Inn at Little Washington, America's first five-star country-house hotel and the first establishment in the *Mobil Travel Guide*'s history to receive five-star awards for both its restaurant and its accommodations. It has been a Beard Foundation Restaurant of the Year, and Patrick has been awarded the foundation's Best Chef/Mid-Atlantic and Out-standing Chef awards. He is the author of *The Inn at Little Washington Cookbook, A Consuming Passion*.

MEATS

Waldy Malouf
LAMB KIBBEH

Sanford D'Amato
SICILIAN SPIEDINI

Philippe Boulot
GIGOT DE SEPT HEURES (SEVEN-HOUR BRAISED LEG OF LAMB)

Jean-Georges Vongerichten
BAECKÖFFE

Thomas Keller
CÔTE D'AGNEAU WITH GLOBE ARTICHOKES AND OVEN-ROASTED TOMATOES

John Ash
MY GRANDMOTHER'S BEEF STEW

Caprial and John Pence
JOHN'S RIBS WITH PLUM BARBECUE SAUCE

David Garrido
PORK AND POTATOES WITH ORANGE JUICE AND COCA-COLA

Andy Husbands
PULLED PORK SANDWICHES WITH COLESLAW

Mario Batali
SALSICCE FRESCHE CON FUNGHI (HOMEMADE SAUSAGE WITH MUSHROOMS)

Noel Cunningham
SAUSAGE AND SAGE PORK LOIN WITH ROASTED BABY CARROTS

Mark Peel
VEAL SHORT RIBS

Waldy Malouf
LAMB KIBBEH

On my father's side my Lebanese grandfather was a Methodist minister in Cambridge, and my grandmother, who lived with us, was Sicilian. I think I had the only Sicilian grandmother who didn't cook much . . . just a few pastries, including rather unforgettable marzipan: she had an artist's off-center sensibility and made bizarre, wildly colored marzipan animals.

When they divorced, my grandfather married a Lebanese woman. About one Sunday a month we'd go to my grandfather's church, and afterward we'd have a midafternoon dinner cooked by my step-grandmother. This lamb kibbeh was always part of that meal. It's a ground meat dish she served either raw or cooked; often she served it both ways. As a young kid, no one expected me to like this Lebanese food. But it became a family joke, because I really did. I even liked the raw kibbeh better. My sister and brother, and even my mother, wouldn't touch it except under duress (many years later they came around), but I looked forward to it every visit.

Their house was exotic in other ways, too. My step-grandmother had lavender water in the bathroom. She wouldn't sit down to eat with us, but stayed in the kitchen, which was how a Lebanese matriarch cooked. To get to know her, and so she could get to know me, I spent a lot of time in the kitchen. (No doubt it was probably pretty boring everywhere else.) She was always doing something with her hands, always preparing food: stuffed zucchini, tabbouleh, phyllo pastries stuffed with nuts (she taught me how to fold those), meats or vegetables braising or stewing in a pot with cinnamon, cumin, black pepper, and coriander.

Eventually my mom, a farm girl from Massachusetts, learned how to make the kibbeh—but only for special occasions like birthdays. Once we moved to Florida, we didn't visit my grandparents as much. Then it was only a couple times a year that we'd have kibbeh, like at Christmas and Thanksgiving, when they'd be untraditional appetizers. My mother learned a few more Lebanese things, like tabbouleh, and she found a Syrian baker near Tampa where we'd get pita bread. So while we really weren't an ethnic family, these remnants did trickle in.

In the fall of 2001, right after the September 11th disaster, I had to fly from my home in Manhattan to Lubbock, Texas—it was my first flight after the towers' collapse. I'd been invited by the Malouf clan to be the guest chef at the annual reunion of distant relatives and cousins. I put off committing to

LAMB KIBBEH Makes 12 pieces

----

1 cup fine-grain bulgur

1 pound lean lamb

1 medium onion, finely chopped

1 teaspoon salt

$1/2$ teaspoon freshly ground black pepper

1 teaspoon Spice Mix, plus extra for garnish

1 cup olive oil

1 lemon, halved lengthwise, and 1 half cut into 4 wedges

1 Place the bulgur in a bowl and cover it with cool water. Soak for 10 minutes. Drain and squeeze out all extra moisture in a clean dish towel.

2 Grind the lamb, onion, salt, pepper, and Spice Mix using either a manual meat grinder or the meat-grinding attachment on an electric mixer.

3 Mix the meat and bulgur together; knead by hand for 10 minutes or use an electric mixer with a dough hook for 7 minutes.

4 Divide the kibbeh into 12 equal portions and shape each piece like a football. Refrigerate for at least 1 hour or up to 24 hours.

5 Heat $3/4$ cup of the olive oil in a cast-iron pan over medium-high heat. (The oil should be at least $1/2$ inch deep.) Fry the kibbeh in batches until brown and crisp on all sides, 7 to 8 minutes. Drain.

6 Arrange the kibbeh on a platter and squeeze the lemon half over the meat. Drizzle with the remaining $1/4$ cup olive oil and garnish with lemon wedges. Sprinkle a light dusting of the Spice Mix on the edge of the platter.

✣ Serve the kibbeh with a simple salad of cucumbers and chopped mint. It can also accompany traditional Mediterranean offerings such as hummus, olives, tabbouleh, or stuffed grape leaves.

SPICE MIX Makes 5 teaspoons

----

1 teaspoon ground cayenne pepper

1 teaspoon ground allspice

1 teaspoon ground cinnamon

1 teaspoon freshly grated nutmeg

1 teaspoon ground cumin

Combine all the ingredients, mixing thoroughly. This mixture can be used to season grilled fish, chicken, and vegetables as well as the kibbeh. Store any extra in an airtight jar in your spice cupboard.

the event for years, not for any particular reason, but owning a restaurant in midtown Manhattan is nothing if not time-consuming. But in the spring of 2001 I had agreed to help. Still feeling raw from the tragedy, I was nervous flying, and I arrived very anxious. But that very night I was a guest at an emotional family dinner with so many dear and even distant relatives . . . and there was kibbeh, which I hadn't eaten for several years, and there were all the traditional dishes that my grandmother used to make on Sundays (she died twenty years ago). Though I'd never been to this place before, it felt so much like coming home. I had a great time with my Texas family.

No matter where you are, the foods of home, even thousands of miles away, can make you feel at home.

Waldy Malouf is chef and co-owner of Beacon, a restaurant and bakery in New York City and in Stamford, Connecticut. His career includes celebrated tenures at the legendary Rainbow Room, La Côte Basque, the Hudson River Club, and the Four Seasons. He is the author of two cookbooks, *The Hudson River Valley Cookbook* and *High Heat,* recently published by Broadway Books. Waldy commits much of his time to hunger-relief efforts and culinary education and works passionately with local farmers, vintners, and other food purveyors to give his food "substance, body, and emotion."

Sanford D'Amato
SICILIAN SPIEDINI

My grandfather moved with his brothers from Sicily to San Francisco. One brother died in California. It was considered a bad omen to remain there, so the rest of the family moved to Milwaukee, which had another large Sicilian community.

When he married in 1919, my grandfather opened a general store—a deli, really—with an Italian slant. He bought a wood-frame house set back a little from the street, and he built a brick storefront in the front yard, enclosing the whole house. That's how storefronts were created at that time, right in the middle of a neighborhood.

They raised their children, built up a viable family business, and then, right after World War II, when my parents were living in Los Angeles, my grandfather called one day and said, "It's time to come home and help your brother run the store." And my dad came back. That's what family meant.

I worked at the store starting when I was

SICILIAN SPIEDINI Serves 4

For the filling

¼ cup extra virgin olive oil

¼ pound pancetta, diced

½ cup finely chopped onion

1½ teaspoons chopped garlic

2 cups fresh bread crumbs

½ cup chopped fresh flat-leaf parsley

1½ cups tomato sauce

¼ pound Romano cheese, grated

** (about 1 cup)**

Kosher salt and freshly ground black

** pepper**

1 Heat the oil in a medium sauté pan over medium heat. Add the pancetta, allowing it to brown slightly. Add the onion and sauté until lightly browned, about 5 minutes. Add the garlic and sauté for 1 minute. Strain in a small strainer, returning the oil to the pan. Place the onion mixture in a small bowl.

2 Brown the bread crumbs in the pan, then add them to the onion mixture along with the parsley, tomato sauce, and cheese.

Taste, adding salt and pepper as desired. Cover and refrigerate in an airtight container for up to 2 days.

For the tomato sauce

¼ cup extra virgin olive oil

1½ pounds mild Italian sausage

** in casings**

2 medium onions, chopped

3 tablespoons chopped garlic

⅓ cup packed fresh basil, chopped

½ cup chopped fresh flat-leaf parsley

** stems, leaves reserved for another use**

2 bay leaves

2 fresh thyme sprigs

½ cup tomato paste

1 cup pork or chicken stock

Two 28-ounce cans peeled plum

** tomatoes in juice, pureed**

3 Preheat the oven to 350°F.

4 Heat the oil in a heavy ovenproof pan and brown the sausages (keeping them whole). Remove and reserve. Add the onions and sauté until browned, about 5 minutes. Add

six. I was allowed to eat all kinds of things in the deli counter. I'd stock shelves, bag groceries, and try to beat my father (who'd use a calculator) adding up a customer's pur-

chases in my head. But even though we kids spent so much time in the store, my father had made a pledge to himself: "I don't care what you kids do in life, but you won't be at the garlic and herbs and sauté for 1 minute. Add the tomato paste and cook for 1 minute. Add the stock and tomato puree and bring to a boil, stirring continuously. Return the sausages to the pot.

5 Cover the pot and place in the oven for 45 minutes or until the sauce is thick. Remove the bay leaves, thyme, and sausages, reserving the sausages for another use. Keep the sauce warm to serve it or refrigerate it in an airtight container for up to 2 days.

For the beef and to assemble the dish

Sixteen 3-ounce slices (3 pounds) trimmed beef strip loin, pounded very thin (see Note)

Salt and freshly ground black pepper

Eight 6- to 8-inch skewers, soaked in water for 30 minutes

2 small onions, quartered, blanched for 10 seconds, and chilled

32 bay leaves, fresh preferred (if dried, blanched first)

$^1/_4$ cup olive oil

6 Preheat the oven to 350°F.

7 Cut the pounded meat pieces in half and season with salt and pepper to taste. Place a tablespoon of the filling on each piece of meat and roll it up like an egg roll: fold up the bottom edge to cover the filling, fold in both sides, and roll the meat toward the top, unfilled edge.

8 Slide 4 meat rolls onto each skewer, placing an onion slice and a bay leaf between pieces. Season with salt and pepper.

9 Heat the oil in an ovenproof skillet over high heat. Brown the filled skewers on all sides. Then place the skillet in the oven and cook the spiedini for 10 minutes.

✢ To serve, ladle tomato sauce onto warm plates and place the skewers on top.

Note: It's easier to cut thin slices of meat if you purchase a single piece of meat and allow it to freeze partially before slicing it into the desired number of pieces. Once the sliced meat thaws, pound it out into thinner slices using wax paper and a kitchen mallet or rolling pin.

this store." He had wanted to be a dentist, but my grandfather never gave him the chance to go to college.

Every night we had dinner behind the grocery. We'd eat in shifts so someone could mind the store. My grandfather was a great cook. My grandmother was a horrible cook. Depending on who was cooking that night, we'd sometimes fill up on Twinkies in the store before dinner.

Grandpa could have opened his own restaurant. He cooked fried artichokes and fennel. Meatballs. Great tomato sauces. Sautéed Sicilian steak with French fries cooked in olive oil. But his best dishes were the spiedini, which he reserved for Sundays or special occasions. Even my mother was persuaded to come over to his house for spiedini.

The basic spiedini is a mixture of leftover tomato sauce and bread crumbs, to which you add pork fat or bacon before wrapping it all in a thin slice of beef. Some regions add raisins and pine nuts to the filling. My recipe is a blend of styles, featuring the flavors my grandfather loved.

In 1989 my wife and I gutted the family store and the house and opened a restaurant in the space. We even sold our own house to help with the finances and moved in above the grocery where I'd spent the first three years of my life. A very odd homecoming. We lived there four years, but we were so busy, I can't even remember how curious it all felt. Where our restaurant kitchen is, right behind the storefront, is right where my father grew up. Our fifty-five-seat dining room fills the grocery store itself. The bathrooms are right where the bathrooms were seventy-five years ago. And when I remember my father saying, "I don't care what you kids do in life, but you won't be at this store," I can only laugh.

We now live across the street from the restaurant, so maybe I haven't totally thwarted his dreams for me.

Philippe Boulot GIGOT DE SEPT HEURES (SEVEN-HOUR BRAISED LEG OF LAMB)

My family owned a farm in Normandy, and so we grew most of our own produce, butchered our own meats, and made our own cream, butter, and cheese from our cows. Farm work took up a great deal of time. In the evenings we'd gather around a big radio for entertainment. I remember the first cars that drove through our village, speeding at all of forty miles per hour! In my teens we finally got a black-and-white TV with one channel to watch. So many of my memories of growing up center around preparing meals.

My grandmother cooked for our big family and all of the farmhands. She had a coal stove, which burned the entire day. While we were in the fields, she'd have something simmering on the stove, which would be ready when we returned at the end of the day. I was raised on these simple simmered dishes: *coq au vin, navarin* of lamb, *civet de lapin* (a braised rabbit dish finished with the rabbit blood), and a favorite rice dish, *teurgoule,* a rice pudding with cinnamon that cooks very slowly.

As a boy, I'd work at my grandmother's side, stirring, cutting, butchering; I learned the basics from her as well as how to properly season food by tasting and how to appreciate this perfectly simple food with its strong regional influences.

When my grandmother prepared lamb, she'd use cubes of the shoulder and neck meat, which tenderize during the long braising. The gelatin in those cuts contributes to the richness of the finished liquid. But when I started working at Maxim's, one of the most classic French restaurants, I learned another way of creating this *braisage,* using a whole leg of lamb and cooking it slowly for seven

GIGOT DE SEPT HEURES (SEVEN-HOUR BRAISED LEG OF LAMB) Serves 8 to 10

One 6- to 7-pound leg of lamb, bone in,
    most of the fat removed
1 1/2 pounds garlic, 1/2 pound smashed
    and minced, 1 pound whole peeled
    cloves
2 ounces fresh rosemary leaves (1 cup)
2 ounces fresh thyme leaves (3/4 cup)
1 tablespoon salt
1 tablespoon freshly ground black pepper
2 cups olive oil
2 medium yellow onions, each cut into
    8 pieces
2 carrots, cut into 2-inch pieces
6 celery ribs, cut into 2-inch pieces
2 ounces (1/3 cup plus 2 tablespoons)
    whole black peppercorns
2 ounces (3/4 cup) whole coriander seeds,
    crushed
2 ounces (3/4 cup) juniper berries
6 bay leaves
1/4 cup tomato paste
2 cups all-purpose flour
1 bottle dry red wine
Fresh pasta or gnocchi as an
    accompaniment

1 Place the lamb in a shallow pan, rub with the minced garlic, rosemary, and thyme, and season with salt and pepper. Cover with plastic wrap and allow to marinate for 24 hours in the refrigerator.

2 Preheat the oven to 400°F. Brown the lamb in the oven, in a heavy roasting pan, for 15 to 20 minutes. (The lamb should take on some color. Raise the temperature to 450°F if necessary.) Remove the lamb from the pan and set it aside. Lower the oven temperature to 300°F.

3 Heat the oil in the roasting pan on top of the stove over medium heat. Add the diced vegetables, garlic cloves, peppercorns, coriander, juniper berries, and bay leaves.

hours—longer than even a hard afternoon of field work.

Now I live in Oregon, where my wife is from, and it has the same microclimate as my town in Normandy. It so often has the feeling of our farm in France; creating this lamb dish fits right in.

Admittedly, it takes some guts to buy an expensive, beautiful, locally raised leg of lamb and just boil it in stock. And for an entire day! But this preparation is a marvel, and so different from a typical rack of lamb. Beyond the seven hours of braising, which you don't really attend to at all, the lamb

Allow the vegetables to brown, 6 to 7 minutes.

4 Stir in the tomato paste and flour. Incorporate well. Deglaze the pan by adding the red wine and 2 quarts water; bring to a boil. Taste and add salt and pepper if necessary.

5 Place the lamb in the braising liquid. Cover the pan with parchment paper and then aluminum foil. Place the roast in the oven for 7 hours.

6 Remove the lamb from the oven and cool in the cooking juices for 45 to 60 minutes. Refrigerate for 24 hours, then remove and discard the congealed fat.

✤ Lift the lamb out of the braising liquid and slice. Bring the braising liquid to a boil, strain, and adjust the seasonings as necessary. Place the sliced lamb in this warm sauce to reheat. Arrange the slices on a warm platter or on individual dinner plates with generous spoonfuls of the sauce. Serve with fresh pasta or gnocchi.

marinates in half a pound of garlic for a whole day before cooking, and it rests in the braising liquid for a whole day after the cooking. The meat becomes like butter, so tender, so intensely flavored. It's almost like creating a confit from the lamb.

This is often the meal I serve when people come to our home. It's ideal for entertaining since most everything is finished the day before and you simply present this fragrant, rich dish in the center of the table. It needs the simplest accompaniments: fresh pasta or potato gnocchi, for example. Or simmer spring vegetables or carrots, turnips, and potatoes in the rich braising sauce.

Having apprenticed with Jöel Robuchon and Alain Senderens in Paris, Philippe Boulot trained and worked at some of the world's finest restaurants and hotels before joining Portland's historic jewel, the Heathman Restaurant, in 1994. Philippe has been guest chef at the James Beard House on numerous occasions and in 2001 was awarded the Beard Foundation's Best Chef/Northwest region.

Jean-Georges Vongerichten BAECKÖFFE

This is a family recipe that I grew up with, and it's still one of my favorite one-pot meals. In Alsace we often used our local baker's oven to slow-cook one-dish meals. The baecköffe (which is the name of a heavy ceramic lidded pot in which the stew is cooked) is the product of a kind of neighborly thoughtfulness that created many of the rituals that were a part of Alsatian life.

In the kitchen, early on Sunday mornings,

my grandmother and mother would set up the dish. I would watch them carefully build the recipe in our baecköffe, preparing each ingredient in turn, never forgetting to season each layer—while my mother would patiently answer my questions about every single gesture she was making.

For a few years I was allowed only to watch as she would peel, slice, and chop, then neatly pile the ingredients on the table. I still remember the first time I was allowed to try my hand at the layering. I can still recall the scent of the fragrant wine and the mellow leeks that permeated the kitchen that day. I can even feel a bit of the pride I had in helping to assemble the very dish that my family would later enjoy for lunch.

Once all the ingredients were assembled in the ovenproof dish, one family member was entrusted with carrying the heavy dish. Ready for church, we walked down the road toward the bakery, leaving the baecköffe in the baker's care. Miraculously, at the end of Mass, the food was ready, perfectly cooked and piping hot from the oven, carefully watched by the baker so there was no risk of burning—even if the sermon ran long. We would pick up our lunch and walk on home to share this wonderful creation that couldn't exist without the attention and teamwork of a mother, her children, and a caring baker.

BAECKÖFFE Serves 4

1 onion, finely chopped

1 carrot, finely chopped

1 leek, finely chopped

2 tablespoons chopped fresh parsley

2 pounds Yukon Gold potatoes, peeled, sliced $^1/_8$ inch thick, and placed in cold water

Salt and freshly ground black pepper

1 lamb shank, boned and trimmed of fat and cut into 2-inch pieces

1 pound boneless lamb shoulder, trimmed of fat and cut into 2-inch pieces

2 slices tomato

$2^1/_4$ cups Riesling wine or more if needed

1 Preheat the oven to 350°F. Mix the onion, carrot, leek, and parsley in a bowl.

2 Drain the potatoes and arrange a layer of slices in the bottom of a 6- to 8-inch-deep baecköffe, cast-iron cocotte, or ovenproof ceramic or glass baking dish. Sprinkle with salt and pepper to taste. Add a layer of the chopped vegetables, season it with salt and pepper, then add a layer of meat, seasoning again with salt and pepper. Repeat the layering process until all the meat and vegetables are used, finishing with a layer of potatoes. Top with the tomato slices.

3 Pour in the wine to cover. Bake for 2 hours; check the potatoes and meat for tenderness. Bake longer if necessary.

✤ Divide the contents of the baecköffe into warm, deep soup plates.

Internationally reputed for his innovative, groundbreaking cuisine, Jean-Georges Vongerichten, originally · from the Strasbourg area of France, has been acclaimed by critics as "formidably gifted," a "residential genius," and the "enfant terrible of modern French cooking." He holds an unprecedented total of twelve stars from the *New York Times* for his four New York City restaurants, JoJo, Vong, Jean Georges, and the Mercer Kitchen. He had restaurants as well in Las Vegas, Chicago, England, and Hong Kong. His cookbooks include *Simple Cuisine*, *Jean-Georges: Cooking at Home with a Four-Star Chef*, and *Simple to Spectacular*.

Thomas Keller CÔTE D'AGNEAU WITH GLOBE ARTICHOKES AND OVEN-ROASTED TOMATOES

This dish, even in this more substantial version, evokes such distinctive memories of my return to Manhattan. This was 1984, after more than a year doing my rounds of stages at various restaurants in Paris. (A stage, which is short for *estagière,* is a position some great kitchens offer where you can observe a master chef: sometimes I learned by helping to cook, sometimes by literally observing.)

I had sold everything before I left New York—I was starting a new chapter in my life. So, upon my return, I had very few possessions. In terms of cooking equipment, I had my knives. I found an apartment. I went out and bought a single Wagner cast-iron skillet. I had no room for cooking in my small apartment, no time for cooking the kind of dishes I suppose I'm known for now, and no time for cleaning up after elaborate meals. I also had no money to spend.

I made this dish frequently over the several months I lived in that apartment. Originally I made this recipe with chicken, so the economy applied to time and money; with the substitution of lamb, it's more expensive. But the simplicity remains: roasting meat and vegetables in one skillet, with a limited amount of energy spent in preparation or in cleanup. And so this one-pot concoction has a simplicity that I still find enormously appealing.

OVEN-ROASTED ROMA TOMATOES Serves 4

8 Roma or plum tomatoes, quartered
1/3 cup extra virgin olive oil
1 bunch fresh thyme sprigs
Gray salt

1 Preheat the oven to 250°F. Bring a large pot of salted water to a boil. Cut and discard the cores from the tomatoes and cut a shallow X on the bottom of each. Immerse the tomatoes in the water for a few seconds to loosen the skin, then plunge them into an ice-water bath. Peel and quarter the tomatoes, cutting from the stem side down.

2 Line a baking sheet with aluminum foil and place a wire rack on top. Arrange the tomato wedges flesh side down on the rack. Drizzle with olive oil and top each slice with a sprig of fresh thyme and grains of gray salt.

3 Roast in the oven for 1 1/2 to 2 hours or until the tomatoes have partially dried but retain some of their juices. Discard the thyme.

CÔTE D'AGNEAU WITH GLOBE ARTICHOKES AND OVEN-ROASTED TOMATOES

Serves 4

Juice of 3 lemons

4 large globe artichokes

Two 6-bone racks of lamb, trimmed

**Kosher salt and freshly ground black
   pepper**

2 tablespoons extra virgin olive oil

16 pearl onions, peeled

4 carrots, split and cut into 1-inch pieces

1 bunch fresh thyme sprigs

1 recipe Oven-Roasted Roma Tomatoes

10 Niçoise olives, pitted and halved

1 Squeeze 2 lemons into a bowl of water just large enough to hold the 4 artichokes; set aside. Prepare the artichokes one at a time. Strip off the bottom leaves. Remove half of each tougher, outer leaf by pulling down on each leaf, leaving the meaty bottom portion of each leaf attached (it will become part of the heart). Leave whole the tender, yellower leaves at the center. Cut off the top two-thirds of the artichoke. Cut away the tough dark exterior leaves of the choke. Spoon out the fuzzy choke, scraping the base. Squeeze lemon juice over the artichoke and submerge it in the lemon water. Repeat with the remaining artichokes. Drain and quarter them just prior to cooking.

2 Preheat the oven to 425°F.

3 Season the lamb with salt and pepper. Heat 2 tablespoons of the oil in a large ovenproof sauté pan over high heat. Sear the lamb for 1 to 2 minutes per side or until the racks are golden brown. Remove the lamb and set aside. Wipe out the excess oil in the pan and add the prepared artichokes, pearl onions, and carrots. Sauté the vegetables until caramelized, 6 to 8 minutes. Set the lamb on top of the vegetables, cover with the thyme sprigs, and place the pan in the oven. Roast for 16 to 20 minutes or until the meat is medium-rare.

4 Transfer the lamb to a tray and cover loosely with aluminum foil to retain heat. Add the Oven-Roasted Roma Tomatoes and olives to the vegetables and cook over medium-high heat until warmed thoroughly. ✢ Arrange the vegetables on warm plates. Slice the racks and place 3 chops on each plate.

John Ash MY GRAND- MOTHER'S BEEF STEW

As I grow older, I become more and more focused on this environmental predicament we face of cultivating, sustaining, and renewing our food sources. How can food be plentiful enough without being poisoned? Our health depends on the health of the things we eat. The seeds for my concerns were planted when I was a child. As I think back on my first experiences of sharing or making food—those first sentient encounters—I see how much they can frame our lives. They don't always, but they have that capacity. Where else do our passions and soapboxes come from? Witnessing so much change can make you an activist.

Comparatively late in life, after he'd served in the World War II, my father decided to become a physician. But first he had to obtain his undergraduate degree. So during those years of study I lived with my grandparents on a cattle ranch in Salida, Colorado, which was then a rather rural area. We were essentially poor mountain folk, but the richness of that place—the *physical* richness—was what I perceived. The geography of those mountains, the streams where my grandfather fished, the gardens my grandmother tended—it all provided for a healthy way of life. And while I had no concept of this at the time, I now see that they practiced biodynamic farming on their ranch.

My grandparents were great observers, with a kind of *Farmer's Almanac* wisdom. How and when the chickens would lose their feathers indicated the changing weather. The precise colors of some tree's turning leaves hinted at how soon cold weather was coming. They had such sensitivity to the natural world.

Even though I was elementary-school age, one of my chores was to help my

MY GRANDMOTHER'S BEEF STEW Serves 4 to 6

2$\frac{1}{2}$ pounds lean boneless stewing beef,
   cut into 2-inch cubes
3 tablespoons olive oil
16 garlic cloves, peeled
2 tablespoons freshly cracked (not
   ground) black pepper or to taste
4 cups canned diced tomatoes in juice
2 cups hearty red wine such as Cabernet
   or Zinfandel
1 cup chopped fresh basil leaves
Salt
Egg noodles, polenta, or roasted
   potatoes, as an accompaniment
1 recipe Gremolata

1 Preheat the oven to 275°F.
2 Pat the meat dry with paper towels. Heat the oil in a large nonreactive Dutch oven or heavy pot over medium-high heat. Brown the meat in several small batches. Drain the fat and return all the meat to the pot. Add the garlic, pepper, tomatoes, wine, and basil and cover with a tight-fitting lid.
3 Place the covered pot in the oven for 8 to 10 hours. (Alternately, keep the pot on the stove over very low heat, simmering very gently. Check occasionally: if the liquid be-gins to boil away, add a little wine or water and turn down the heat.) Cook until the meat is very tender.
4 Transfer the meat to a deep platter or tray and keep warm. Degrease the cooking liquid if needed and add salt to taste. Return the meat to the hot braising liquid. Reheat over medium heat before serving.
✤ Accompany the stew with buttered wide egg noodles, polenta, or roasted potatoes. Place any of these in deep soup bowls, ladling the stewed meat on top. Sprinkle the Gremolata over all.

GREMOLATA Makes about $\frac{1}{2}$ cup

----

3 large garlic cloves
1 cup packed fresh flat-leaf parsley leaves
2 to 3 tablespoons finely grated
   lemon zest
$\frac{1}{2}$ teaspoon salt or to taste

Place the garlic in a food processor and chop finely. Add the parsley and lemon zest and pulse to finely chop it all. Be careful not to turn it into a paste. It should be light and airy. Add salt to taste. Alternately, grind the ingredients in the order given with a mortar and pestle.

grandmother cook for the ten or twelve farmhands. She almost never used what she called "receipts." She made cakes without measuring—she just had a feel for the texture of each dough or mixture. (And at that altitude, baking can be a real issue, especially using a wood-burning stove.)

Of course, what *I* wanted was to be out on the *other* range, where all the men were, but I did like cooking with her, which involved big lunchtime meals consisting of many dishes. (Supper, which we ate later in the evening, was much simpler, like soup or stew or some leftovers.)

And we were always "putting food by," since there's such a short growing season in that area. Her preserves and jams were unsurpassed: we'd fill a huge copper bucket with blackberries or strawberries and set the bucket out in the hot sun. Not only was she conserving fuel by letting nature do the work, but the sun's heat gave the fruit an intense flavor since the enzymes slowly softened the fruit.

Her "receipt" for beef stew circled back to me as an adult. I may not have all the ingredients right, but her beef stew continues to be one of my most requested recipes. She used lots of red wine making this; where this European notion came from so many years ago, way out there in the Colorado hills, I don't know. But she always had wine for special occasions or for Sunday dinners, which reinforced the specialness of gathering together. She would pour me some, too, watered down a bit.

This recipe is a variation of an ancient Italian recipe called *peposo,* which is so named because it uses a lot of pepper. It's a very simple recipe. What's seductive about it is the longer you wait, the more delicious it becomes. Slower cooking breaks down collagen in the meat, making it even more succulent. And the long cooking mellows the black pepper. Start this in the morning and your house will smell delicious the entire day, making you hungrier and hungrier. If you still have a slow cooker, now is the time to drag it out!

Traditionally this was served over day-old crusty bread topped with the braising liquid. You could also serve it with roasted potatoes, polenta, or pasta.

Note: This rich, earthy recipe calls for a wine with deep earth flavors that also can stand up to the pepper. It's a classic definition of the flavors of a young California Cabernet or Zinfandel.

John Ash is the founder of John Ash & Co. restaurant in Sonoma County. His three books are *American Game Cooking,*

Caprial and John Pence
JOHN'S RIBS WITH PLUM BARBECUE SAUCE

My parents and my grandparents are all southern, so we always had ribs around the house. Someone was always barbecuing. My father hosted huge Fourth of July parties on our gentleman's farm: six acres, chickens and horses, six children. I'll always remember that July heat and watching my father hover over the fire as he cooked for 150 hungry guests.

When Caprial and I started in the restaurant business, hosting a barbecue seemed like the natural choice for a party. All you have to do is tell one person that you're cooking ribs, and twenty people will show up. It's a curious thing about ribs! Caprial's birthday is July Fourth, so we have an added thing to celebrate. Each year we simply announce the date of the party, everyone shows up with a potluck dish, and we cook up something like seventy pounds of St. Louis ribs, which is a lot of meat to haul.

But here's another curious thing about great ribs: you eat a hamburger, and you've eaten it, and you're done. But ribs put you in some kind of trance state, and you eat rib after rib, and you don't even know if you're full. You almost can't stop!

I insist on putting a rub on the ribs before barbecuing them; it's an idea I adapted from a way of smoking salmon. The salt and sugar penetrate the meat and give it an intensity that barbecue sauce alone can't do.

As for the sauce, I'm always varying it. This plum sauce is a favorite, though my daughter Savannah loves one I do with pureed cherries. I've used other fruits. I like improvising, keeping in mind the basic elements of sweet, hot, salty, smoky, tangy that I love in barbecue sauces.

(It's true, I make a big deal about each year's sauce, and Cappy loves to kid me: "You have so many ingredients—you don't need *half* that many." So this year, just to prove it, she made a four-ingredient sauce—orange juice, soy sauce, garlic, and ginger—*baked* the ribs in foil in the oven, and then dabbed the ribs afterward

JOHN'S RIBS WITH PLUM BARBECUE SAUCE Serves 6

- -

5 pounds pork ribs, St. Louis style
  if possible
1 cup John's Cure
Smoking chips
1 recipe Plum Barbecue Sauce, divided

1 Remove the thin membrane from the back of the ribs. Coat the ribs with John's Cure. Place the ribs in shallow pans, cover, and refrigerate for 24 hours.

2 Prepare a grill with hot coals only on one side; the other side should be empty. Soak the smoking chips in water for 30 minutes.

3 Put a small handful of the soaked chips in a small disposable tin container and set this on top of the coals. Place the ribs on the side of the grill rack that has no coals beneath. Cover with the lid. Let the ribs cook for 2 hours; begin to baste them with half the sauce every 15 minutes or so for the next 2 hours or until the ribs are tender. You will have to replace coals and chips at least once during the cooking process.

4 Move the ribs to the hotter side of the grill with the coals below. Continue to baste and allow the sauce to caramelize, 10 to 15 minutes. Remove the ribs from the grill.

✣ Before serving, separate the ribs by slicing through the meat. Serve warm with the remaining sauce on the side.

JOHN'S CURE Makes about 3¾ cups

- -

2¼ cups packed light brown sugar
1 cup kosher salt
3 tablespoons onion powder
3 tablespoons garlic powder
3 tablespoons ground mace
3 tablespoons ground allspice
1½ teaspoons ground cloves

Combine all the ingredients in a food processor and pulse to blend. Store in an airtight container for 6 months. The rub can be used for chicken, steaks, or fish.

with her glaze. It was a sacrilege! An insult to my southern heritage! But, sorry, ancestors, they were also delicious.)

I get five grills going in our backyard. We have a double lot, so there's room for my kettle grill, my Brinkman smoker, and a stainless-steel Dacor grill that's three feet across. I cook on gas, mesquite—with that many ribs to grill, you can't be too particular.

By five o'clock the guests arrive, and we have several tables crammed with potluck items: Asian-style dishes, traditional dishes

PLUM BARBECUE SAUCE

Approximately 1 quart

----

2 tablespoons extra virgin olive oil

1 medium onion, diced

2 celery ribs, diced

4 garlic cloves, chopped

6 fresh plums, pitted and diced

2 tablespoons grated fresh ginger

1 tablespoon chili powder

1 cup white wine

1 tablespoon ground cumin

1 cup chicken stock

1/4 cup hoisin sauce

1/4 cup tamarind sauce (available at Asian markets)

1 teaspoon chipotle chile powder

1 bay leaf

One 12-ounce bottle cherry soda

1/2 cup ketchup

1 tablespoon smoked paprika

1 tablespoon plum vinegar (available at Asian markets)

1 tablespoon dry mustard

Salt

1 To prepare the sauce, heat the oil in a large sauté pan over high heat until very hot. Add the onion, celery, and garlic and sauté for 3 minutes. Add the plums and ginger and sauté for 2 to 3 minutes. Add the remaining ingredients. Lower the heat to medium and simmer the sauce for 30 to 60 minutes. Cool slightly.

2 Puree the sauce in a blender in small batches. Taste and season with salt if necessary.

✣ The sauce can be refrigerated in an airtight container for 2 to 3 weeks.

like corn bread and beans, trays of sushi, coolers of margaritas, desserts galore, and birthday cake, just to make it official.

After everyone has had his fill, and a little extra, the sun begins to set. There's only one part of the festivity left: I run out and tell my neighbors to move their cars. We set off tons of fireworks in the middle of the street—and now that my son's older, he's taken over the display. He can take over the rib cooking, too, if he'd like—or at least help.

Caprial and John Pence are the owners of Caprial's Bistro and Caprial & John's Kitchen, a restaurant and a cooking school in Portland, Oregon. They also cohost a cooking show on PBS, *Cooking with Caprial and John.*

David Garrido PORK AND POTATOES WITH ORANGE JUICE AND COCA-COLA

One of my first cooking jobs was working in the pantry at Charlie's 517 in Houston. The chef who hired me offered $3.25 an hour and told me that he expected "creativity." I barely knew how to make hollandaise. At night I'd read magazines, and then I'd go to work to create something I'd never made before and wait for the chef to approve it. Or he'd bring out some wonderful ingredient and I'd experiment, trying to prepare such a new thing. The combinations often surprised me, and once in a while they made me recognize some flavor from my mother's or my grandmother's kitchen.

When you first taste something, especially when you're young, you can't imagine how it was created. But once you start cooking, you can go back to those tastes and try to rediscover them . . . crack their codes. One particular combination triggered a memory I had of my grandmother's pork and potato dish, which I just loved. She made it with Coca-Cola, orange juice, poblanos, and chiles—and what kid is going to resist a dish made with Coke and orange juice? My mother made me this recipe for all my birthdays, and now it has become a favorite of my own two sons.

My grandmother's poblano mole was also a mystery to me until I learned to cook. She comes from Puebla, about an hour from Mexico City, a city famous for mole: garlic, onions, tomatoes, bittersweet chocolate, poblano chiles—a complicated combination of flavors. She'd always make me *pambazos,* a light hamburger bun filled with chicken simmered in her poblano mole. I'd stay with her during the summers. She lived near the bullfighting arena, and on Sundays, during the contests, I'd often go up to the roof of her house and watch the fights. While crowds of people cheered in the arena, my grandmother taught religion

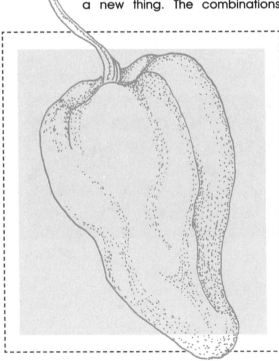

PORK AND POTATOES WITH ORANGE JUICE AND COCA-COLA Serves 4 to 6

1 pound pork tenderloin, cut into 2-inch cubes
Salt
2 tablespoons all-purpose flour
3 tablespoons olive oil
2 large Yukon Gold potatoes, cut into 2-inch cubes
1 cup onion in large dice
2 poblano chiles, seeded and cut into large dice
1 red bell pepper, seeded and cut into large dice
2 cups fresh orange juice
2 cups Coca-Cola
Brown rice and wilted fresh spinach leaves, as an accompaniment

1 Season the pork with salt to taste and lightly dust the cubes with the flour.

2 Heat the oil in a Dutch oven or a medium-size heavy pot over high heat. Add the pork and potatoes to the hot oil and sauté until golden brown, about 4 minutes. Add the onion, poblano chiles, and bell pepper. Continue cooking until the onion is translucent, 3 to 5 minutes. Add the orange juice and Coca-Cola. Reduce the heat to a simmer and cook until the liquid has reduced to sauce consistency, 40 to 50 minutes. (If the sauce has not reduced in this time, strain and reduce the liquid separately over high heat until thickened.)

✣ Before serving, reseason with salt if necessary. Accompany the stew with brown rice and wilted fresh spinach leaves.

classes inside her house for some of the very poorest people in the neighborhood. Along with the Bible studies (which was also a chance to teach literacy), she made food for everyone, sending her "students" home with some of the food as well.

When I became a chef, my father, who is a military diplomat, a consul for the Mexican government, well, he didn't say a word. To him a chef was like a housekeeper, someone you never saw. Obviously I don't agree with that, but I did understand that cooking alone was only partly satisfying. Inspired by my grandmother's example, I've found that giving to my community has filled that role.

A few times a year I cook at the Austin Children's Shelter for two or three dozen children who have been taken away from their families. On Thanksgiving, and again at

Christmas, we cook up big meals for everyone. And my sons have been joining me in the kitchen for years now. Even when they were too young to understand exactly why these children are living at a shelter, they understood enough to be at my side, reaching into the turkey to stuff it or measuring out the chopped pork or passing around bowls for kids to have seconds. It's a tradition that's very important to us all, feeding these kids . . . some who are just a year or two old, some who are just leaving elementary school. And what kid isn't going to love a dish made with Coca-Cola and orange juice? None that we've been lucky enough to serve.

The son of a Mexican diplomat, David Garrido was born in Canada, reared in Mexico, Puerto Rico, and Costa Rica, and schooled in Switzerland. He spent his early career in Texas, working with two of the state's most acclaimed chefs: Stephan Pyles in Dallas and Bruce Auden at San Antonio's Fairmont Hotel. In 1991 David became executive chef at Jeffrey's and is at work on a cookbook commemorating Jeffrey's twenty-fifth anniversary. In 1998 he helped develop and launched the Josephine House. With food writer Robb Walsh, David is the author of *Nuevo Tex-Mex*.

Andy Husbands PULLED PORK SANDWICHES WITH COLESLAW

I opened Tremont 647 with Chris Hart, my best buddy from high school. Our names were next to each other in the alphabetical seating arrangement in homeroom, and we hung out together, often causing trouble. High school wasn't exactly where I applied myself; it wasn't until culinary school that I realized I could be smart.

But after a year in the restaurant together, I bought out Chris—as a business partnership, it just wasn't working. Months after that I realized how incredibly sad I felt about his leaving. While family has always been a source of love, friends have become more and more important. So Chris's absence really was like a breakup.

One day, after not seeing one another for too long, we decided we'd enter the Pig 'n' Pepper BBQ Competition, an annual event like those older national cook-offs such as the Kansas City Royale, the Jack Daniels', or Memphis in May. We had worked at Jack and Earl's Dixie Barbecue at the event years earlier, serving the thousands of visitors who come to watch the competition. We packed a few things and headed off to Carlisle, Massachusetts, for the Columbus Day weekend event.

PULLED PORK SANDWICHES WITH COLESLAW

Makes 8 sandwiches

For the sauce

3/4 **cup white vinegar**

4$^1/2$ **teaspoons sugar**

2 **tablespoons ketchup or favorite barbecue sauce**

1$^1/2$ **teaspoons kosher salt**

1 **tablespoon yellow mustard (such as French's)**

1 **teaspoon freshly ground black pepper**

For the pork

1 **cup apple cider**

1 **cup apple cider vinegar**

3 **pounds boneless pork butt or shoulder**

1 **recipe Pulled Pork Spice Rub**

8 **white sandwich buns**

1 **recipe Celeriac Coleslaw**

1 Combine all the sauce ingredients in a lidded jar and shake well. The sauce can be stored in the refrigerator for several days or until needed.

2 Preheat the oven to 275°F. Combine the cider and cider vinegar together in a spray bottle.

3 Place the pork in a shallow pan or bowl and liberally smear the Pulled Pork Spice Rub over the pork. Transfer the pork to a baking rack on a sheet pan (with sides) and place in the oven. Cook the meat for 4 to 4$^1/2$ hours. After the first 2 hours, mist the meat with the cider mixture every half hour. The finished meat should read 195°F on a meat thermometer.

4 Allow the meat to cool slightly (20 minutes), then shred it by hand; use rubber gloves to avoid staining your hands. Immediately pour the sauce over the shredded pork and toss well.

✢ Open each sandwich bun, fill one side with the pulled pork, and top with a heaping spoonful of Celeriac Coleslaw. Serve the extra slaw as a side dish.

PULLED PORK SPICE RUB

Makes 1 cup

----

3 **tablespoons paprika**

1/4 **cup packed light brown sugar**

1/4 **cup granulated sugar**

1$^1/2$ **teaspoons cayenne pepper**

2 **tablespoons kosher salt**

1 **tablespoon ground cumin**

1$^1/2$ **teaspoons chili powder**

1 **tablespoon freshly ground black pepper**

Combine all the ingredients, mixing thoroughly. Store in an airtight container in a cool place.

CELERIAC COLESLAW

Makes about 8 cups

$^3/_4$ pound green cabbage, shredded
(4 cups)

$^1/_4$ pound red cabbage, shredded
(1$^1/_2$ cups)

$^1/_2$ pound celeriac root, peeled and cut
into matchsticks

1 cup julienned red onion (1 medium
onion)

$^2/_3$ cup shredded carrot

1 tablespoon minced garlic

$^1/_2$ cup finely chopped fresh parsley

1 cup mayonnaise

$^1/_4$ cup whole-grain mustard

1 teaspoon salt

1 teaspoon freshly cracked black pepper

1 teaspoon cayenne pepper

3 tablespoons sugar

Juice and freshly grated zest of 2 lemons

2 tablespoons apple cider vinegar

1 Toss together the cabbages, celeriac, red onion, carrot, garlic, and parsley in a large mixing bowl.

2 Combine the remaining ingredients in a small mixing bowl and blend well. Pour this mixture over the cabbage and toss to incorporate. Cover and refrigerate until ready to eat, up to several hours ahead.

Were we ever unprepared! Everyone else had these efficient portable tents, mobile fireplaces, well-appointed RVs, nice overnight gear—and we had the trunk of my car with a tarp, a small offset smoker, and a couple cases of beer. Everyone else had teams of four or six, and Chris and I had—well, Chris and I. We had arrived at 10:00 P.M. Everyone else had been there since noon.

And it rained. And the field was muddy. And it was very cold.

We pulled the car onto our designated site, stretched our tarp to form a makeshift lean-to, and set up camp underneath just as an official came over to inform us that we had to move the car: it presented a fire hazard.

Uncle Jed's Barbecue took us into their site to get warm. We were dead tired. We were arguing about everything. So, cold and wet and grousing, we started the meats smoking and even argued about how to do that: when to fire the meats, what temperature to run the smoker, which spices to use, when to apply the mustard . . .

Meanwhile, we downed the beers. We tended the fires, drank more, laughed ourselves silly, and just bonded until we both passed out in the middle of the night. (When my wife showed up in the morning, she couldn't even find us. The tent had collapsed on top of us.)

Finally, we got to serious cooking. It's all double-blind judging, with each entry—chicken, ribs, pulled pork, and brisket—presented in a large Styrofoam clamshell for the six judges. You get green leaf lettuce and parsley for presentation. That's it. I can't even use my $40,000 culinary education! The judges consider taste first, then tenderness, then appearance. Each team has a ten-minute window to turn in the first dish, and then each of the next three dishes follow at half-hour intervals. And everyone tries to deliver each entry at the last possible minute so the meat will be hot.

There were about thirty teams. The judges tasted everything and then started to announce the winners, starting with fifth place in each category. Chris and I would have been happy with fifth place. In any category. They announced all the fifth places. All the fourth places. Disappointment was setting in, and then, amazingly, we won third place in pulled pork—and even a trophy. We started hugging and jumping around like the crazy best friends we had been in school.

It's been ten years of competitions. Now Chris and I are a lot more prepared, and we've even been all-around grand champions a few times, winning the most total points.

This sandwich is pretty much what Chris and I cook up in the pulled pork category. Since you're not competing, add on my favorite coleslaw as well; the fresh crunch of the celery root counters the spicy pork. Serve it up at a summer party. You don't need the rain, cold, mud, or even the beer for serving—just the friends.

Andy Husbands is chef-owner of Tremont 647 and Sister Sorel, two of the hippest restaurants in Boston's South End. Andy recently opened Rouge, serving New American South cuisine and southern hospitality. Andy's commitment to his community includes serving on both local and national advisory boards for Operation Frontline, which engages chefs to teach cooking and nutrition to low-income families; he also cochairs Share Our Strength's Taste of the Nation fund-raising event. His honors include not only *Wine Spectator* Awards of Excellence but also a shelf of trophies won by his barbecue team, the PBR Social Club.

Mario Batali SALSICCE FRESCHE CON FUNGHI (HOMEMADE SAUSAGE WITH MUSHROOMS)

Our family would always divvy up the holidays—Easter, Thanksgiving, Christmas Eve, Christmas Day, and New Year's—between the western and eastern sides of the state, as well as along the sides of the family. One holiday at Aunt Marty and Uncle Dick's in Yakivegas (Yakima is so much fun that all of the cousins call it Vegas). One at Aunt Cheri's at Grandma and Grandpa's old ranch. And every other turn at our house.

When the blackberries, black raspberries, and salmonberries lined the sides of Dash Point Road that stretched between Sacajawea Junior High and our arch-rival Illihi, we'd drive along in our yellow Cutlass Supreme and spend an entire summer day picking berries. Mom would choose the spot, and then out we piled, for as long a berry-picking session as the car could support. Back at home we'd make jam and pies and freeze the remaining berries; Mom would bake a fresh, hot blackberry pie every Sunday until we ran out of berries far into the following spring.

Toward the end of summer the whole team of aunts and uncles and cousins would go into production again, this time making what we called our antipasto: baby onions, mushrooms, tuna, peppers, olives, and a tomato sauce that we'd bottle up into twenty or thirty large mason jars and process in a water bath just like we would prepare dilly beans, pickles, and asparagus at other times of the year.

In October all of the uncles (now the job belongs to all the cousins) would compete with Grandpa Laframboise and buy raw olives from Mexico or California. Each family would cure them a little differently. Grandpa would cure his with lye, that bottle with the red devil and skull and crossbones on it, and his olives would be ready as soon as November. But the rest of the family either salt-cured or cracked and brined the olives. These wouldn't be ready until Christmas, when we'd all sample one another's finished olives, arguing over whose came out the best. To this day, most of the mail I exchange with cousins Vance, Derek, and Adam finish with the cryptic note "respect the olive." And we'd have our own home-cured olives for the rest of the year.

New Year's Eve or New Year's Day was also the time for sausage making. With the same family spirit, my brother, my sister, and my parents would go into production, making seventy to a hundred pounds of sausage. This was inspired by my father's side of the family, since my grandfather was a

SALSICCE FRESCHE CON FUNGHI (HOMEMADE SAUSAGE WITH MUSHROOMS) Makes 2 dozen
$1/4$-pound sausages, serving 10 to 12

For the sausage

4 pounds boneless fresh pork shoulder, coarsely ground

2 pounds pancetta, coarsely ground

$1/4$ cup kosher salt

2 tablespoons freshly ground black pepper

$1/2$ cup dry white wine

8 feet casings (sheep or pig)

For the sauce

$1/4$ cup plus 2 tablespoons extra virgin olive oil

1 medium red onion, thinly sliced

3 pounds button mushrooms (or other locally available mushrooms), sliced or quartered depending on size

1 tablespoon hot red pepper flakes

2 tablespoons dried oregano

One 6-ounce can tomato paste

1 cup dry red wine

1 In a large bowl, combine the ground pork and pancetta with your hands and mix well. Add the salt, pepper, and white wine and mix thoroughly. (Mix very quickly not to over-work the fat; melting too much of it will change the texture of the sausage.)

2 Set up the sausage stuffer and place the casing over the funnel feeder. Stuff the sausages into the casing, twisting every $3^{1}/2$ to 4 inches. (To stuff the sausages by hand, quickly form $1/4$-pound logs and stuff them into the casing. Be careful not to overhandle the sausage meat.) Prick the sausages all over with a needle and set aside in a cool place.

3 To make the sauce, heat the oil in a large heavy sauté pan over medium heat until it is smoking. Add the onion, mushrooms, hot pepper flakes, and oregano and cook for 8 to 10 minutes, stirring constantly. Add the tomato paste and cook for 15 to 18 minutes, until the paste turns a dark color. Add the red wine and simmer for 10 minutes. Remove from the heat and set aside. (This can be done several hours in advance.)

4 Heat a large skillet over medium heat and place the sausages in the pan. Cook until golden brown all over, 7 to 9 minutes, shaking the pan occasionally to keep the sausages from sticking to the bottom. Add the cooked sausages to the mushroom mixture and bring to a boil. Lower the heat and simmer for 25 minutes. Add water as necessary, $1/4$ cup at a time, to keep the mushroom mixture looking like a ragù.

✛ To serve, arrange 2 sausages on warm dinner plates with a large spoonful of the mushroom sauce.

prosciutto guy. We ground the pork and pancetta in a hand grinder. And then Dad, the master seasoner, added one thing or another according to his whim or some secret recipe that I never saw. We'd toss a spoonful of the finished sausage into a skillet and fry it up quickly for a taste test. We'd pack most of the sausage into casings, but we'd also leave some of the sausage loose for meat sauces.

It was a whole day of work, of course, though some of the time was taken up with watching the bowl games. Our annual dream was that the Washington Huskies would end up in the Rose Bowl. But nearly every year, it was that Woody Hayes from Ohio State who ruined our chances. We hated him. For us that bowl game was as exciting as opening Christmas presents. So throughout the day we'd stuff sausages and snack our way through the different bowl games, cheering and booing our teams— Orange Bowl, Rose Bowl, and even the distant-sounding Hula Bowl.

Over the next few months we'd have sausages to slice and fry with roasted peppers. We'd also leave sausages whole and smother them under a tomato sauce. Or we'd chop them for a meat sauce to put over pasta. The sausages never quite lasted in the freezer until summer, though we always harbored this idea that they would

have been great to grill on the barbecue. But since they're easy enough to make, it's worth making even a few pounds of sausage just for summer grilling.

Mario Batali's restaurants include his flagship Babbo Ristorante e Enoteca, as well as Lupa, a Roman-style trattoria, and Esca, a seafood trattoria. He is also a partner in Italian Wine Merchants. Among his culinary accolades, Mario was named "Man of the Year" in the chef category by GQ in 1999, received a 2002 Beard Best Chef/New York City Award, and the 2001 D'Artagnan Cervena Who's Who of Food & Beverage in America, a lifetime achievement award. Mario hosts his own programs, *Molto Mario* and *Mario Eats Italy*. He has three cookbooks to his credit: *Simple Italian Food*, *Mario Batali Holiday Food*, and *The Babbo Cookbook*.

Noel Cunningham
SAUSAGE AND SAGE PORK LOIN WITH ROASTED BABY CARROTS

My mom was an incredible cook, and all my friends hung out at our house in Dublin. When I moved away from home at

SAUSAGE AND SAGE PORK LOIN WITH ROASTED BABY CARROTS Serves 6 to 8

For the stuffing

4 tablespoons (¹/₂ stick) unsalted butter

¹/₂ pound bulk pork sausage

4 celery ribs, diced

1 large yellow onion, diced

1 teaspoon minced garlic

¹/₄ cup fresh sage leaves, minced

3 fresh thyme sprigs, leaves minced

2 large eggs

2 cups chicken or vegetable stock

1 medium loaf dried bread, cut into
   ¹/₂-inch cubes (8 cups of cubes)

Salt and freshly ground white pepper

For the pork loin

One 2¹/₂- to 3-pound pork loin, trimmed
and butterflied

Salt and freshly ground white pepper

¹/₄ cup vegetable oil

1 large onion, sliced

2 celery ribs, halved

1 pound baby carrots with 1 inch
   of stem attached

1 For the stuffing, melt the butter in a large sauté pan over medium heat and add the sausage, celery, and onion. Cook until the meat is no longer pink and the vegetables are translucent, about 7 minutes. Crumble the sausage into medium bits.

2 Whisk the garlic, herbs, eggs, and stock together in a large bowl. Add the bread cubes and the cooked meat. Season with salt and pepper, mix well, and refrigerate.

3 To prepare the pork loin for stuffing, open

seventeen, my younger brother's friends took their places at the table. My mom simply loved kids and loved to whip up something for whoever arrived at her table.

My whole family worked in the restaurant business: cooking, bartending, managing, waiting tables. Any time we gathered for a meal, the conversation was food and the food business. My mom was a waitress, fulltime, in addition to raising four kids. My dad was a chef; he almost never cooked at home—sometimes on Sundays he'd make some sort of meat, cooking it perfectly rare, and we'd all protest, *"We're not cannibals!"* and then my mother would finish cooking the meat until it was well done so we could eat our portions.

Each of us kids had a favorite dish that she'd make special for us. My little brother loved her steak fries, and my sister loved her steak pie. David, my other brother, loved her pastries, like rhubarb pie. And on Fat up the loin (the meat should be of even thickness) and pound the meat in any thick areas to create an even surface. Season with salt and pepper.

4 Cover the surface with a thin layer of the stuffing, leaving a 2-inch strip on one side without any filling. Roll the loin starting with the covered side and secure with butcher's twine. Season the outside of the loin with salt and pepper. Place the extra stuffing in a buttered gratin dish and bake along with the roast.

5 Preheat the oven to 375°F.

6 Heat the oil in an ovenproof casserole or a large sauté pan over medium heat. Season the meat with salt and pepper. Brown the pork on all sides. Add the onion slices, celery, and baby carrots (remove the carrots when tender, 25 to 30 minutes). Roast the loin for 40 minutes or until the internal temperature reaches 160°F.

7 Remove the pork from the pan and cut away the twine. Place the roast on a platter and cover with aluminum foil to keep it warm.

8 To prepare the sauce, remove any excess oil from the pan and deglaze the remaining pan drippings with 2 cups water. Scrape the bottom of the pan to loosen any browned bits. Let the sauce reduce by half and then strain.

✣ Slice the roast and arrange the carrots around the platter. Spoon the reduced juice over the meat. Offer the additional stuffing on the side.

Tuesday she made these very thin crêpes with orange and lemon and sugar, and we'd all eat them as quickly as she could make them. But the dish she made for me was this stuffed pork loin.

I'd come home to Ireland from that "pagan country" England, where I was working at the Savoy Hotel, and I was always greeted with this wonderful roast. I'd walk in the door, and the whole house would smell of this fantastic dish. It was the smell of sausage and sage, but it was really the evidence of love: my mother had been in the kitchen thinking about my coming home.

One evening, the only way I could get home to Dublin was to take a boat across the Irish Sea. Now that's not the most calm crossing you can undertake, and I got home at seven the next morning. I walked in, and there was the pork roast, and there were all my friends waiting. No bacon and eggs and tea—just the pot roast!

This is pretty much my mother's recipe, finessed a little. Our biggest regret is that my mom didn't write down a single recipe. She never counted, measured, weighed a single ingredient. In her whole life, she never looked at a cookbook. Yet the dishes she made over and over always tasted the same, always delicious.

My mother figured out how to get this pork loin crisp on the outside and sumptuously juicy on the inside. When you eat this, in your belly you just feel like you've been loved. That's it: I could taste the love she put into the food. And *that* you don't find in cookbooks.

Born in Dublin, Ireland, Noel Cunningham became the youngest non-French sous-chef ever at the Savoy. He is now chef-owner of Strings restaurant in Denver, Colorado. Noel is known for his compassion and generosity in the Denver community and nationwide. Fifteen years ago he helped to organize the very first Taste of the Nation event for Share Our Strength in response to the famine in Ethiopia. He has been a board member of that organization as well as an unflagging advocate in his community, sponsoring programs ranging from Quarters for Kids to Operation Frontline's nutrition education classes.

Mark Peel
VEAL SHORT RIBS

What can I say? These are the flavors that I love. You start with short ribs, which are a tough meat, but with a long, slow braising they'll become so flavor-rich and tender that the meat will just slide from the bone. The finished meat is the most satisfying, delicious food, especially paired with greens that are similarly cooked for a long time. Kale, collards, turnip, and mustards develop such a deep flavor this way. This combination is just the ideal comfort food.

Not that I ever had such a thing when I was growing up. Sometimes it's childhood foods that remain your comfort foods; sometimes you find them later. No, when I was young, my mother never had this kind of time to prepare food. She was a single parent with three kids and few resources. Her parents had died when she was a child; my father's parents did not live close by. So my mother had about half an hour to prepare dinner. It might be nice to say that her specialty was lasagne, since she made that often, but it was simply a thrifty and easy-to-assemble dish that could provide some leftovers and save time later in the week. And she did make a fantastic macaroni and cheese that was nothing like the ready-made box version.

VEAL SHORT RIBS Serves 6 to 8

5 pounds (30 pieces) veal short ribs

2 tablespoons salt

2 teaspoons freshly ground black pepper

1/2 cup vegetable oil

1 onion, diced

1 celery rib, diced

1 carrot, diced

1 bottle dry white wine

1 quart chicken stock

1 cup veal stock or water

2 heads garlic, cloves peeled

12 to 15 fresh thyme sprigs

Sautéed dandelion greens or stewed shell
    beans, as an accompaniment

1 Place the short ribs on one or more trays and pat dry. Season with 2 tablespoons salt and 2 teaspoons pepper. Refrigerate, covered, for 24 hours or up to 2 days.

2 Place a large skillet over medium-high heat and add 2 tablespoons of the oil. When the oil is hot, sear the ribs in batches, browning on all sides except for the bone side. Transfer the ribs to a large roasting pan with 2-inch sides and brown the remaining ribs, adding more oil as necessary. Set aside.

3 Preheat the oven to 350°F.

4 Lower the heat under the skillet and add the onion, celery, and carrot. Scrape the bottom of the pan so that the liquids released from the vegetables will deglaze the pan. Increase the heat to evaporate the

I found this method of cooking ribs when I first ventured out to get a job; I fell into cooking by accident, working as a dishwasher in Sonoma County. I started tasting things there—things I'd never had before. So the first sample I had of this wonderfully cooked veal (which was beyond the budget when I was living at home) was at Ma Maison. Michel Maupuy, the sous-chef, often served osso buco as a lunch special, and I remember being so startled and amazed at the tenderness and richness the meat obtained

after that long, slow braising. These ribs have something of that same quality.

Now I often make these ribs at home. It doesn't take all that much attention, really. And it can sit, it can be reheated, it can serve a whole family gathering. Serve the ribs with your favorite cooked green—I happen to love quickly sautéed dandelion greens (give them a quick blanching in boiling water first). Stewed shell beans are also delicious since they can absorb some of the rich broth as well. And if you want to add liquid and caramelize the vegetables. When the vegetables have turned golden brown, add the white wine, stir once or twice, and cook until almost all of the wine has evaporated and the vegetables are almost dry, 15 to 20 minutes.

5 Add the chicken and veal stocks to the vegetables and bring to a boil. Taste the liquid for seasoning and add the garlic cloves. Remove from the heat.

6 Pour the liquid and vegetables into a large roasting pan. Place the ribs, bone side down, in the pan. The liquid should cover all but a third of the meat. Add or remove water as necessary. Place the thyme sprigs across the top of the meat.

7 Cover the pan with plastic wrap (to create a steam oven), then cover with aluminum foil. Place in the oven and cook for 2 hours. Remove both covers and bake for 10 more minutes or until the ribs brown. Remove from the oven, carefully transfer the ribs to a tray, and increase the oven temperature to 425°F.

8 Strain the broth through a fine-mesh strainer into a tall container. Let the juices settle for 15 minutes, then skim off the fat with a ladle.

9 To glaze the ribs, return them, bone side down, to the roasting pan. Pour in enough strained broth so that half of each rib is submerged. Cook for 15 minutes. Remove from the oven and reseason the cooking broth with salt and pepper.

another course, start with Nancy's Caesar salad; to me it's just a crispier serving of the same comfort. Use whole romaine lettuce leaves and plenty of grated Parmesan, and make a classic Caesar dressing with a mortar and pestle, using plenty of garlic and some diced red onion.

What's key is simply having a few dishes—no matter how rich or "gourmet" they may be—whose very reappearance makes you happy, happy just being at the table with your family.

Mark Peel is executive chef and owner of Campanile; both he and his restaurant have received several nominations and awards from the Beard Foundation. He served for three years as head chef at Spago, a year at the celebrated Chez Panisse, and in 1989, opened Campanile restaurant. Mark is the co-author of *Mark Peel and Nancy Silverton at Home: Two Chefs Cook for Family and Friends* and *The Food of Campanile.*

SALADS AND SIDE DISHES

Susanna Foo
PANKO-CRUSTED GOAT CHEESE WITH TOMATO
AND ASPARAGUS SALAD

Debra Paquette
ROASTED BEET AND CRANBERRY SALAD

Thierry Rautureau
WILD MUSHROOM SALAD WITH A BALSAMIC CARAMEL

Pano Karatassos
TWO GREEK VEGETABLES

Frank Stitt
GRILLED JUMBO ASPARAGUS WITH HAM-HOCK VINAIGRETTE

Greg Higgins
THREE PICKLES

Frank Brigsten
OYSTER DRESSING

Kevin Von Klause
THREE BEANS

Susanna Foo PANKO-CRUSTED GOAT CHEESE WITH TOMATO AND ASPARAGUS SALAD

Before we moved to Taiwan in 1948, my mother had lived in Inner Mongolia, a region of China that's not exactly known for its cooking. It's a very rustic, poor part of the country (the weather resembles Chicago's) with a very short growing season. So there aren't many native vegetables. My mother grew up eating daikon, napa cabbage, root vegetables such as sweet potatoes and radishes, the occasional venison, and goats, which her family raised. Mongolian cooking is a slower, simmering style compared to the faster, wok-tossed or steamed cuisine that people often associate with Chinese foods.

My mother often talks about the wonderful goat cheese she ate as a young girl. Besides mutton occasionally (slow-cooked with lots of leeks and garlic to soften its scent), there was usually goat's milk (often warm, which also has a rather *distinctive* smell), and goat cheese. Most people can't imagine cheese in a Chinese cuisine, but in this region of China, with its cold temperature, goat's milk provided essential nutrition.

When my parents came to visit me in Florida—this was 1972—they had never been overseas. But they wanted to meet their grandchildren: our first child had turned two, and I had just given birth to our second child. At the time, my husband was an assistant professor and I took care of the kids and the house.

Curiously the climate in Taiwan is similar to Florida's, and many of the things in the market seemed similar to my mother. She was delighted to find the same fresh peanuts she loved in Taiwan. And she even thought the cabbages in this country were better than any she knew in Taiwan.

To welcome my parents, I bought some very strong goat cheese, thinking it would especially please my mother; I don't think she'd tasted goat cheese in twenty-five years. As it turned out, she thought this cheese was so *mild*, at least compared to what she had eaten as a child. Still, it brought back many memories of the kitchen she'd known as a girl and how she'd coat the goat cheese with flour and panfry the slices.

When you eat goat cheese like this, the contrast of the crispy outer crust and the hot creamy inside startles your mouth. These slices are wonderful hors d'oeuvres or an ideal accompaniment to a salad such as this one with asparagus and arugula. Of course, this is quite a departure from an Inner Mongolian dish. (I don't think my

PANKO-CRUSTED GOAT CHEESE WITH TOMATO AND ASPARAGUS SALAD Serves 4

1/2 **pound jumbo asparagus (8 to 10**
   spears), peeled and cut into 2-inch
   pieces on the diagonal
One 10- to 11-ounce log of mild
   goat cheese
1/2 **cup all-purpose flour**
2 eggs, slightly beaten
1 cup panko (Japanese bread crumbs,
   available at Asian markets)
1/2 **cup vegetable oil**
1 cup baby arugula or watercress
2 small ripe tomatoes, sliced (8 pieces)
1 recipe Balsamic Vinaigrette

1 Blanch the asparagus pieces by immersing them in a small saucepan of boiling water for 30 seconds. Plunge the drained pieces into a bowl of cold water and allow to chill. The asparagus can be prepared in advance and refrigerated.

2 Slice the goat cheese into 8 pieces, dipping the knife into hot water between cuts to make neat slices. Set them on a plate.

3 Use 3 separate bowls to hold the flour, eggs, and panko. Coat the goat cheese in the flour and shake off any excess flour. Dip each slice into the eggs and then into the panko. Gently place each slice on a plate. Refrigerate until ready to fry.

4 Heat the oil in a nonstick skillet over medium heat. Add the slices to the hot oil and fry until lightly browned, about 2 minutes. Turn and brown the other side. Remove the slices and drain on a stack of paper towels. (This step can be done in advance; the cheese can be held in a warm oven until ready to serve.)

✢ Divide the arugula or watercress among 4 chilled plates. Top each with 2 tomato slices and some asparagus pieces. Spoon the vinaigrette, including the garlic slivers, over all. Place 2 pieces of warm goat cheese atop the vegetables.

BALSAMIC VINAIGRETTE

Makes 2/3 cup

----

2 garlic cloves, thinly sliced
1/2 **cup extra virgin olive oil**
3 tablespoons balsamic vinegar
1 teaspoon kosher salt
Freshly cracked black pepper

Combine the garlic and oil in a small heatproof glass bowl and cover with a paper towel or plate. Microwave on high for 1 minute. (This will mellow the sharpness of the garlic.) Whisk in the remaining ingredients. Refrigerate the dressing in a sealed jar.

mother had ever eaten tomatoes, let alone arugula or asparagus!)

For this dish I prefer a French goat cheese such as the mild, creamy Chevrion (plain). I also like using panko, Japanese bread crumbs, which are coarser than plain bread crumbs and create a deliciously crunchy crust when fried.

Susanna Foo was born in Inner Mongolia, China, and raised in Taipei, Taiwan. She emigrated to the United States in 1967. In 1987 she opened Susanna Foo Chinese Cuisine in Philadelphia, where she reinterprets classical Chinese dishes with French techniques. Her first cookbook, *Susanna Foo Chinese Cuisine*, was heralded with rave reviews and awarded the Beard Foundation award for Best International Cookbook; the following year, Susanna herself became the first chef in Pennsylvania to win a Beard Foundation Award for Best Chef/Mid-Atlantic region.

Debra Paquette
ROASTED BEET AND CRANBERRY SALAD

I am a beet fanatic. The queen of beets. Honestly. Beet soups, beet relishes, beet risotto, beet BBQ sauce, beet broth, beet chips, beet salads, roasted beets, beet lipstick (yes, sometimes at the restaurant, I grab a beet and apply a little color to my lips before running out to chat with the guests). The other day I ate a few roasted beets and happened to look in the mirror: my tongue was so red, with such an exuberant color, I couldn't resist doing my Kiss imitation of Gene Simmons, making my staff laugh like crazy. (I also get them to scream occasionally. When we get beets with especially long, rattail-looking roots, I can't resist: I hide their tails in inconspicuous places and wait. . . .)

I also adore cranberries, another brilliant red globe, particularly in winter, when there's nothing bright and red to serve (I don't really like importing strawberries and raspberries), and I have a salad that combines beets with these cranberries that I stew in a simple syrup steeped with Indian spices. It's inspired by my love of jams, preserves, and the whole range of chutneys. The berries are crunchy and tart inside, sweet and fragrant outside, and are great flavor boosters on all kinds of dishes, from grilled fish to roasted meats. Since cranberry season is so short, I end up buying every bag off the shelf at our local Kroger's. (The cashiers are probably thinking to themselves, "Oh, that poor lady's whole family must have kidney infections!")

ROASTED BEET AND
CRANBERRY SALAD Serves 6

For the cranberries

3/4 pound fresh or frozen cranberries

1/2 cup sugar

**1 1/2 tablespoons pickling spices, ground
(or left whole and strained before
adding the cranberries)**

1/3 cup bourbon

1/2 teaspoon salt

For the beets and salad

3 medium beets

6 to 7 tablespoons vegetable oil

Salt and freshly ground black pepper

2 oranges

1 cup pecans

1 cup plain fresh bread crumbs

1/2 cup all-purpose flour

1/2 cup whole milk

1 1/2 pounds mixed salad greens

1 recipe Walnut Tabasco Dressing

1 recipe Sage Goat Cheese

**1/2 pound applewood-smoked bacon,
diced, cooked until crisp, and drained**

1 Rinse the cranberries. (If using frozen, remove the fruit from the freezer 15 minutes before cooking.)

2 Combine 1/4 cup water, the sugar, pickling spices, bourbon, and salt. Bring to a simmer over medium heat and cook for 10 to 15 minutes or until the syrup coats the back of a spoon. (Strain out the pickling spices if using them whole.) Add the cranberries; continue to cook over low heat for 8 to 10 minutes or until you hear the cranberries begin to pop. Remove from the heat and cool. Set aside. This step can be done ahead of time; cover and refrigerate the berries.

3 Preheat the oven to 400°F. Peel and cut the beets into 1/4-inch slices. Toss the beets with 1 to 2 tablespoons of the oil and season with salt and pepper to taste. Transfer the slices to a sheet pan lined with parchment paper and cover with aluminum foil. Bake for 25 to 30 minutes, until the beets are tender but firm; a fork should poke through easily. Remove the foil and cool. (The beets can be done 1 day in advance and refrigerated.)

4 Using a sharp paring knife, cut off and discard the peel and pith from the oranges. Cut between the membranes to release the segments into a small bowl and set aside.

5 Grind the pecans and bread crumbs together in a food processor. Add a pinch of salt and pepper. Set out 3 shallow bowls. Place the bread-crumb mixture in one. Place the flour with 1/4 teaspoon salt and 1/2 teaspoon pepper in the second. Pour the milk into the third.

6 Heat 3 to 4 tablespoons of the remaining oil in a skillet over medium heat. Dip a beet slice into the flour, then the milk, and then into the bread-crumb mixture, pressing to make sure the mixture adheres. Panfry the slices in batches until golden brown on both sides, 2 or 3 minutes per side. Drain on paper towels.

✛ To arrange the salad, toss the greens with a pinch each of salt and pepper and the Walnut Tabasco Dressing. Place the greens in the center of each plate and sprinkle with the Sage Goat Cheese, bacon, and cranberries. Alternate the warm beet slices with the orange segments around the edge of the plate.

WALNUT TABASCO DRESSING
Makes $\frac{1}{2}$ cup

----

3 tablespoons walnut oil (other nut oils may be substituted, adding their own unique flavors)

4 teaspoons Tabasco sauce

$\frac{1}{3}$ cup maple syrup or honey

Whisk the ingredients together in a small bowl. The dressing can be prepared several days in advance and refrigerated in an airtight container.

I should say that my two sons' favorite beet recipe is my beet brownies. Roasted beets have the most sugar, so you can puree them with flour, chocolate, and butter. These brownies take a little longer to bake because of the extra moisture, but that makes them extra moist, deep, and dark. There's no explaining how good they are; you just have to try them. Serve them to friends, but don't tell them about the beets until they've eaten their first one.

Their other favorite beet dish is a Mediterranean salad I do with Parmesan cheese, capers, and beets layered on lettuces. Their grandmother was here one night, and she actually had to tell my boys, "*No more beets* until you finish your dinner." (And this is the same mom who had served us the infamous canned beets, with vinegar and raw onions, when I was a youngster—and never once did she make us kids eat them. We ignored the beets . . . and then she and Dad got to eat the whole bowl themselves!)

Even our dog likes beets! I was chopping some fresh veggies at home last week, and a zucchini slice fell on the floor. Our black Lab, Murphy, just sniffed at it. But then, to my astonishment, when I gave her a roasted beet that was sitting on the counter, she loved it. I gave her one, then another, then another! And you know how owners can

SAGE GOAT CHEESE Serves 6

2 tablespoons unsalted butter

12 small fresh sage leaves, chopped

6 ounces mild soft goat cheese

1/4 teaspoon salt

1/2 teaspoon freshly cracked black pepper

1 Melt the butter in a small sauté pan over medium heat. Add the sage and sauté for 2 minutes or until the leaves turn light brown. Watch closely: the leaves will burn very easily. Cool completely.

2 Crumble the goat cheese and mix in the sage, salt, and pepper. Cover and refrigerate until ready to serve. This step can be done 1 day in advance.

BEET BROWNIES Makes 24 brownies

2 medium beets (or one 8-ounce can of
    beets)

1 tablespoon vegetable oil

1/2 pound (2 sticks) plus 1 tablespoon
    unsalted butter

1/2 pound semisweet chocolate

2 cups sugar

3 large eggs

2 teaspoons vanilla extract

1 cup all-purpose flour

Pinch of salt

1 cup chocolate chips, optional

1 cup walnuts, coarsely chopped,
    optional

1 To roast fresh beets, preheat the oven to 400°F. Toss the beets with the oil, wrap in a double layer of aluminum foil, seal tightly, and transfer to a sheet pan. Bake for 50 to 60 minutes until the beets are tender but firm; a fork should poke through easily. Unwrap, cool, and peel. (Canned beets are ready to use.)

2 Preheat the oven to 350°F. Grease an 8 X 10-inch pan with 1 tablespoon of the butter.

3 Melt the remaining butter and the chocolate in a medium heavy saucepan over very low heat, stirring constantly. (Alternately, microwave it in a microwaveable container on the low setting for a total of 1 1/2 minutes, stirring every 30 seconds.) Set aside to cool slightly.

4 Place the beets and sugar together in a food processor and puree. Add the eggs and vanilla and blend well. Add the beet puree to the melted chocolate and then stir in the flour, the salt, and the chips and nuts if desired.

5 Pour the batter into the prepared pan and bake for 30 to 35 minutes or until a toothpick inserted in the center of the brownies comes out clean. Remove from the oven and transfer to a cooling rack. Cut the brownies when cool. Store in an airtight container.

look like their dogs: we had matching red tongues. You can't beat that!

But I also committed a major mother boo-boo. I sent my older son to school one day with beets in his lunch box. Good roasted beets, just as tasty and nutritious as can be. (He also had salmon and other stuff the teachers themselves would drool over.) And then, the following time I served beets at home, he wouldn't touch them. Not one. Same thing the next time I cooked beets. Finally, I figured something was up. True enough, his buddies at school had given him one brutal verbal *beeting,* razzing the daylights out of him for having these funky red vegetables in his lunch box. It took him a year to get over the humiliation. But now the beet prince has a red tongue once again.

Debra Paquette is chef and co-owner, with her husband, Ernie, of Zola in Nashville, Tennessee, a restaurant they opened in 1998 that features her own style of Med-American cuisine. A 1978 graduate of the Culinary Institute of America, Debra has been featured on the Discovery Channel's *Great Chefs* series and has been named, four times, Nashville's Best Chef. For several years Zola has been the recipient of *Wine Spectator*'s Award of Excellence.

Thierry Rautureau WILD MUSHROOM SALAD WITH A BALSAMIC CARAMEL

I grew up in a town of two thousand people near the Loire. When I was very young, my father would wake my brother and me extra-early during the fall mushroom season, and we'd walk for a couple miles to the pastures where the cows grazed. We were so eager to get started: mushrooms had sprung up while we were sleeping! Stepping right between the cows (they were much taller than we were, of course—but we were used to cows), we'd search for parasol mushrooms, or the *petit rose,* a small field mushroom. I'd get so excited finding the first cap. And then another. And one bigger than any my father had found so far! And then a whole cluster of them together! We picked each mushroom carefully, leaving the bottom of the stalk attached to the ground just as my father had taught us.

On a good morning we'd come home with fifty big mushrooms and dozens of the littler button mushrooms, and my mother would cook them in the simplest ways: just sautéed in butter for an omelet or with sautéed potatoes. They were treats of the moment. Once in a while we'd forage in a

WILD MUSHROOM SALAD WITH A BALSAMIC CARAMEL Serves 4

----

2 tablespoons 25-year-old balsamic vinegar (see Note)

1/4 cup extra virgin olive oil

Salt and freshly cracked black pepper

2 tablespoons unsalted butter

3 cups wild mushrooms (a mix of chanterelle, lobster, coral, matsutake, shiitake, oyster, etc.)

1/4 cup minced shallots

1 teaspoon minced garlic

1 teaspoon chopped fresh thyme leaves

3 cups micro greens (miniature lettuces, sprouts, and herbs available at specialty markets) or a mix of wild greens (watercress, arugula, red oak lettuce, etc.)

1/4 cup toasted pecans, coarsely chopped

1/2 cup mild goat cheese, such as chèvre

1 recipe Balsamic Caramel

1 Place the vinegar in a small mixing bowl and whisk in the olive oil. Season with salt and pepper to taste and set aside.

2 Melt the butter in a small skillet, raise the heat to high, and cook the butter until it turns golden brown, about 2 minutes. Add the mushrooms and sauté over high heat until nicely browned. (The size and variety of mushroom will determine cooking time—from 2 to 6 minutes.) Add the shallots and cook until translucent, about 2 minutes. Add the garlic and thyme and cook for an additional 1 to 2 minutes.

✛ To serve, toss the greens with 2 to 3 tablespoons of the dressing and arrange in the center of individual plates. Spoon the cooked mushrooms around the greens. Top the greens with a few pecans and a sprinkling of the goat cheese. Drizzle the Balsamic Caramel over the mushrooms.

Note: To approximate the taste of the 25-year-old balsamic vinegar, combine 2 cups good-quality balsamic vinegar with 3 tablespoons sugar and reduce, using the method for the caramel, until 1/2 cup of liquid remains. When cooled, store in a clean, airtight bottle.

nearby forest for cèpes, which were harder to find but so wonderful.

My first fall in Seattle, I was utterly unprepared for the bounty and range of mushrooms—everyone was gathering mushrooms. Strangers came to the restaurant offering us lobster and coral mushrooms, cauliflower mushrooms, cèpes, matsutakes, chanterelles, bluefoots, wild oysters—I cooked and cooked and never exhausted the possibilities.

My sons, Ryan and Adrian, have become great mushroom enthusiasts. I've taught them how to walk and look carefully and how not to just pick anything that looks like a mushroom.

One morning, after a long night at the restaurant, we all drove to a friend's home on the sound, and I ended up sleeping in until about ten o'clock, when my sons bounded into the room. "Daddy, get up, look! Chanterelles! Lots of them! Come on, we have to go get *more!*" They had a sack filled with three or four pounds of chanterelles, and they'd gone out on their own and found them all by themselves. They were just beaming.

So we spent part of the afternoon on the deck brushing and cleaning the mushrooms, but we had a nice bottle of wine, and friends to talk with, and everyone had the best time. For dinner we had a version of this wonderful mushroom salad.

Recently the seventeen kids in Ryan's fifth-grade class came to our restaurant to learn about mushrooms and to meet "the chef in the hat." I bought seven varieties, and the class prepared each mushroom, taking turns washing, brushing, and slicing. Then we trooped into the kitchen, and I sautéed each batch with butter, shallots, a little thyme, and some chives at the finish.

As you'd suspect, some kids started off, "Oh, Mr. Rautureau, I don't like eating mushrooms," but out of the entire class, only one kid didn't actually enjoy them.

BALSAMIC CARAMEL

Makes 2 tablespoons

----

1 cup balsamic vinegar

$^1/_4$ cup sugar

1 Place the vinegar and sugar in a small heavy saucepan. Stir until the sugar dissolves.

2 Reduce the liquid by half over medium-high heat. Lower the heat to medium and reduce the liquid to 2 tablespoons by gently swirling the pan to keep the liquid from burning. The mixture should have the thickness and color of molasses. Cool slightly and pour into a small container. Reheat just before drizzling on the salad.

Thierry Rautureau, "The Chef in the Hat," creates "Northwest Contemporary Cuisine with a French accent" in his Seattle restaurant, Rover's, a "country house" in Madison Valley consistently praised with accolades from both local and national press. A five-time nominee for the Beard Foundation's Best Chef Award, Thierry won the honor in 1998. He and his restaurant have been featured on PBS, the Discovery Channel, and the Food Network.

Pano Karatassos TWO GREEK VEGETABLES

My father came from Greece, my mother's parents came from Greece, and my mother was the first in her family to be born in America. They lived in such a tightly knit Greek neighborhood in Savannah, it might have been Greece.

Greek Easter was the celebration my mother most loved. On Saturday she would make a simple soup, *magiritsa*, from the lamb's organ meats, romaine lettuce, lemons, and eggs, which we'd all eat right after the midnight services. It was always served with the hard-boiled eggs, which we'd eat only after we played the traditional game: each person hitting an egg against someone else's to see whose egg would last the longest without cracking. The winner is supposed to have the best luck for the coming year.

Then, for Easter dinner, we'd have the roast lamb, *arni aromatiko*, with roasted potatoes and two special vegetable dishes—this stewed eggplant and the artichokes and favas. It's a Greek custom and a peasant tradition to enjoy these vegetables with the lamb. They're wonderfully rich with olive oil and fragrant with dill and onions. We'd also have green beans with chopped tomatoes and onions; a Greek

BRAISED ARTICHOKES WITH FAVA BEANS AND DILL Serves 12

----

12 large globe artichokes

$1/2$ cup fresh lemon juice, plus

1 lemon, halved

1 cup extra virgin olive oil

2 medium Vidalia onions, sliced

2 heads garlic, peeled and slivered

2 cups dry white wine

2 quarts vegetable stock

1 bunch fresh thyme (10 to 12 sprigs)

1 cup freshly peeled and shucked
fava beans

1 cup pearl onions, peeled

Salt and freshly cracked black pepper

$1/4$ pound chopped fresh dill ($3/4$ cup
loosely packed)

1 To clean the artichokes, remove 2 or 3 rows of the tough outer leaves. Cut the top inch from the crown and rub with the lemon half. Cut away all but 2 inches of the stem and rub with the lemon half. Spread open the inner leaves of the artichoke and, with a spoon, dig into the middle of the choke and remove the hairy fibers. Squeeze $1/2$ teaspoon of lemon juice into each artichoke.

2 Heat the olive oil in a large braising pan over medium heat. Add the sliced onions and garlic and cook until tender, about 5 minutes. Add the cleaned artichokes and cook for an additional 3 minutes. Add the wine, stock, $1/2$ cup lemon juice, and the thyme. Cover and cook for $1 1/2$ hours. The artichokes should be completely tender but not falling apart.

3 Remove the pan from the heat and cool the vegetables in the broth. Remove the artichokes and strain the broth, discarding the onions, garlic, and thyme. Place the artichokes back in the broth.

4 To prepare the final dish, reheat the artichokes in the broth with the fava beans and pearl onions. Cook over medium heat until the beans and onions are tender, about 25 minutes. Season with salt and pepper to taste.

❖ Transfer the vegetables to a serving dish and sprinkle with dill.

---

salad, *eliniki salada,* with feta, dried oregano, olives, and tomatoes (no lettuce). For sweets, we'd have *karythopita,* a syrup-soaked walnut cake, *baklava, koulourakia,* a crescent butter cookie piled high with sugar, and the *pasxalina koulourgia,* the traditional Easter cookie, a crispy, shiny, twisted dough that you eat with the hard-boiled egg and a cup of coffee.

I served in the navy for three years, ten

MELITZANES STIFADO (EGGPLANT STEW) Serves 8

3 cups extra virgin olive oil

10 small eggplants, Italian or Japanese, cut diagonally into 1/2-inch-thick pieces

Salt and freshly ground black pepper

2 Vidalia onions, sliced

2 cups canned tomato sauce

1/3 cup loosely packed fresh flat-leaf parsley leaves, chopped

1/2 cup loosely packed fresh dill leaves, chopped

1 Heat the oil in a deep medium skillet over medium-high heat until almost smoking. Add the eggplant pieces in batches, cooking on both sides until tender, about 2 minutes. Transfer the pieces to a tray lined with paper towels. Sprinkle with salt and pepper to taste.

2 Remove and discard all but 2 tablespoons of the oil. Add the onions and sauté until browned and caramelized, about 15 minutes.

3 Layer the eggplant in a saucepan with the onions and tomato sauce. Cook over medium-low heat for 35 to 40 minutes, until the vegetables become very soft and the juices reduce to a syrup.

✣ Transfer the stew to a serving dish. Add the parsley and dill and reseason with salt and pepper if necessary.

months, and seventeen days. I was stationed aboard ship on the West Coast. Once a year I'd be able to come home, and it was always for Easter. My mother would prepare the roasted lamb, the artichokes and favas, and the stewed eggplant, and they'd be waiting for my arrival. One year I had to take my leave two weeks *before* Easter. For my mother there was no question of what to do: she prepared an early Easter supper for me . . . and then she made the whole supper again for the rest of the family when the holiday arrived.

My mother lived a great, long life, and few things gave her more pleasure than cooking for her children. She recently passed away at the age of ninety-one; I was lucky enough to be with her, cooking for her, during her last weeks. I made nothing as robust and substantial as these vegetables, and yet everything I cooked returned something of the gifts she gave me.

Pano Karatassos of Atlanta, Georgia, is one of the country's premier restaurateurs. He is founder and president-owner

----

Frank Stitt GRILLED JUMBO ASPARAGUS WITH HAM-HOCK VINAIGRETTE

Mother's mother, Grandmother White, lived with Granddaddy White just outside town on a forty-acre farm. And what a farm it was! Chickens, quail, guinea hens, beehives, grapevines, asparagus beds, corncribs (with those old-fashioned dried corn grinders), potato houses that doubled as homes for baby chicks, a couple of Jersey cows, and two fine mules that my grandfather plowed with until he was seventy. I remember he would pull my brother and me bumpety-bump with those mules on a sled through the cornfield for the best ride of our young lives. Corn stalks became rifles

to us, and dirt clods were the most explosive of hand grenades.

Sometimes, early mornings, Granddaddy would let us watch him milk the cows; later in the day we would be amazed at how his mules would slurp up buckets of water we'd drawn from the well. The kitchen table was close to a coal-burning stove, and, most mornings, Eulalha would roll out biscuits on a flour-sack cloth—all the jams were thick and full of plump little nuggets, and the honey came with the comb. And, of course, summertime lunch on the farm was a feast—almost vegetarian except for the fatback and bacon: we had green beans layered and cooked with onions and potatoes; field corn cut not too close and scraped for the treasured creamed corn; fried okra cooked in a cast-iron skillet; sliced tomatoes; cucumbers and onions with vinegar; turnip greens with little turnip roots and pickled peppers; butter beans; pinkeye peas; sweet corn on the cob; corn bread; boiled okra— God, that was wonderful. A feast, and all from Grandmother's garden.

One of my fondest memories of the farm is that phone call I'd get in middle May from Grandmother White telling me the first asparagus of the season was just popping through the ground. Since I was about ten, asparagus has been my specially loved food. My grandmother's asparagus bed

GRILLED JUMBO ASPARAGUS WITH HAM-HOCK VINAIGRETTE Serves 4

For the ham hocks

2 ham hocks

1 medium yellow onion, quartered

1 carrot, cut into 3-inch pieces

1 celery rib, cut into 3-inch pieces

2 whole garlic cloves

For the vinaigrette

2 tablespoons apple cider vinegar

1 shallot, minced

1 teaspoon honey

$1/4$ teaspoon sea salt

$1/4$ teaspoon freshly ground black pepper

2 tablespoons chopped fresh parsley

6 to 8 chives, snipped

3 tablespoons olive oil

Reserved cooked ham

For the potatoes

8 very small new potatoes

Pinch of sea salt

1 tablespoon olive oil

For the asparagus

16 to 20 fresh jumbo asparagus, trimmed, peeled, and blanched (see Note)

2 tablespoons olive oil

1 bunch fresh watercress

1 Place the ham hocks, onion, carrot, celery, and garlic in a medium saucepan and cover with cold water. Bring to a boil. Reduce the heat and simmer for 3 hours.

2 Remove the hocks from the water and cool. Pick off the meat (discard the fat and bones) and shred it. Set it aside.

3 Combine the first 7 ingredients for the vinaigrette in a mixing bowl. Whisk in the olive oil and adjust the seasonings. Add the reserved meat.

4 Place the potatoes in a small saucepan and cover with cold water. Add the salt and bring to a boil. Reduce the heat and simmer until the potatoes are tender, about 10 minutes.

5 Drain and halve the potatoes. Drizzle with the olive oil, cover, and set aside.

6 Prepare a medium-hot grill.

7 Drizzle the asparagus with the olive oil and char the spears for 2 minutes or until grill marks appear.

✤ To serve, toss the asparagus, potato halves, and watercress with the vinaigrette and arrange on individual plates.

Note: When using large or jumbo asparagus, snap or cut off the woody, lower quarter of each stalk. Use a vegetable peeler to strip the remaining stalk—below the leafy tip—of its fibrous outer layer.

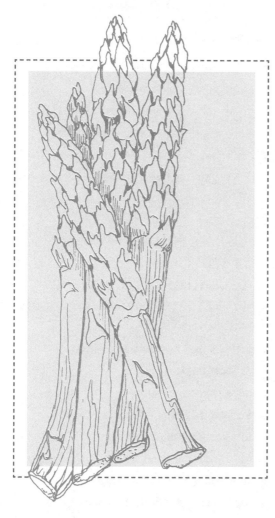

table about the earthy and vibrant taste of just-picked asparagus. Now we usually settle for the none-too-small pleasure of eating asparagus many days old. Maybe, someday, someone else will invite me to help pick her asparagus come spring. —FS

Frank Stitt of Birmingham, Alabama, is the chef-owner of Highlands Bar & Grill, Bottega, and Chez Fonfon. He is the 2001 recipient of the Beard Award for Best Chef/Southeast and is Share Our Strength's founding chef in Alabama, organizing the city's Taste of the Nation event for more than ten years.

Greg Higgins
THREE PICKLES

The world is divided into pickle people and those who aren't. How this is I don't know, but some folks love that vinegary taste on their palate, and some just don't. I grew up in a family that made pickles, and the three recipes here are pretty much my mother's and my grandmother's. (I did add the chipotle chile to the dill pickles, since I like that extra heat.) Preserving food was clearly a tradition in my family, and making pickles today harkens back to that

was set slightly to the side of her huge garden, just south of the chicken house. It was her pride and joy. By inviting me there, she honored me above all the other children in our family (because of my unabashed hunger for fresh asparagus and butter). In a good year we could pick enough for the whole family's lunch in just a few minutes. It was our rite of spring.

There is something elusive yet unforget-

CHOW CHOW Makes eight

1-pint jars

For the brine

$1/4$ cup kosher salt

3 cups sugar

3 cups apple cider vinegar

1 teaspoon ground turmeric

$1/4$ cup minced fresh ginger

3 tablespoons mustard seeds

2 tablespoons celery seeds

1 tablespoon hot red pepper flakes

For the vegetables

4 onions, cut into $1/4$-inch dice

6 green tomatoes, cut into $1/4$-inch dice

6 green bell peppers, cut into $1/4$-inch dice

6 red bell peppers, cut into $1/4$-inch dice

3 carrots, cut into $1/4$-inch dice

3 cups fresh corn kernels (5 to 6 ears)

Eight 1-pint canning jars with lids, sterilized

1 Combine $1^{1}/2$ cups water with all of the brining ingredients in a large nonreactive stockpot. Bring to a boil and reduce to a simmer. Add the vegetables and simmer over medium heat, stirring frequently. Cook the vegetables until al dente, 15 to 20 minutes. Taste and adjust the seasoning if necessary.

2 Ladle the vegetables and brine into the sterilized jars, leaving $3/4$ inch of head-space. Wipe the rims and put on the lids, lightly tightening them. Allow the jars to cool to room temperature. Tighten the lids completely when cool. Refrigerate any jars that do not vacuum-seal. Sealed jars will keep for 1 year in cool, dark storage conditions.

HIGGINS BREAD AND BUTTER CHIPS

Makes ten to twelve 1-pint jars

For the pickles

6 quarts small cucumbers, sliced $1/8$ inch thick

6 large onions, julienned

6 red bell peppers, julienned

1 cup kosher salt

For the pickling solution

2 quarts apple cider vinegar

8 cups packed light brown sugar

1 teaspoon whole cloves

2 tablespoons celery seeds

2 tablespoons whole allspice

$1/4$ cup mustard seeds

1 tablespoon ground turmeric

Ten to twelve 1-pint canning jars with lids, sterilized

1 Mix the vegetables and salt together and place in a colander. Drain for 3 to $3^{1}/2$ hours. Rinse and drain the vegetables.

2 Combine all the ingredients for the pickling solution in a large nonreactive pot. Bring to a gentle boil and simmer for 10 minutes. Add the vegetables to the hot liquid and bring to a full boil. Remove from the heat.

3 Ladle the vegetables and pickling solution into the sterilized jars, leaving $^3/_4$ inch of headspace. Wipe the rims and put on the lids, lightly tightening them. Allow the jars to cool to room temperature. Tighten the lids completely when cool. Refrigerate any jars that do not vacuum-seal. Sealed jars will keep for 1 year in cool, dark storage.

SMOKY DILL PICKLES

Makes eight 1-quart jars

----

1 gallon apple cider vinegar

$^1/_2$ cup light corn syrup

$^1/_2$ cup sugar

7 cups kosher salt

$^1/_2$ cup pickling spices

One 7-ounce can chipotle chiles packed in adobo, pureed (adobo included)

1 tablespoon ground turmeric

16 pickling dill sprigs with seed heads

48 garlic cloves, peeled

8 quarts small-to-medium firm pickling cucumbers

8 wide-mouth 1-quart canning jars with lids, sterilized

1 Combine 1 gallon water, the vinegar, corn syrup, sugar, salt, pickling spices, pureed chiles, turmeric, dill sprigs, and garlic cloves in a large nonreactive stockpot and bring to a boil. Reduce the heat and simmer for 5 minutes. Add the cucumbers and cook until the liquid comes to a hard boil. Remove from the heat.

2 Transfer the cucumbers, garlic cloves, and dill sprigs to the sterilized jars. Cover with brine, leaving $^3/_4$ inch of headspace. Wipe the rims and put on the lids, lightly tightening them. Allow the jars to cool to room temperature. Tighten the lids completely when cool. Refrigerate any jars that do not vacuum-seal. Sealed jars will keep for 1 year in cool, dark storage conditions.

simpler technology, before excessive transportation and refrigeration.

All summer long my mother put up foods. We lived in upstate New York, and my mother was raising five kids under the age of thirteen by herself—her husband, my father, had died and we were living in Eden, a farming town outside of Buffalo. It had one stoplight everyone called "the light," and at that intersection we had our post office, our bank, and our grocery.

My mother didn't drive. She didn't have a job. She hadn't graduated from high school. She had limited resources, living on my father's social security. As soon as she could, she learned how to drive, and then she commuted an hour each way to Buffalo to earn a teaching degree. Eventually she was certified and went on to get her master's. But along the way she raised a great bunch of kids—all of us have successful careers now—and she put up thousands and thousands of canned goods.

We had a special root cellar with racks for all of Mother's pickle crocks and jars. In the cool, dark basement, hundreds of jars lined the shelves. This was as much about stretching food dollars as it was about making the kind of homespun American foods she liked. In tomato season we'd do twenty bushels of tomatoes, canning a full year's supply of chile sauce and stewed tomatoes and ketchup (it always embarrassed me a little when friends would come over and see we didn't have a bottle of Heinz, but our homemade brand).

Every summer, as one item after another came into season—strawberries, then blueberries, then pickling cukes, then peaches— we'd follow my mother from one "U-pick" place to the next. We five kids were a small labor force! (Of course, we ate as much as we picked.) Then, back home, we'd gather around the table and hull or pit or peel or whatever the fruit or vegetable required so that mother could start canning.

Her thriftiness went far beyond produce. Every year we placed an order for a whole cow with Harold Greely, who ran the butcher shop at the general store. And then we'd have a freezer filled with white packages, each labeled with a single word: "chuck" or "ground" or "ribs." Once or twice a week, one of us kids would be instructed to run down to the freezer and pick out a package. We were amazed at the variety of meals Mother prepared from that one cow.

The pickles and relishes and ketchup all played a huge part in enhancing the simple farmhouse cooking she'd do, and they came from our long line of Pennsylvania Dutch ancestors. These condiments are aspects of the seven sweet and seven sour tastes that enhance the traditional, and rather bland, Pennsylvania Dutch dishes.

The Chow Chow is perfect for simply roasted or grilled chicken; it's great with pork or a fish like halibut as well. The Smoky Dill Pickles go on or alongside a great burger—or some other sandwich that could use a hot and puckery burst every few bites. And if I were to pick one favorite for the Higgins Bread and Butter Chips, it would have to be homemade pastrami on rye.

Even if you don't count yourself among us pickle people, you ought to put up a few jars of these for your lucky friends.

Greg Higgins is chef-owner of Higgins Restaurant & Bar in Portland, Oregon. Since 1994 Greg has used Pacific Northwest ingredients with traditional French techniques, incorporating an eclectic range of influences from around the world. A Beard Foundation Award winner for Best Chef in his region, Greg is an active supporter of Chefs Collaborative, committed to sustainable cuisine. He promotes the foods of his region throughout the year, contributing to gourmet benefits and cookbooks, as well as appearing on various television programs.

Frank Brigsten
OYSTER DRESSING

My father was fifth-generation New Orleansian. He sold brick back in the early sixties, and most of the homes around here were built with his brick. And like anyone who grows up here, Dad had cravings for certain foods. When he married my mother, Miss Ernie—a girl from the Alabama countryside—she had to learn to make his favorite New Orleans classics: red beans and rice, gumbo, fried catfish, and grits. I never appreciated this hankering until I came home from my first real tour of Europe, when the first thing I wanted to eat was Miss Ernie's catfish. Just catfish, right in season, shook up with cornmeal in a brown paper sack, overfried until it's utterly crispy, and then smothered in creamy grits.

I remember coming home from school, sleepy and hot and just snoozing on the couch and then waking up to these vivid smells of my mother preparing dinner. She'd have her cast-iron skillet sautéing onions, celery, and bell peppers—Louisiana mirepoix—and those smells triggered my appetite. "Food memories" like this one guide me in the dishes I like to cook today. They're primal tastes. And I think New Orleans has the most depth and character of any regional

OYSTER DRESSING Serves 6

4 tablespoons ($^1/_2$ stick) unsalted butter

6 cups finely diced celery

8 cups (6 bunches) thinly sliced scallions, both white and green parts

4 cups (2 bunches) finely chopped fresh flat-leaf parsley

1 bay leaf

1 teaspoon minced garlic

1$^1/_2$ teaspoons salt (depending on saltiness of the oysters)

$^1/_4$ teaspoon freshly ground black pepper

2 cups (3 to 4 dozen) freshly shucked oysters and their liquid

4 cups $^1/_2$-inch cubes of stale French bread

2 cups oyster liquor from shucking the oysters or chicken or turkey stock

1 large egg, beaten

1 Preheat the oven to 350°F.

2 Melt 2 tablespoons of the butter in a large heavy sauté pan over medium heat. Add the celery, scallions, parsley, and bay leaf. Cook, stirring constantly, until the vegetables soften and dull in color, 15 to 20 minutes.

3 Lower the heat to medium and add the garlic, salt, and pepper. Cook, stirring, for 1 minute. Add the remaining 2 tablespoons butter and the oysters (not the liquid). Cook, stirring occasionally, for 3 to 4 minutes.

4 In a mixing bowl, combine the bread and the oyster liquor with your hands, squeezing until it becomes soft and mushy. Add the egg, and blend thoroughly. Gradually temper the egg/bread mixture by adding in the hot vegetable mixture, $^1/_4$ cup at a time. Thoroughly blend after each addition. This will keep the egg from scrambling. Fold the warm egg mixture into the oyster mixture and toss to blend.

5 Transfer the oyster dressing to an oiled sheet pan or shallow baking dish. The dressing should be no more than 1 inch deep. Bake for 1 hour. Stir the mixture and bake for 1 more hour. Serve right away or cool and refrigerate in an airtight container. The dressing can be made up to 2 days in advance; the extra days will enhance its flavor.

Note: This dressing is great with roast turkey, but it also works wonderfully with chicken, veal, pork, or fish. Alternately, it can be the basis of a great baked oyster casserole: layer a shallow baking dish with the dressing. Add a layer of fresh oysters and top with seasoned bread crumbs and grated cheese. Bake at 450°F for 30 minutes, until bubbling hot, and serve.

cuisine in America—and the wealth of seafood at its heart is part of the reason. People only think of New Orleans as hot: a hot summer, and hardly any spring or fall, but we do have four seasons: crab season, shrimp season, oyster season, and crawfish season.

Until I was twenty-one, my father could never get me to eat raw oysters; I couldn't get past the texture. Then one evening, after I'd graduated college, some bar had a twenty-five-cent oyster special, and I downed something like three dozen raw oysters. Now they're my favorite food, and in New Orleans you can find them year-round.

The taste of oysters is almost entirely determined by the water they're in. We have a marshy delta here with brackish water, and as the Mississippi River rises and falls, the salt concentration changes. Oysters will taste different—sweeter, plumper, saltier—from one season to the next and from one inlet to the next.

Here's my favorite of all oyster recipes: shuck and eat. Don't do or add a thing. The next best thing is this oyster dressing; the cooking process concentrates the oyster flavor and reduces the oyster liquor. The Brigsten family could manage Thanksgiving without a roast turkey, but not without oyster dressing.

To this day there is a running joke at our holiday table. Mom is never completely satisfied with the dressing if she makes it. "I don't like it this year; the oysters weren't very good." But if someone else makes the dressing, then it's always "Now this is the best I've ever had."

Frank Brigsten began his culinary career in 1973 and worked for the next seven years at Commander's Palace and K-Paul's under Paul Prudhomme. In the late eighties Frank started his own venture, Brigsten's, in a small cottage in Uptown New Orleans and quickly gained his own deserved reputation. He has been named one of the Top 10 New Chefs in America by *Food & Wine* and Best Chef/Southeast region by the Beard Foundation. *Zagat* has voted Brigsten's its Top Cajun Restaurant.

Kevin Von Klause
THREE BEANS

I grew up in Borger, Texas, a boom-and-bust town depending on the oil industry. It was a very small world, surrounded by prairie and grassland, but I could look out

TEXAS PINTO BEANS

Serves 12 to 15

----

1 pound dried pinto beans

1 tablespoon salt

4 slices smoked bacon, chopped

1 medium Vidalia onion, diced

3 tablespoons chili powder

1 tablespoon freshly ground black pepper

3/4 cup Coca-Cola

1 Rinse the beans and pick out any foreign matter. Place the beans in a large container with a lid. Add 1 quart cold water and cover with the lid. Soak the beans overnight in the refrigerator. You may also place the rinsed beans in a stockpot and cover them with several inches of cold water. Over high heat, bring the water to a boil, then turn the heat to low and simmer the beans, uncovered, for 5 minutes. Remove the pot from the heat, cover, and allow the beans to soak for 1 hour.

2 Drain the beans and place in a large heavy pot with water to cover them by 2 inches and add the salt. Bring to a boil over high heat, then lower to a simmer. Cook for 2 hours or until the beans are almost tender, adding small amounts of water, if necessary, to keep the beans moist.

3 Fry the bacon until crispy. Add the bacon bits and drippings, onion, chili powder, pepper, and cola to the beans. Stir thoroughly. Cook for an additional 30 minutes or until the beans are completely tender.

my bedroom window and see the oil refineries everywhere, building after building, their towers all lit up—I imagined it was a great city filled with exciting things to do.

You could smell Borger long before you could see it. We'd be out at recess, and the air was like rotting pineapples: butane, butanols, butadiennes, all a part of the carbon black and synthetic-rubber manufacturing. It blackened the city.

Everyone was involved with oil. We lived with my mother's parents, and my grandfa-ther worked with his team of mules grading roads for new wells. Being a sharecropper, he also worked in the fields starting in third grade, when his father died. My grandmother, Minnie Lee, was one of thirteen—and the oldest girl—so she took care of the babies.

Now, beans were always important vittles. Nutritious, cheap, easy to obtain—and you could cook up a bunch and feed lots of folks. Minnie Lee worked incredibly hard. Never a speck of dust in the house. She washed her *washing machine,* which was

WANDA LEE'S BAKED BEANS

Serves 12 to 15

----

1 pound dried Great Northern white beans

2 teaspoons salt

$^1/_2$ pound bacon, cut into thin strips

1 cup diced onion

1 cup diced green bell pepper

1 cup ketchup

$^1/_4$ cup plus 1 tablespoon yellow mustard

$^1/_4$ cup packed dark brown sugar

2 tablespoons Worcestershire sauce

2 cups reserved cooking liquid

1 teaspoon freshly ground black pepper
   or to taste

1 Rinse the beans and pick out any foreign matter. Place the beans in a large container with a lid and add 6 to 8 cups cold water and 1 teaspoon of the salt. Soak the beans for 12 hours or overnight in the refrigerator. (For a quick-soak method, see the first step in Texas Pinto Beans.)

2 Drain the beans and place them in a large heavy pot with cold water to cover by 1 inch. Add the remaining teaspoon of salt. Place over high heat and bring to a boil. Reduce the heat, cover the pot, and simmer for 1 hour. Add small amounts of additional warm water if necessary.

3 Drain the beans over a bowl and reserve the bean broth. You should have 2 cups. If not, add water to make up the difference.

4 Preheat the oven to 350°F.

5 Heat a large Dutch oven or ovenproof pot over medium heat. Add the bacon strips and sauté until some fat has been rendered and the bacon turns translucent. Add the onion and green pepper and cook until soft, about 5 minutes. Add the ketchup, mustard, brown sugar, Worcestershire sauce, reserved cooking liquid, and pepper. Stir and bring to a simmer for 2 minutes. Add the cooked beans and mix well.

6 Bake, uncovered, for 30 to 40 minutes or until the beans have browned lightly and the liquid has been absorbed.

her main appliance. She ironed everything from tea towels to Grandfather's khaki uniform that he wore out in the dirt.

On especially busy days, like when she waxed the floor or made pies, she'd cook up beans. She'd take some drippings from the can on the back of the stove, coat a very hot skillet, and pour in her corn bread batter—we had it every day. And there would be her butter beans in a pot on the stove. Whenever you came in, you'd just help yourself to a warm bowl. My brother

MINNIE LEE'S BUTTER BEANS Serves 10 to 12

- **1 pound dried lima beans**
- **1 pound smoked ham hocks**
- **2 fresh or dried bay leaves**
- **2 teaspoons salt**
- **Freshly ground black pepper**
- **2 teaspoons chopped fresh thyme**
- **1 teaspoon chopped fresh rosemary**
- **1 teaspoon chopped fresh sage**
- **1 teaspoon chopped fresh parsley**
- **Corn bread, as an accompaniment**

1 Place the beans, ham hocks, bay leaves, and salt in a medium pot and add enough water to cover the beans by 2 inches.

2 Place over high heat and bring to a boil. Lower the heat, cover the pan, and simmer for 1 hour and 15 minutes, until the beans are tender. Add water as needed to keep the beans covered while cooking.

3 Discard the bay leaf. Remove the ham hocks and allow them to cool.

4 Trim the meat from the bones and fat, chop it, and add it to the beans. Discard the bones and fat. Season with salt and pepper to taste and add the fresh herbs.

✣ Serve warm with hot, buttered corn bread.

Roger would eat a huge bowl with this big spoon—he reminded me of Jethro Bodine on *The Beverly Hillbillies.*

The pinto beans are from Mama Klause, my dad's mother from Louisiana. During the Depression no one had money, and Coca-Cola was almost exotic—a luxurious ingredient! Sugar was being rationed, and cola was one way to add sweetness. She certainly didn't invent the dish, but Mama Klause did teach it (and lots more) to my mother, who had just turned sixteen and eloped with her son. Both families were none too pleased, but my parents, who are just in

their midsixties, are very much in love after more than fifty years.

People just get a reputation for their beans. My mother, Wanda Lee, can't go anywhere—a barbecue, office party, holiday meal—without bringing her baked beans. She's made this dish hundreds of times. This recipe's originally from an English woman, an air force bride stationed at Amarillo. With the Worcestershire sauce and mustard, it was distinctly British.

And now I live in a genuinely big city, Philadelphia, that's filled with excitement, but there isn't a day that I don't think about living in the country again. Whatever else I love to cook, beans will always have stories to tell about me.

Kevin Von Klause has been chef and co-owner with Judy Wicks of the White Dog Café in Philadelphia for sixteen years. Under his spoon the White Dog's kitchen has combined the "down home" cooking of the Café's early years with his own wonderfully fresh and natural "modern American" cuisine. His use of organic and humanely raised foods from local farms is both his trademark and passion. The Café has a four-part mission of service: to staff, customers, the environment, and the local and global community. The White Dog hosts local and international tours, table-talk discussions, block parties, and community service days.

DESSERTS

Jody Adams
MUSTARD GINGERBREAD

Joyce Goldstein
CHOCOLATE-DIPPED CUSTARD-FILLED ÉCLAIRS

Deborah Madison
RAISIN SQUARES

Gale Gand
A COOKIE PLATE

Cory Schreiber
BLUEBERRY ROLY-POLY

Nancy Silverton
COCONUT CUPCAKES

Charles Dale
PINEAPPLE UPSIDE-DOWN CAKE WITH COCONUT CRÈME ANGLAISE

Marcel Desaulniers
CHOCOLATE APPLESAUCE CAKE WITH JACKED-UP CARAMEL APPLE SAUCE

Donna Nordin
CHOCOLATE MAYONNAISE CAKE WITH PEANUT-BUTTER-CUP ICE CREAM AND FUDGE SAUCE

Christopher Gross
ALMOND CHEESECAKE WITH CHAMPAGNE-HONEY SAUCE

Hubert Seifert
MALLORCAN ALMOND CAKE

Paul Minnillo
BEGGAR'S PURSE WITH CARAMELIZED PEARS

Robert Helstrom
APPLE TART WITH BROWN-BUTTER CUSTARD AND CRÈME FRAÎCHE

Stan Frankenthaler
TWO BAVARIANS

Rick Bayless
PEACH ORCHARD COBBLER

Seth Bixby Daugherty
MULBERRY CRUNCH

Ann Amernick and Frank Ruta
CLEVELAND PARK CREAM CAKE

Gary Danko
PORT-ROASTED FIGS WITH LICORICE ICE CREAM

Charlie Trotter
DYLAN'S CHOCOLATE–PEANUT BUTTER GANACHE TART

Jody Adams
MUSTARD GINGERBREAD

My first memories of working in a kitchen are with my older sister, Ginny. We weren't raised on fancy foods, but everything at home was cooked from scratch. My parents, both Depression-era children, were librarians; books and food were the primary things we shared. They spent money on sabbatical years in England or summers on the cape, and things like televisions never entered into the picture (which might have made sense of the once-a-year, frozen TV dinners, which we loved having).

My mother also liked entertaining, and we kids loved being the hired help. At a very young age we helped cook. But it was at Christmas that Ginny and I took over the kitchen. Starting in mid-December, we'd bake like mad until we'd exhausted all the ingredients in my mother's pantry. We were competitive partners in a race to see who could make the most varieties. We made springerle cookies with a special carved rolling pin, spritz cookies, pecan puffs, candied-fruit cookies, powdery pfeffernüesse, my grandmother's refrigerator cookies with a cherry balanced on each one, and lots of things from *The Joy of Cooking*. Ginny would do a few more complicated things such as cinnamon stars that involved whipping egg whites.

During those hours everything about family life seemed easy. Instead of being told what to do, we had a mission all our own that we wanted to carry out—we were keeping our traditions going.

We'd freeze packages of the cookies and deliver plates of them all around our neighborhood. We were lucky: we knew most of the families on our block. And there were lots of girls my age. Every Christmas, for something like eight years, all the girls would put on a play in someone's attic: *A Christmas Carol* or *Amahl and the Night Visitors,* or something the older girls would write. We'd begin our rehearsals around Thanksgiving, and on Christmas Eve we'd invite all the parents to come up to what we considered our huge stage up there in the eaves. And after the play we'd serve everyone the Christmas cookies we'd baked.

This Mustard Gingerbread recipe is inspired by an unusual recipe that Ginny brought home from home ec one year when we were in elementary school. It's probably the only recipe from that period worth remembering. Our school had little kitchens, and each week we'd make something—mostly sweets. And a lot of fritters, corn and apple and even fish fritters.

But this gingerbread was fabulous. The

MUSTARD GINGERBREAD

Makes 9 squares

---

8 tablespoons (1 stick) plus 1 tablespoon unsalted butter at room temperature

1$^1/_2$ cups plus 1 tablespoon unbleached all-purpose flour

1 tablespoon dry mustard

2 tablespoons ground ginger

$^1/_2$ teaspoon ground cloves

1 teaspoon baking soda

$^1/_2$ teaspoon kosher salt

$^1/_2$ cup dark molasses

$^1/_2$ cup packed dark brown sugar

$^1/_2$ cup granulated sugar

1 extra-large egg

2 tablespoons diced crystallized ginger

1 recipe Ginger-Lemon Crème Fraîche

1 Preheat the oven to 350°F. Butter and flour an 8-inch square pan using 1 tablespoon each butter and flour. Tap out any extra flour.

2 Cut the remaining butter into 8 pieces and place in a mixing bowl. Add the mustard, ginger, cloves, soda, and salt. Pour $^1/_2$ cup boiling water over the ingredients and stir until the butter melts.

3 Whisk together the molasses, sugars, and egg in a large mixing bowl. Stir in the butter mixture and then the flour. Mix until combined.

4 Pour the batter into the prepared pan. Sprinkle the top of the gingerbread with the crystallized ginger. Bake for 30 to 35 minutes or until a toothpick inserted in the center comes out clean.

5 Cool on a wire rack for 10 minutes. Invert the pan onto a plate and then back again onto the cooling rack. Serve warm or cold with Ginger-Lemon Crème Fraîche.

GINGER-LEMON CRÈME FRAÎCHE

Makes 1$^1/_4$ cups

---

2 tablespoons grated fresh ginger

1 cup crème fraîche

1 teaspoon freshly grated lemon zest

$^1/_4$ cup packed dark brown sugar

Whisk all the ingredients together in a mixing bowl and refrigerate.

recipe probably came from a Colman's mustard promotion booklet, but the idea of mustard in a sweet bread stuck in my head. You hardly know the mustard is included, but without it the gingerbread isn't nearly as addictive.

Later, in high school, when all us girls were on diets, Ginny concluded that dipping carrots in Dijon mustard was much better than eating iceberg lettuce with Russian dressing (which was full of fat, of course). So mustard has loomed in my memory. It's an intense flavor; mustard, ginger, capers, anchovies—these are potent flavors, like a ready-made reduction of a stock or sauce. All the great cuisines have potent flavors at their base. Not only are they memorable, but tasting these flavors often recalls the people and places connected to them.

The actual gingerbread recipe, even though it became a family favorite, was lost years ago. I've re-created this version for Ginny from my memory's palate. I have so many memories of that incredibly safe and nurturing kitchen, baking with my sister. My very feelings of home.

Jody Adams, chef of Rialto at the Charles Hotel in Cambridge, Massachusetts, describes her food as "intensely flavored, honest, and straight-forward, with respect for tradition, seasons, and fresh local ingredients." Jody has received a Beard Foundation Award for Best Chef/Northeast, as well as recognition from such publications as *Bon Appétit*, *Esquire*, *Food & Wine*, and the *Boston Globe*. She is the author, with her husband, Ken Rivard, of *In the Hands of a Chef: Cooking with Jody Adams of Rialto Restaurant*.

Joyce Goldstein
CHOCOLATE-DIPPED CUSTARD-FILLED ÉCLAIRS

When I was a little girl, I was madly in love with my father. On special occasions he would take me to lunch at Longchamps on Fifth Avenue and 12th Street in New York City. (It is long gone, as is my father, who died when I was twelve.) It was not a classic French restaurant despite the name, but it was cool and dark, and we sat on banquettes; it seemed very sophisticated and glamorous to a small girl from Brooklyn. We always had the same waiter, named Georges. He was from Canada, of middle years, and slightly balding. He doted on me as he knew how special these lunches were. I was supposedly a "problem eater." Actually I thought I was being a discerning and critical young diner.

In honor of our ritual lunches, I always ordered roast turkey with chestnut dressing. Later I would carefully look over the pastry cart selections as though I might make a wild choice, pretending to consider the napoleon or the strawberry tartlette, but, after much consideration, I always would end my meal with the chocolate éclair. Not the kind filled with whipped cream, but the one filled with creamy vanilla custard.

CHOCOLATE-DIPPED CUSTARD-FILLED ÉCLAIRS

Makes 12 large éclairs or 30 mini-éclairs

For the éclair shells (pâte à choux)

6 tablespoons unsalted butter, cut into bits

1 cup bread flour

Pinch of salt

4 large eggs at room temperature

1 Preheat the oven to 400°F and line 2 baking sheets with parchment paper.

2 Bring 1 cup water and the butter to a boil. At the boiling point, quickly stir in the flour and salt, continuing to stir until a ball of dough develops and a thin coat of flour forms on the bottom of the pan, 1 or 2 minutes.

3 Transfer the hot dough to an electric mixer fitted with the flat paddle attachment. Add the eggs, one at a time, mixing after each addition.

4 When the mixture develops a glossy, pasty consistency, spoon the dough into a large pastry bag fitted with a plain $1/2$-inch tip. Pipe the dough into 3-inch-long ovals about 2 inches apart on the prepared baking sheets.

5 Bake large éclair shells for 15 minutes; bake smaller shells for 10 minutes. Reduce the heat to 350°F and bake the large éclairs an additional 25 to 30 minutes and the small éclairs an additional 10 to 15 minutes. The shells should be puffed and golden, with a dry center. If not, leave the shells in the oven with the door ajar for an additional 10 minutes.

6 Transfer the éclairs to a cooling rack. Cooled shells can be kept in an airtight container for 1 day. Frozen shells will keep for several weeks. To recrisp the shells, toast them in a 350°F oven for 10 minutes.

For the vanilla custard filling

$2^1/2$ cups whole milk

8 large egg yolks

$3/4$ cup sugar

$1/2$ cup flour

2 teaspoons vanilla extract

1 tablespoon unsalted butter

7 For the custard, bring the milk to a boil in a heavy saucepan over medium-high heat.

8 Whisk together the yolks and sugar in a large mixing bowl. Beat in the flour.

9 Slowly whisk $1/2$ cup hot milk into the egg mixture. Carefully add the remaining hot milk and combine. Return all to the pan and cook over medium-low heat, stirring, until the custard thickens. Remove from the heat.

10 Add the vanilla and the butter. Mix until the butter is completely melted.

11 Cool the mixture over an ice bath. Cover the surface of the custard with plastic wrap

and refrigerate. The vanilla custard can be made 1 day in advance.

For the fudge glaze

1 cup heavy cream

3 ounces unsweetened chocolate

1 cup sugar

1 tablespoon light corn syrup

1 teaspoon vanilla extract

12 Combine all the glaze ingredients except the vanilla in a small heavy saucepan. Stir over medium heat until the sugar dissolves and the chocolate melts.

13 Clip a candy thermometer to the side of the pan and cook until the liquid reaches 224°F. Off the heat, mix in the vanilla and allow the glaze to cool slightly.

14 To assemble the éclairs, either poke a hole in one end of each shell and pipe in the custard using a pastry bag fitted with a $^1/_4$-inch tip or slice each shell in half horizontally and sandwich a dollop of custard between the halves. Dip the tops of each shell in the chocolate glaze. Éclairs should be refrigerated if not served immediately.

It remains my favorite dessert. On my birthday I never want cake, preferring chocolate éclairs. After I had children I continued the tradition: while my daughters are more flexible about desserts, my son, Evan, shares my addiction to chocolate éclairs and requests them for his annual fete. The year he turned forty, we threw a big party. I baked ninety mini-éclairs and watched his children eat them, three at a time. I suspect that our tradition will continue, and it gives me enormous pleasure imagining this legacy starting anew in what would be my father's great-grandchildren.

Now, admittedly, I am not crazy about baking. I'm a line cook at heart. I love high-energy cooking and improvisation at the stove. Baking triggers my natural impatience and my resistance to measuring and precision. But for chocolate éclairs, I call upon discipline that I don't usually have. I measure with care. I follow the recipe exactly. I slow down. I know that the care I take will produce wonderful results and bring great pleasure to my family.

Joyce Goldstein, former chef-owner of Square One restaurant in San Francisco, for which she won a Beard Award, served as visiting executive chef at the Culinary

Institute of America in St. Helena, California. Her many books include *Sephardic Flavors*, *Enoteca*, *Food and Wine Pairing*, *Kitchen Conversations*, *Taverna*, *Mediterranean Kitchens*, and *Cucina Ebraica: Flavors of the Italian-Jewish Kitchen*.

Deborah Madison
RAISIN SQUARES

Leafing through the cookbooks I've written over the years, I notice that nearly every recipe has to do with a person, a meal taken somewhere, or an exchange of recipes. Lately the story often has to do with a garden, a farm, or a farmers' market, because I like knowing how food is grown and who grew it. In fact, for me the best meal is always the one where I know where everything on the table comes from. A lot of my favorite food memories have to do with events like this one: I'm looking out the window of a Scottish inn at a forlorn winter garden (cabbages, potatoes) and a lake. Eventually my friend and I are presented with a platter holding a fish, cabbage, and potatoes. A perfectly local meal.

When thinking of family dishes that stand out for me, my father's Concord grape pie leaps to mind—it's still a favorite—and my grandmother's raisin squares. My grandmother lived in Hartford, Connecticut, while we, part of her extended family, lived in California. Every winter a Lord & Taylor box would arrive packed with layers of these little confections, their tops dusted with cinnamon sugar. Unlike other cookie care packages, this one did not arrive as a box of crumbs and fragments but as a treasury of sturdy, whole pieces; it was their moist, soft nature that kept them cohesive. Had they not been sent to a household of six people, and had they not been my father's absolute favorite, they could have lasted a whole lot longer than they did. I know this because I make raisin squares every year myself, and in our household of two they keep quite nicely. They are perfect in the afternoon with a cup of Earl Grey tea or a glass of sherry.

My grandmother's recipe called for quite a bit of sugar, which I have been steadily reducing over the years, to the point where I leave it out altogether. After all, raisins are pretty much concentrated sugar. I know she used raisins out of the box, and, on the few occasions I cooked with her, she always insisted, "Wash them! You don't know whose hands have touched them!" I always thought that rather silly since those hard little raisins seemed so inert. Whether one should

RAISIN SQUARES Makes 24 squares

For the filling

1 pound raisins, rinsed

Zest and juice of 1 lemon

3 to 4 tablespoons sugar, optional

1 tablespoon all-purpose flour

1 cup finely chopped walnuts

For the dough

**8 tablespoons (1 stick) unsalted butter,
softened**

$^1/_2$ cup plus 1 tablespoon sugar

1 teaspoon vanilla extract

2 large eggs at room temperature

2 cups unbleached all-purpose flour

1 teaspoon baking powder

$^1/_4$ teaspoon salt

3 tablespoons sour cream

2 teaspoons ground cinnamon

1 Place the raisins, lemon zest, and sugar if desired in a food processor fitted with a steel blade. Start the machine and add 1 cup boiling water. Make a coarse puree.

2 Scrape the raisins into a small saucepan and add the lemon juice, flour, and walnuts. Cook over medium heat, stirring, until the mixture is thick, about 5 minutes. Set aside to cool.

3 To prepare the dough, use an electric mixer fitted with a flat paddle to cream together the butter and $^1/_2$ cup sugar until light and fluffy. Add the vanilla, 1 whole egg, and all but 1 tablespoon of the white of the second egg.

4 Sift together the dry ingredients in a small bowl. Set the mixer on low speed. Gradually add the dry mix to the butter mixture, alternating with the sour cream. The dough may become stiff and difficult to work. Remove it from the mixer and finish incorporating the flour by hand until the dough is smooth. Place it in a plastic bag and press the dough into a rectangle. Refrigerate for 30 minutes or until firm.

5 Preheat the oven to 350°F. Lightly butter a 9 X 12-inch baking pan.

6 Divide the cold dough into 3 equal pieces. Roll out the first piece into a 9 X 12-inch rectangle and place it in the pan. Trim the dough if necessary. Spread half of the cooled filling over the dough. Repeat the process for a second layer.

7 Roll out the third piece of dough and lay it neatly on top, brushing it with the reserved egg white. Combine the remaining tablespoon of sugar and the cinnamon and sprinkle the mixture over the egg-washed surface.

8 Bake for 40 minutes or until the top is crisp and lightly browned.

9 Cool completely and cut into 24 squares. Store in a tin layered with wax paper.

wash raisins or not, her belief that you *should* lodged in my mind. I find that I do give them a rinse, which also helps to soften them up.

I like interesting varieties of raisins, preferably moist ones, and my favorites are the red and gold Flame raisins I've found at some California farmers' markets. Otherwise I might choose Monukka or a mixture of dark raisins and currants. I don't think my grandmother put in the walnuts, either, but I think they only make the squares taste better. —DM

Deborah Madison is the founding chef of the renowned restaurant Greens and is the author of the bestselling *Vegetarian Cooking for Everyone*, an encyclopedic compendium that won two Julia Child/IACP Awards as well as a Beard Foundation Award. Her other books include *The Savory Way* (winner of two Julia Child/IACP Awards), *This Can't Be Tofu!*, *The Greens Cookbook*, and, most recently, *Local Flavors: Cooking and Eating from America's Farmers' Markets*. She lives with her husband in Santa Fe, New Mexico.

Gale Gand
A COOKIE PLATE

My mother, Myrna, learned to cook from her mother, Elsie Grossman, who, as a Hungarian, came from a great baking tradition. Maybe cooking *is* genetic. And my grandmother's pecan cookies came from the Hungarian generation before her. This is where my theory of "Eternal Life Through Your Recipes" comes from: you live forever through your recipes if you take the time to pass them down.

Myrna was the best baker I've known. She had really cold hands—poor circulation, I guess (that much *is* genetic, because I have cold hands, too)—and that's ideal for working with crusts and butter. She made perfect crusts—I'd watch her put a lattice top over a cherry pie, and her cool hands worked so quickly, none of the dough would be limp.

But Myrna was forever trying to improve her baking. We'd travel to folk festivals—my father was a folk singer—visiting diners where my mother would order eight different slices of pie. And she'd reverse-engineer each one while we were eating, eventually asking the server what made the best ones so good. The answer was always lard. Even though my mother was Jewish, she "converted" to a half-lard, half-butter crust (with

HUNGARIAN PECAN COOKIES Makes 4 dozen cookies

----

^{1}/2 pound (2 sticks) unsalted butter, softened

1 teaspoon vanilla extract

2^1/2 cups confectioners' sugar

2^1/4 cups all-purpose flour

1 cup finely chopped pecans

1 Preheat the oven to 350°F and lightly grease 2 cookie sheets.

2 Combine the butter and vanilla in the bowl of an electric mixer. Add ^{1}/2 cup of the confectioners' sugar and mix to incorporate. Slowly add the flour and pecans and mix just to combine. Place the remaining 2 cups confectioners' sugar on a plate and set aside.

3 Roll small balls of dough (^{3}/4 inch in diameter) and arrange them on the prepared cookie sheet, 1^1/2 inches apart.

4 Bake for 15 to 20 minutes or until golden brown.

5 Remove the cookies from the oven and immediately place them deep in the sugar. Let them cool slightly, 3 to 5 minutes, then roll each cookie in the sugar until well coated. Place the cookies on a wire rack to cool completely. Store in airtight containers.

COCONUT CHOCOLATE MACAROON TOWERS

Makes 3 dozen cookies

----

^{3}/4 cup sugar

Scant ^{1}/2 cup egg whites (from 3 to 4 large eggs)

^{3}/4 pound (2^1/2 cups) unsweetened flaked coconut

2 ounces semisweet chocolate, melted

1 Preheat the oven to 350°F and line 2 cookie sheets with parchment paper.

2 Combine the sugar, egg whites, and coconut in a bowl. (The recipe can be made to this point and refrigerated for up to 3 days.)

3 Measure out teaspoonfuls of the coconut mixture and place them 1 inch apart on the cookie sheets. (Have a damp cloth nearby to wipe your fingers.) Pinch the mounds with your fingers to create a pyramid shape. Chill for 30 minutes.

4 Bake for 10 to 12 minutes or until light golden brown on the edges. Let cool completely on the pans. Carefully remove the cookies and dip each tip into the melted chocolate. Place back on the tray and allow the chocolate to set. Store in airtight containers.

MINT CHOCOLATE CHIP MERINGUES Makes 7 dozen tiny drops

- **1/2 cup egg whites (from 3 to 4 large eggs)**
- **2/3 cup sugar**
- **1/2 teaspoon mint extract (not mint oil)**
- **2 ounces unsweetened chocolate, finely chopped or grated**
- **2 ounces semisweet chocolate, chopped**

1 Preheat the oven to 350°F and line 2 cookie sheets with parchment paper.

2 Place the egg whites and sugar in the bowl of an electric mixer and place it over gently simmering water. Heat until warm to the touch, stirring constantly, about 2 minutes.

3 Place the egg mixture in the electric mixer fitted with the beater attachment. Whip the egg whites until they form stiff peaks and appear glossy. Add the mint extract and continue beating for 10 more seconds. Fold in the chopped unsweetened chocolate.

4 Spoon the meringue into a pastry bag fitted with a 1/2-inch plain or star tip. Pipe bite-size drops onto the prepared sheets.

5 Bake the meringues for 25 to 30 minutes or until they are a milky, coffee color. To test, remove one drop from the pan and allow it to cool. It should be dry and crisp through to the center. Cool completely.

6 Place the semisweet chocolate in the top of a double boiler over gently simmering water. Stir to melt. With the tines of a fork, drizzle the chocolate onto the meringues. Allow the chocolate to set. Store in airtight containers for up to 3 days.

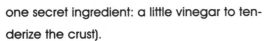

one secret ingredient: a little vinegar to tenderize the crust).

I baked alongside her as much as I could. There was always a hunk of pie dough left over from trimming, and Myrna had a six-inch pie plate just for that. She'd roll out the scraps, press them into the tin, sprinkle it with cinnamon and sugar, and then draw my monogram with a rope of dough. The moment she pulled it from the oven, she'd splash cold milk onto the browned crust, and we'd share this little tasty shell. I have that Pyrex pan, and now, when I bake with Giorgio, my six-year-old son, I put his initials, which are the same as mine, in the bottom crust.

Gio's made three pies so far. I stand behind him to help with the rolling of the dough—just like helping a child swing a baseball bat—steadying the ends of my great-grandmother's rolling pin. The first time we were pushing the dough together, I started thinking how many crusts this rolling pin must have rolled out in four—and now five—generations. Thousands. Thousands of pies, I figured, and I had to wipe tears from my eyes. My mother and her mother and her mother, all living on through this rolling pin and these special recipes.

For instance, my son knows my mother—she's been gone ten years now—only as the person who made fried matzo and chicken paprikash and *palacsinta* (the Hungarian pancake). He knows my aunt Jimmy (her real name was Sylvia) through her terrific apple crisp. Maybe you wonder what people will say about you in your obituary, but in my family we think of what five dishes people will remember us by. Don't we get to visit with family members we've lost when we cook their dishes?

Luckily for me, my mother annotated her cookbooks, and I have so many of her recipes, including her Hungarian pecan cookies. This was an all-day project we'd start weeks before Christmas: mixing dough, shaping the individual balls, baking sheet after sheet of cookies, and sugaring each one separately. Myrna's secret is to roll the cookies in the sugar while they're still scorchingly hot. Because you have to work quickly, it's a job for extra hands: someone takes the cookies off the baking sheet and sets them in the powdered sugar (that would be Myrna), and then someone rolls the cookies around so the sugar can seep in (that would be me, with the messier job).

We'd make plates and plates of the cookies. Eventually we'd tuck them in neat little rows inside empty stationery boxes with plastic lids that Myrna would have saved up. (My mother wrote her two sisters and her mother every week.) And then we'd take them down to Peoria on a visit to my cousins. The butter stains on the cardboard box became a sign of something delicious to come.

I've added two other simple recipes here in case you'd like to be known for *three* delicious cookies.

Gale Gand, executive pastry chef/partner of Tru in Chicago, caught the eye of a *Life* magazine photographer while she was six years old making mud pies. Forty-some years later, she's still attracting attention for her desserts. The recipient of a Beard Award for Outstanding Pastry Chef, Gale appeared in Julia Child's book and PBS series *Baking with Julia*. Her previous culinary experience includes Charlie Trotter's, Gotham Bar & Grill, Stapleford Park Hotel, a five-star hotel near London, and Trio. Gale is the host of the Food Network's *Sweet Dreams* and the author of four books, including *Gale Gand's Just a Bite*.

Cory Schreiber
BLUEBERRY ROLY-POLY

Although I grew up among the vast farmlands of Oregon, surrounded by agriculture and gardens, the most abundant fruit garden I knew was my great-grandmother Elizabeth's in an entirely urban neighborhood known as Brooklyn on the east side of the Willamette River. You could see downtown Portland from her yard. Her house was encircled by six fruit trees that she and my great-grandfather had planted when they moved into the house around the turn of the century. When I came into the family, Elizabeth was already in her eighties, and those trees were only twenty years younger than she was.

I especially remember her Calimyrna fig tree and the Italian plum, but she also grew Concord grapes, wild and thorny blackberry brambles, and bushes of plump jumbo blueberries. Everyone had blueberry bushes: it's the volcanic soil and the fact that the temperature never gets extremely hot during the summer. I'd wander around the backyard, picking and grazing on this world of flavors.

Some of the fruit that wasn't consumed right as we picked it would find its way into this bygone dessert, a roly-poly. It's a flaky pastry that could sit on the oven counter for a day or two within easy reach of hungry grandchildren. We'd finish off the roly-poly so that it, in turn, could become part of our roly-poly little bodies that my great-grandmother just loved to pinch.

Her husband, my great-grandfather Louis Charles, founded a wholesale seafood shop, City Oyster Company, in 1907. With his handcart, he'd deliver fish and shellfish to farmers' markets and stores around town. As a sideline the shop served oyster stew and oyster cocktails. In the 1930s they expanded the shop into a full seafood restaurant. My cousins own the restaurant now; at ninety-five years old, it's a well-loved seafood house, but it's also like a maritime museum, since they have a century's worth of oyster plates and photographs.

Sometime after my great-grandmother died, I wanted to create a cookbook to celebrate the restaurant and our family, and I went looking for her recipes. They had nothing to do with the restaurant—Great-grandma Elizabeth's recipes were mostly sweets like gingerbread or pantry items like pickles and chow chows. Each recipe was carefully noted in her elegant penmanship. She even had a letter from "Betty Crocker" signed in 1929 by this fictitious Pillsbury character. Elizabeth wasn't a blue-ribbon prize cook, but she loved to bake, particularly those German desserts she grew up on,

BLUEBERRY ROLY-POLY Serves 8

7 tablespoons unsalted butter, cold

2 cups plus 1 tablespoon all-purpose flour

2 teaspoons baking powder

$1/2$ teaspoon salt

$3/4$ cup heavy cream

$1^1/2$ cups fresh or frozen blueberries
   (see Note)

6 tablespoons sugar

1 recipe Sliced Orange Sauce

Unsweetened whipped cream or ice
   cream, as an accompaniment

1 Preheat the oven to 350°F. Use 1 tablespoon each butter and flour to grease and flour two 8- to 10-inch loaf pans. Set aside.

2 Sift together 2 cups flour, the baking powder, and the salt in a mixing bowl. Cut in 4 tablespoons of the remaining cold butter using a pastry blender, 2 knives, or a food processor fitted with a steel blade. The mixture should resemble crumbs.

3 Add the heavy cream and mix until the dough comes together to form a ball. Turn the dough onto a floured surface and knead 4 to 5 times. Cut the dough in half and roll each piece into an 8 X 10-inch rectangle, $1/4$ inch thick.

4 Melt the remaining 2 tablespoons butter and brush half on each surface of the dough. Top each piece with $3/4$ cup blueberries and 3 tablespoons sugar.

5 Roll up each rectangle like a jelly roll. Each pastry should be approximately 8 inches long. Place seam side down in the bottom of the prepared pans.

6 Bake for 35 to 40 minutes, until the crust is golden brown. Allow the pastries to rest for 10 minutes before removing them from the pans and setting them on wire racks to cool completely.

✣ Cut the pastries into 2-inch pieces and serve with Sliced Orange Sauce. Unsweetened whipped cream or ice cream can also complement the roly-poly.

Note: If using frozen berries, do not allow the berries to thaw before rolling them in the pastry dough.

which helped her pass along the story of where our family came from originally.

I chose this roly-poly out of all her recipes partly because of its name, but also because it's so simple: a roulade of pastry with a light fruit filling. While I could have added crème fraîche to the dough or liqueur to the fruit, I find greater pleasure in

SLICED ORANGE SAUCE

Makes 1 1/2 cups

1/2 cup sugar

2 tablespoons cornstarch

1/4 teaspoon salt

1/3 cup fresh orange juice

1 vanilla bean, split and scraped,
　 or 1 teaspoon vanilla extract

3 tablespoons unsalted butter, cut into bits

2 oranges, peeled, halved lengthwise,
　 seeded, and sliced as thinly as possible

1 Combine the sugar, cornstarch, and salt in a medium saucepan. Stir in 1 1/2 cups cold water, the orange juice, and the vanilla bean. (If using vanilla extract, add it *after* the sauce has cooked.) Mix until smooth.

2 Cook the sauce over medium heat, stirring constantly, until it thickens, 5 to 7 minutes. Remove from the heat, add the butter, and mix until incorporated.

3 Cool the sauce slightly and add the orange slices. Remove the vanilla bean if used. Serve the sauce at room temperature.

✤ The orange sauce will keep for 3 to 4 days in the refrigerator. Heat slightly to reincorporate the butter into the sauce before serving.

being respectful of this venerable dessert and setting it down here just as Great-Grandmother Elizabeth recorded in her handwriting. What can you expect? I'm a fifth-generation Oregonian who lives in her son's—my grandfather's—very house.

Cory Schreiber opened Wildwood Restaurant and Bar in Portland, Oregon, nine years ago and rapidly became a leader in the region's bustling culinary scene. He won the Beard Award in 1998 for Best Chef/Pacific Northwest, a fitting tribute to a man who cherishes the land, its peoples, and its produce much in the same way as Beard, a native Oregonian himself, did. Cory's family has been involved in the Pacific Northwest oyster business since the mid-1800s. He is the author of *Wildwood: Cooking from the Source in the Pacific Northwest.*

Nancy Silverton
COCONUT CUPCAKES

Starting with kindergarten and lasting until sixth grade, all of us mothers are roped into providing the school birthday party treat. I'm on my last of three rounds: our daughter, Vanessa, is in college now, Ben just turned seventeen, but my youngest, Oliver, is in third grade. Last year, for his birthday, Oliver wanted coconut cupcakes for

COCONUT CUPCAKES

Makes twenty-two 3-inch cakes

For the cupcakes

2$\frac{1}{4}$ cups sugar

1 tablespoon freshly grated nutmeg

$\frac{1}{2}$ pound (2 sticks) unsalted butter

$\frac{1}{2}$ cup cream of coconut powder
   (available in the Thai section of
   Asian markets)

1$\frac{1}{2}$ cups unsweetened coconut milk

1 tablespoon almond extract

3 cups self-rising flour

8 large egg whites

For the topping

2 large egg whites

1 cup unsweetened shredded coconut
   (thick strips preferred)

2$\frac{1}{2}$ tablespoons sugar

1 Preheat the oven to 350°F. Fill 3-inch-diameter muffin tins with paper liners (as many as needed for holding twenty-two cupcakes).

2 Blend together $\frac{3}{4}$ cup of the sugar and the nutmeg in a small bowl and set aside.

3 To make the batter, cream together the butter, coconut powder, and 1 cup of the remaining sugar in an electric mixer fitted with a flat paddle.

4 Mix together the coconut milk and almond extract. Alternate additions of the flour and the coconut milk to the butter mixture, beating until smooth.

5 In a separate bowl, whip the egg whites and remaining $\frac{1}{2}$ cup sugar until they form soft peaks. Fold a third of the whipped egg whites into the batter to lighten it. Add the remaining egg whites and fold until thoroughly combined.

6 Fill the tins two-thirds full with batter. Sprinkle each cupcake with $\frac{1}{2}$ teaspoon of the sugar-nutmeg mixture.

7 To make the topping, stir together the egg whites, shredded coconut, and sugar in a small bowl. Evenly spread the topping on each cake.

8 Bake for 30 to 40 minutes, until a toothpick poked in the middle of the cake comes out clean and the tops are golden.

✤ Cool the cupcakes and then remove them from the muffin tins.

his school party. (For whatever reason, this flavor has regained a certain popularity.) Typically, kids want a commercial cake frosted with their favorite cartoon character at the time; the second most popular choice is a giant box of doughnuts.

Now, I remember one year when Vanessa decided that her mom, the fancy baker, should bake her a cake for her school birthday party. I did, and promptly several of her friends told her point-blank that it was the most terrible cake that they'd ever had. It was a chocolate cake—low and dense and bittersweet—clearly not sweet enough for elementary-school taste buds. I was shell-shocked.

So when Oliver asked me to bake cupcakes, I took it as a real challenge. I decided the simpler the better this time. Yet I was determined not to make coconut cupcakes that were simply boxed yellow-cake mix with coconut in the frosting. I wanted the cake itself to possess the coconut flavor. After a little experimenting, I made a batter with coconut milk and coconut powder (something I found at a Thai grocery) and a little almond extract that seems to increase the coconut sensation. I also found some long, unsweetened threads of dried coconut, which have so much more flavor than the dull, dried flakes.

These can be easily embellished with kid-friendly sprinkles. Or you can frost the cupcakes with the familiar white-mountain frosting and sprinkle with strips of toasted coconut.

Oliver's class did like the cupcakes. And what's more, I like them, especially with just the little crunch of the egg white and toasted coconut "crust" on top.

Nancy Silverton is pastry chef and owner of Campanile restaurant and owner and baker of La Brea Bakery, both in Los Angeles. Among Nancy's books are *Desserts*, *Nancy Silverton's Breads from the La Brea Bakery*, and three coauthored with her husband, including *Mark Peel and Nancy Silverton at Home* and *The Food of Campanile*. Her food, restaurant, bakery, and cookbooks have received a multitude of distinctions and awards over the last fifteen years.

Charles Dale PINEAPPLE UPSIDE-DOWN CAKE WITH COCONUT CRÈME ANGLAISE

From the age of two to seven, I was raised with four other children in the palace of Prince Rainier in Monaco. My father served as the prince's adviser. Not your typical elementary-school experience.

But everything changed when Charles de Gaulle convinced himself that my father, whom he had hired, was a spy—if Monaco wanted to be a French protectorate, my family had to leave immediately. We went on a six-month trip around the world, and one stop was Freeport, Grand Bahama, which at the time was nominally developed.

PINEAPPLE UPSIDE-DOWN CAKE WITH COCONUT CRÈME ANGLAISE Serves 8

----

1 fresh pineapple, peeled, cored, and
  sliced into eight $1/2$-inch-thick disks,
  or 8 slices canned, juice reserved
4 tablespoons ($1/2$ stick) unsalted butter
1 cup packed light brown sugar
$7/8$ cup granulated sugar
1 cup all-purpose flour
1 teaspoon baking powder
3 large eggs, separated
$1/4$ cup pineapple juice
Pinch of salt
1 recipe Coconut Crème Anglaise
  (or whipped cream)

1 Preheat the oven to 350°F.

2 Halve 7 of the 8 pineapple rings.

3 Melt the butter and brown sugar in a heavy 10-inch skillet or pie pan over medium heat. Remove the pan from the heat and stir to make an even mixture.

4 Place the whole pineapple ring in the center of the pan and arrange the half-rings around it in concentric half-circles.

5 In a small bowl, combine the granulated sugar, flour, and baking powder.

6 Place the egg yolks in a mixing bowl and beat until thick and pale yellow. Stir in the pineapple juice. Mix in the dry ingredients.

7 Whisk the egg whites and a pinch of salt in another mixing bowl. Whip until they form soft peaks. Gently fold the egg whites into the batter and pour over the arranged pineapple slices.

8 Bake for 45 to 55 minutes or until a toothpick inserted in the middle of the cake comes out clean. Remove the cake from the oven and cool for 15 minutes. Place a large plate over the pan and invert. Let the cake cool completely before cutting into 8 slices.

✣ Place a wedge of the cake onto individual plates and serve with cold Coconut Crème Anglaise or whipped cream.

APRICOT VARIATION

In Colorado, we have fabulous apricots in June and I like to make this cake substituting fresh apricots for the pineapple. Place 24 apricot halves, skin side down, in the brown sugar and butter mixture. Substitute water for the pineapple juice. And for the Crème Anglaise, replace the coconut milk with $1\frac{3}{4}$ cups whole milk.

My parents met someone who'd bought the only hotel there, the Lucaya (the Indian name for the island), and my father's company decided to remodel it, build a port, and see if they could contract a cruise ship to go back and forth between it and Florida:

COCONUT CRÈME ANGLAISE

Makes 2$\frac{1}{2}$ cups

- -

$\frac{1}{2}$ cup whipping cream

One 13$\frac{1}{2}$-ounce can Thai lite
    coconut milk

1 teaspoon vanilla extract

6 large egg yolks

$\frac{1}{3}$ cup sugar

1 Combine the cream, coconut milk, and vanilla in a heavy saucepan and bring to a boil over high heat.

2 Whisk the egg yolks and sugar together in a mixing bowl. Continue to beat until the mixture is very thick and pale yellow. Add 1 cup of the hot cream to the warmed egg mixture, whisk together, then add to the saucepan.

3 Cook over low heat, stirring constantly. The sauce should become very thick. Do not allow it to boil. Strain the sauce through a fine-mesh strainer into a bowl placed over an ice bath. Cool the sauce completely, then pour it into an airtight jar. The sauce can be refrigerated for up to 2 days.

they basically hoped to put the Bahamas on the map.

The island was utterly unspoiled, with such natural beauty. I'd go out fishing, and we'd hit a pocket of yellowtail or snapper and reel as fast as we could: I'd toss the line in and have another fish in seconds. (Now if you fish for four hours and bring back three fish, you're lucky.)

When we returned to the island to live, our house was a trailer in the middle of the woods for an entire year while our permanent residence was being built. I loved it, but the changes were almost baffling. My parents adapted to island life, but they brought along their European customs. We had a Jamaican housekeeper, and my mother gave her this recipe for pineapple upside-down cake. It was my grandmother's dish—she was Swedish—and we often had this for dessert on the island. But while the dessert sounds tropical, it's not typical to the island: at that time, pineapples weren't even native. But what I loved about this dessert is how caramel would form on top of the cake, magically appearing after the pan was inverted.

She'd also make an upside-down cake with canned apricots. This was the early sixties. In the Bahamas, nothing much grew besides coconuts. Picture sand and rock, mostly, with tropical flowers and palm trees, but no livestock and very few people. And certainly no restaurants: we ate our meals at home.

I started cooking after graduate school. I was an amateur cook first, and over the years I'd cook up a storm for friends and family. Pineapple upside-down cake became a mainstay. It keeps very well—refrigerated, it will hold for three days.

Colorado has some of the same unspoiled nature of the Bahamas in the sixties. There's trout fishing here, but we have wonderful, fresh apricots in June: our luscious fruit. So I had to offer you an apricot variation for this cake as well.

Born in Nice, France, raised both abroad and in the States, Charles Dale earned degrees in romance languages and art history at Princeton, traveled as a troubadour and songwriter, but eventually apprenticed himself to Alain Sailhac of Le Cirque. He subsequently worked with Georges Masraff in Paris, Daniel Boulud in New York, and Jean-Paul Lacombe in Lyon. In 1990 Charles opened Renaissance Restaurant in Aspen, and in 1993 the Rustique Bistro. He is coauthor of *The Chefs' Guide to America's Best Restaurants* and the forthcoming *Haute Rustic Cuisine*.

Marcel Desaulniers
CHOCOLATE APPLESAUCE CAKE WITH JACKED-UP CARAMEL APPLE SAUCE

I came by my passion for chocolate honestly. My mother, even at eighty-three years old, is a chocophile. When we were growing up, chocolate was never a forbidden fruit; it was always around, and we learned to love it. My mother was widowed at thirty-seven with six kids. She'd work all day at a dry cleaner's, and then she'd come home, make us dinner, and then iron her kids' school uniforms all evening: the six of us went to parochial schools, and my five sisters had pleated skirts and starched blouses.

But my mother would also bake something each night. A pot of fudge . . . chewy chocolate caramels dipped in chocolate . . . chocolate chip cookies . . . or an amazing cake made with cocoa, not baking chocolate, that she called her Heavy-Duty Chocolate Cake. Baking was like the cocktail she never had: a way to unwind.

And certainly it wasn't easy raising six kids in Woonsocket, Rhode Island, a textile mill town that by the 1950s had seen much of the industry move farther south. I'd like to remember our family as having all kinds of

CHOCOLATE APPLESAUCE CAKE WITH JACKED-UP CARAMEL APPLE SAUCE

Serves 16

1/2 pound (2 sticks) unsalted butter, cut into 16 pieces, plus 2 teaspoons, melted

2 1/2 cups all-purpose flour

1 teaspoon baking powder

1 teaspoon baking soda

1/2 teaspoon ground allspice

1/2 teaspoon freshly grated nutmeg

1/2 teaspoon salt

1 1/4 cups sugar

4 large eggs

6 ounces semisweet baking chocolate, coarsely chopped, melted, and slightly cooled

1 recipe Quick Applesauce

2 tablespoons apple brandy

1 teaspoon vanilla extract

1 recipe Jacked-Up Caramel Apple Sauce

1 Preheat the oven to 350°F. Coat a 9 1/2-inch nonstick fluted tube pan with the 2 teaspoons melted butter. Set aside.

2 Sift together the flour, baking powder, baking soda, allspice, nutmeg, and salt. Set aside.

3 Place 1/2 pound butter and the sugar in the bowl of an electric mixer. Mix on low speed for 1 minute. Increase the speed to medium and beat for 2 minutes. The mixture should be soft. Scrape the sides and add the eggs one at a time, scraping the bowl after each addition. Beat on medium speed for 30 seconds.

4 Add the melted chocolate and beat on medium speed for 30 seconds. Add half the flour and mix on low speed; add 1/2 cup of the applesauce and mix again. Repeat with the remaining flour and applesauce. Add the apple brandy and vanilla. Mix on low speed for 5 seconds, then beat on medium speed for 15 seconds, until combined.

5 Spoon the batter into the prepared pan and bake for 50 to 60 minutes or until a toothpick inserted in the center of the cake comes out clean. Cool the cake on a rack for 15 to 20 minutes, then invert onto a cake plate to cool completely.

✤ Slice the cake with a serrated knife warmed in hot water and then dried. Wipe, heat, and dry the knife after each cut. Top each wedge of cake with 3 tablespoons warm Jacked-Up Caramel Apple Sauce.

✤ The cake will keep for 2 or 3 days in a tightly sealed plastic container at room temperature. (The "crumb texture" will be lost with refrigeration.)

QUICK APPLESAUCE Makes 1 cup

$^1/_2$ cup apple juice

2 tablespoons packed light brown sugar

1 teaspoon ground cinnamon

3 medium Red Delicious apples

1 Place the apple juice, brown sugar, and cinnamon in a medium saucepan over medium heat and stir to dissolve the sugar.

2 Peel, core, and cut each apple into about 8 pieces, placing each in the cooking liquid to prevent browning. Cover the saucepan, bring to a boil, then lower the heat, letting the mixture simmer for 20 minutes or until the apples are tender.

3 Drain the apples in a colander placed over a bowl. Puree the apples in a food processor for 30 seconds with 2 tablespoons of the cooking liquid. Cool and set aside.

great European chocolates that I have come to love, but it was Bakers' chocolate in that red box at home, and Hershey's cocoa, and Nestlé chocolate chips. Still, I never thought we were deprived as kids: because we had *chocolate.* Not just cookies, but cookies with *chocolate.* And cake that was utterly *chocolate.* This was luxury and indulgence.

I started working in restaurants during my high school years, and I'd often sit at the table and watch my mother bake; I certainly could have helped, but my mother was happiest cooking by herself. I'd participate in the aura of baked chocolate just by being there, having real conversations with her.

Soon after I graduated from the Culinary Institute of America, I was drafted into the marines. I served for two years, part of that time in Vietnam. I have done a pretty good job of removing most of my Vietnam service from my immediate consciousness, despite having attended three marine reunions in the last eight years. But I do remember that in December of 1966 my unit, India company 3/26, was operating near Quang Tri. We were living in foxholes. It rained constantly. Christmas had come and gone without fanfare. A few days later mail arrived from the States, including a package from my mother. I somehow knew what it would contain, so I announced that chocolates had arrived from home as I tore away the string and brown wrapping paper. I wasn't disappointed: she'd sent some two dozen cookies and a pound of chocolate fudge, none the worse for the long journey—better than that, they tasted as if Mom had stayed up late the night before to prepare these treats (although two or three weeks had certainly passed). I was a fire team leader and shared the package with the three men under my supervision. As best as I can recall, they all praised Mrs. D's way with chocolate.

A few other packages arrived from my mother while I was in country, but that first package, a few days after Christmas, is what I remember best more than thirty-five years later.

After my discharge I worked in New York restaurants for a while before moving to Williamsburg, Virginia. And it was here, starting the Trellis in 1980, that I decided to showcase chocolate in our desserts.

Now, apples have never been at the top of the chocolate-and-fruit affinity list. Pears, bananas, raspberries, or figs all seem to elbow the apples out of the chocolate possibilities. But I wanted to create a dessert that connected these two tastes, and in this recipe, applesauce finds an unsurpassed partnership with chocolate.

I use Captain Apple Jack apple brandy, distilled in Virginia, where I live. Of course there's the estimable Calvados from France, too, but ordinary apple brandy works fine here. Indeed, try an ounce or two of the brandy heated in a cup of apple cider to accompany this dessert. Then all you'll need is a snowstorm.

JACKED-UP CARAMEL APPLE SAUCE Makes 4 cups

----

2 cups sugar

1 teaspoon fresh lemon juice

$^3/_4$ cup heavy cream

4 tablespoons ($^1/_2$ stick) unsalted butter

1$^1/_2$ cups walnuts, toasted and coarsely chopped by hand

2 medium Red Delicious apples

$^1/_4$ cup apple brandy

1 Place the sugar and lemon juice in a large heavy saucepan. Cook over medium-high heat, stirring constantly, and caramelize the sugar to a light golden brown color, 8 to 10 minutes. Watch vigilantly: the color will quickly change from white to golden brown; a burned color and taste can follow within seconds. Immediately remove from the heat.

2 Gradually add the cream to the hot sugar and whisk vigorously. (Adding it slowly will prevent too much steaming and spattering.) Add the butter and whisk to incorporate. Stir in the walnuts.

3 Dice the apples (do not peel) into $^1/_4$-inch pieces, stirring the apple bits into the sauce as you dice them to keep the flesh from browning. Pour in the apple brandy and stir well. Serve immediately or cover and refrigerate. Reheat in a double boiler.

Donna Nordin
CHOCOLATE MAYONNAISE CAKE WITH PEANUT-BUTTER-CUP ICE CREAM AND FUDGE SAUCE

My parents were married sixty-two years ago, on June 30, 1940, in Escondido, California. My dad will turn eighty-three very soon, and my mom will be eighty. She was just a hair under the legal marrying age of eighteen in California, and even though they had permission from all the parents, they had to run away across the border to Winterhaven, Arizona, where they were married at a courthouse.

My mother's sisters and sisters-in-law threw her a shower shortly after their return. Everyone was asked to bring a three-by-five card with a favorite recipe to help the new bride. Each guest wrote out a recipe in longhand on an index card's pale blue lines, and each card was tucked inside a handmade wooden box with a lovely blond grain. The box is only four inches deep; it wasn't meant for hundreds of recipes—just the staples for making dinners and entertaining.

She also received a cookbook as a shower gift: *The American Woman's Cookbook* from 1939. I have it now, still filled with all the newspaper recipes she clipped and tucked into its pages. The inside cover depicts a whole tray of petits fours in greens and pinks—I don't think we ever made those, but inside there is the Swiss Steak I made when it was my turn to cook family dinner (my sister and I each took one night a week). There is the Noodle Goulash we loved. The Cheese Mayonnaise Sandwich, with a recipe for making your own mayonnaise . . . and the Russian Sandwich (cream cheese, pimientos, chopped olives, and mayonnaise on that tinned Boston brown bread). Just looking through the book reminds me of so many things.

CHOCOLATE MAYONNAISE CAKE WITH PEANUT-BUTTER-CUP ICE CREAM AND FUDGE SAUCE

Makes 9 to 12 servings

----

1 cup mayonnaise (not Miracle Whip)

1 teaspoon vanilla extract

1 cup granulated sugar

2 cups all-purpose flour

2 teaspoons baking soda

$1/4$ teaspoon salt

$1/4$ cup unsweetened cocoa powder or 2 ounces unsweetened chocolate, melted

Confectioners' sugar, optional

1 recipe Peanut-Butter-Cup Ice Cream

1 recipe Fudge Sauce

1 Preheat the oven to 350°F and grease an 8-inch square pan.

2 In a mixing bowl, combine the mayonnaise with 1 cup boiling water. Mix well and add the vanilla, granulated sugar, flour, baking soda, salt, and cocoa. Pour the batter into the prepared pan and bake for 35 to 40 minutes.

3 The cake is done when a toothpick poked in the center of the cake comes out clean. Let it cool on a wire rack. If desired, dust with confectioners' sugar.

✤ Place a slice of cake in a shallow bowl. Top with a scoop of Peanut-Butter-Cup Ice Cream and drizzle both with Fudge Sauce.

PEANUT-BUTTER-CUP ICE CREAM Makes $1^1/2$ pints

$1^2/3$ cups whole milk

1 cup creamy peanut butter

$1/2$ cup plus 3 tablespoons sugar

2 teaspoons vanilla extract

$1^1/2$ ounces bittersweet chocolate, chopped

1 Combine the milk, peanut butter, and $1/2$ cup of the sugar in a saucepan over low heat. Stir the mixture until smooth. Remove from the heat and stir in the vanilla.

2 Cool the mixture over an ice bath. Freeze in an ice cream maker according to the manufacturer's instructions. (The finished ice cream will be soft enough to swirl in the chocolate from the final step.)

3 In a small bowl, over a pot of simmering water, melt the chocolate with 3 tablespoons water and the remaining 3 tablespoons sugar. Stir until smooth.

4 Once the chocolate mixture has cooled, swirl it into the finished ice cream. Cover and freeze until firm and ready to serve.

FUDGE SAUCE Makes 2 cups

----

1 cup whole milk

1 tablespoon light corn syrup

1 pound bittersweet chocolate, chopped

1 teaspoon vanilla extract

Combine the milk and corn syrup in a small saucepan over medium heat, cooking until it begins to simmer. Remove the pan from the heat, add the chocolate, and stir until the sauce is smooth. Stir in the vanilla, transfer the sauce to a lidded jar, and refrigerate for up to 2 weeks.

This recipe box was so modern, really, since my grandmother's generation didn't use recipes typically. When I wanted to make a wonderful piecrust like my grandmother's, I'd have to watch and follow along beside her in the kitchen. She just couldn't write down a recipe. It was all the feel of the dough. Or the taste. She would sample the final crust and say, "That wasn't quite short enough" or "It's all right, but it's a little short." (I had no idea what she was talking about: pie had nothing to do with height!)

When I was ten or eleven, I found my mother's recipe box—I can picture the drawer in which it resided—because I decided to bake something myself. The Peanut Butter Cookies were the first thing I tried. When I thought I'd graduate from cookies to cake, I found this Chocolate Mayonnaise Cake in the box, and I can clearly remember asking my mother, "What's mayonnaise doing in a cake? Are you sure this is a cake?" And she explained to me about wartime cooking, about the shortage of eggs and shortening during the Depression, and how the mayonnaise provided both—premeasured, even!

We didn't finish the cake with powdered sugar or frosting, since it's so moist. A tall glass of milk was all I needed. But now I like to serve this cake with a peanut-butter ice cream and a drizzle of classic fudge sauce. Maybe years from now some young girl will look at *these* recipes and think "how old-fashioned and strange." And that will be true, because what we eat is so connected to place and time and the people who were right there, right then, with us.

Donna Nordin is the owner and chef of Café Terra Cotta in Tucson, Arizona. She was instrumental in developing the concept of southwestern cuisine and now oversees the quality and creation of the dishes at the restaurant. Donna attended Cordon Bleu Cooking School in Paris in the early 1970s and started her career teaching cooking in San Francisco. While traveling as an instructor, she met her husband, who owned a cooking school, and settled in Tucson, opening Café Terra Cotta in 1986.

Christopher Gross
ALMOND CHEESECAKE WITH CHAMPAGNE-HONEY SAUCE

I ate practically nothing as a kid. Not vegetables. Not potatoes, except Tater Tots and occasionally fries. Not Jell-O, even though my father tried to convince me it was a Popsicle without a stick. (I did eat Popsicles.) Not my grandmother's baking, and she was a great baker: pecan pies, walnut pies, cakes, apple pies—all I would eat was plain chocolate cake. At big holiday dinners I ate plain noodles and white turkey meat. I couldn't even look at the can-shaped cranberry with the wiggling bands.

When we moved to Phoenix, I was twelve, and my one desire was motocrossing. (It's still a passion.) But at twelve, to earn money for my first cycle, I took a restaurant job. And that led to cooking jobs in Arizona and California and, eventually, to London as I tried to build up my résumé.

After a year in England, I took the *Michelin Guide* and looked at all the one-, two-, and three-star restaurants in and around Paris. I photocopied all the certificates of where I'd worked and stuffed them into envelopes. I wrote a lousy letter that basically said, "Please hire me. I'll do prep work, dishes— anything," and had a chef friend translate it into French. I mailed off a hundred letters. I got one interview.

Chez Albert had fourteen tables. They prepared both modern and classical French foods. The old guy who owned the place figured me to be British, but after a few weeks he learned that I was American: suddenly getting me working papers through the Commonwealth was not possible.

One day, I am working at my station, and the chef, who knew very little English, starts shouting at me, *"Christopher, go! Go! Go now!"* I look down at my work, and I see that I haven't done anything that would warrant getting fired. But I figure that's it, I blew it. I race upstairs, change clothes, and resign myself to finding another job. But on my way out the door, someone on the staff who knows a bit more English explains that the work inspector has arrived and that I could come back around five o'clock. I am so relieved. But every so many weeks, I have to dash out of the restaurant for a few hours.

During my time in France, I learned this champagne and honey sauce, which is wonderful on many desserts; on this almond cheesecake, it's perfection.

ALMOND CHEESECAKE WITH CHAMPAGNE-HONEY SAUCE Makes 8 individual cakes or one 8-inch cake

----

1 pound plus 2 ounces cream cheese

1 cup sugar

3 ounces (6 tablespoons) crème fraîche

3 ounces (6 tablespoons) heavy cream

1 large egg

1 teaspoon vanilla extract

$^1/_2$ cup sliced almonds, toasted

1 recipe Champagne Honey Sauce

Fresh strawberries or raspberries for garnish

1 Preheat the oven to 210°F. Line eight 3-inch-diameter ramekins or one 8-inch cake pan with plastic wrap.

2 Beat the cream cheese on medium speed in an electric mixer until smooth. Scrape the bowl and add the sugar; mix again until smooth. Scrape the bowl again and continue to mix until the batter is smooth and creamy.

3 Adjust the mixer speed to low and add the crème fraîche and heavy cream. Scrape the bowl and mix for 30 seconds. Add the egg and vanilla and mix just to incorporate.

4 Fill the ramekins two-thirds full or no more than 2 inches high with the batter (if using a cake pan, fill with all of the batter). Sprinkle with almonds. Place the prepared ramekins or pan on a baking tray. Place the tray in the oven and fill the tray with as much boiling water as possible.

5 Bake the ramekins for 80 to 90 minutes. The single cake pan will take up to 10 minutes longer. The center of the finished cake should be firm. Remove from the oven and cool. Refrigerate for several hours before unmolding.

✤ Carefully invert the cake(s) and remove the ramekins or the pan. Remove the plastic and gently invert the cake(s) again on a serving plate or dessert plates. Top with the Champagne Honey Sauce and garnish with fresh berries.

CHAMPAGNE-HONEY SAUCE
Makes $^1/_2$ cup

$^1/_3$ cup plus 2 tablespoons honey

1 cup champagne

1 fresh mint sprig, leaves sliced into thin strips, optional

Heat $^1/_3$ cup of the honey in a small saucepan over medium heat. When the honey begins to bubble, add the champagne and reduce the liquid to $^1/_2$ cup. Cool slightly and add the remaining 2 tablespoons cold honey and the mint if desired. Pour into a jar and refrigerate until ready to serve or for up to 1 week.

The cheesecake itself was an accident. I had a traditional crustless cheesecake that I used to bake in small, individual rings in a water bath. But one day one of my chefs unmolded some that he'd prepared, and the cheesecakes sagged. I tasted one, thinking they were just undercooked, but I realized he had used a mousse recipe that had similar ingredients. Its warm, molten taste was terrific. So we added eggs to the original recipe and baked this cheesecake at a very low temperature so the mixture wouldn't rise too much like a soufflé. The result is this smooth cheesecake that's so creamy because there's no starch in the recipe.

Sometimes I make a chiffonade of mint leaves to swirl into the glaze before applying it. The green threads make a bright decoration, and you don't need more than a small sprig of fresh mint. (Simply roll the leaves into a bundle and slice through the layers to create thin strips.)

I think even as a kid I would have liked this dessert. It has a purity and a plainness, but also an elegance and subtlety. And the mint doesn't really count as a vegetable, does it?

Among his many accolades, Christopher Gross was named one of America's 10 Best New Chefs by *Food & Wine* magazine and Best Chef/Southwest by the Beard Foundation. In 1997 Christopher was the first chef in Arizona to be given the Robert Mondavi Culinary Award of Excellence. His earlier restaurants included both Christopher's and Christopher's Bistro, which received superior reviews in periodicals such as *Gourmet*, *Wine Spectator*, *Bon Appétit*, the *New York Times*, and *Connoisseur*. His current venture, opened in 1998, is Christopher's Fermier Brasserie within Biltmore Fashion Park, featuring fresh, French-inspired fare created from local and regionally farmed ingredients.

Hubert Seifert
MALLORCAN ALMOND CAKE

My wife, Helga, and I lived on Mallorca for some time. It may be the most beautiful place in the world with its white beaches, rich valleys, windmills, and rocky coasts, but for people who come from a place with four seasons, even all that splendor can be a little . . . monotonous? April goes directly into the summer without a spring. There's hardly any fall, and there's no winter, really. I mentioned this once to some friends in a Mallorcan café. They'd asked us how we liked their country, and though we

MALLORCAN ALMOND CAKE

Makes one 12-inch cake

----

12 large eggs, beaten

2 1/2 cups granulated sugar

9 cups ground almonds

Freshly grated zest of 1 lemon

2 tablespoons confectioners' sugar

1/2 teaspoon ground cinnamon

Almond liqueur, such as amaretto,
    optional

1 Preheat the oven to 350°F. Line the bottom of a 12-inch springform pan with parchment paper and lightly oil the pan with cooking spray.

2 In a large bowl, whisk together the eggs and granulated sugar until smooth. Gradually add the ground almonds and mix to incorporate. Stir in the lemon zest. Pour the batter into the prepared pan.

3 Bake for 1 hour and 15 minutes or until a toothpick poked into the center of the cake comes out clean. Allow the cake to cool completely on a rack.

4 Remove the sides of the pan. Place a plate on top of the cake and invert. Remove the bottom of the pan.

5 Combine the confectioners' sugar and the cinnamon. Sprinkle over the surface of the cake.

✤ Serve thin slices of cake with a dousing of almond liqueur if desired and offer espresso or cappuccino.

professed our love of the foods, the landscape, and the people, we admitted that we missed the seasons. "What are you missing?" he asked us. Though it seemed strange to him, I answered "winter." And he said, "Winter will come very soon," and he told us this story.

One of the Spanish princes lived on Mallorca, and he met a French princess on his travels and brought her back to the island to live with him. But by the time winter came around, the princess longed to return home and left for France. The prince could not bear to lose her, so he traveled to the mainland and bought all the young almond trees he could find. Every one. Hundreds of thousands. And he had them planted back on Mallorca. At the year's end, he sent word to the princess: "Come back to the island and stay through the holidays, and I promise you will have your winter." At the end of January, when the prince knew that the time was right, he drove the princess up the tallest mountain—a thousand feet into the air—so they could oversee the valleys of Mallorca. And when the princess looked out, the landscape below her was as white as snow: all of the almond trees were blooming, and the valley was filled with white blossoms as though thick snowflakes had settled on everything.

Once, Helga and I returned to Mallorca after visiting family in Germany, where it had been snowing and cold. As we started our descent into Palma, I experienced a little of that princess's astonishment: we hadn't been to the island for maybe ten years, and in ten years you forget so much. So I looked out the window and I said to Helga, "It's been snowing here! Look how white!" I couldn't remember ever seeing snow in Mallorca. But, of course, as we flew in closer, I saw that it was the blossoming almond trees. Millions and millions of trees in full bloom. When we landed and the cabin doors opened, the air that rushed in was almond perfume! Thick like amaretto. You could bite the air. And the minute I stepped outside, that smell was like a movie starting behind my eyes, and I started to remember all these names and tastes and places of Mallorca—they just rushed back into my mind with that almond scent.

The cooking of Mallorca is simple and pure with influences from its long history of occupation by Romans, Arabs, and Spaniards. Almonds can appear in almost any dish, and of all the recipes I learned while in Mallorca, I have many favorites. Try making an almond aioli sometime: replace the egg yolk with riced potatoes and beat in equal parts almond oil and corn oil in place of the olive oil. A little garlic and lemon juice, and it's fantastic. I make an almond ice cream where the "cream" comes from simmering the almonds. But my favorite may be this almond cake, which is simply almonds and sugar bound with eggs. It's dense and fragrant and, in restaurants, the waiter will come around with almond liqueur

and start pouring it on the cake until you say "when." You can get tipsy on one slice!

But with its beauty, with its perfumes, and with the warmth of its people, Mallorca is intoxicating in every way.

Hubert Seifert, born in Aachen, Germany, began his culinary career at fourteen in one of Germany's most renowned restaurants. Hubert arrived in America in 1979, working as a private chef before opening Gourmet Market in Columbus, Ohio, a fine-dining restaurant and prepared foods market. He is now chef and co-owner, with his wife, Helga, of Spagio, Spagio Cellars, and Aubergine, a private dining club. Hubert donates much of his time to the community, supporting the March of Dimes, American Lung Association, Hospice of Ohio, and the James Beard House.

Paul Minnillo
BEGGAR'S PURSE WITH CARAMELIZED PEARS

I travel to Europe a few times each year as part of my work for Continental Airlines; I'm the chef for their Cleveland hub, and I help with their first-class, international food. But what you see in Italy, the country where my relatives are from, is a tradition of making and sharing in food that goes back for thousands of years. And beyond any one dish or ingredient, what immigrants to this country brought with them—what they hoped to preserve in their new homeland—is the importance of a family meal, of taking time to sit down together and share in great food, great wine, great company. In Italy, France, Spain—that's what eating is supposed to be about. I was brought up in Cleveland with this European tradition. We didn't have grand cuisine, but we dined rather than rushed through meals.

Before my father served in World War II, he'd owned a local grocery store for twenty years. And, later, my family owned a restaurant, Minnillo's, as well as the Greenhouse, where I eventually started working. So food has always been the focus for our family; what's on the table was always something to talk about at the table. For starters, anyway.

I first learned to make this beggar's purse when I apprenticed as a chef in London. It sums up the essence of a glorious meal, enclosing some of my favorite elements in one dessert. In this version it captures a season as well: up here, near Lake Erie, we have a window from mid-September to October, when local farmers have Bartlett pears. The fruit is so sweet, they speak for themselves. But my passion for cheese is

BEGGAR'S PURSE WITH CARAMELIZED PEARS Serves 4

----

1 bottle Muscat (Muscat de Beaumes de
   Venise preferred)

1 cup granulated sugar

Two 3-inch cinnamon sticks

6 ripe Bartlett pears, peeled, cored,
   and halved

$^1/_4$ pound mascarpone cheese

$^1/_4$ cup confectioners' sugar, plus extra
   for dusting

1 teaspoon almond liqueur such as
   Amaretto

8 sheets phyllo dough

8 tablespoons (1 stick) unsalted butter,
   melted

$^1/_2$ cup chopped toasted walnuts

1 Combine the wine, sugar, and cinnamon in a nonreactive saucepan and bring to a boil. Reduce the heat and add the prepared pears. Poach until the pears are soft, 10 to 15 minutes. Transfer the fruit to a cooling rack. Once cool, dice the pears and pat dry.

2 Increase the heat to high and reduce the wine sauce to 1 cup. Allow to cool.

3 In a small bowl, combine the mascarpone, confectioners' sugar, and almond liqueur.

4 Preheat the oven to 375°F and line a sheet pan with parchment paper.

5 To assemble the purses, cut the phyllo dough in half, making 16 total pieces. To keep the dough from drying or cracking, keep the unused sheets covered with a towel. The goal is to create a star with 16 points by staggering the orientation of each rectangular sheet. Orient one sheet of dough on a work surface and brush it lightly with butter. Consider it a clock face. Place the second sheet on top of the first, shifted about "five minutes" later. Brush it with the butter. When you place the third sheet, orient it "five minutes" later still, then butter it. Place the fourth sheet another "five minutes" later and butter it.

6 Layer $^3/_4$ cup chopped pears, 1 tablespoon walnuts, and 2 tablespoons mascarpone mixture in the center of the layered phyllo. Gather the sides of the dough to form a pouch and lightly pucker the top edges to form a seal. Transfer the beggar's purse to the sheet pan. Repeat the process for the remaining 3 pouches.

7 Bake for 8 to 10 minutes or until the dough is golden brown.

✤ Pour the sauce into the center of each plate and place 1 pouch on top. Sprinkle with the remaining walnuts and dust with confectioners' sugar. Arrange the extra pear pieces around the purses.

such (we even age our own cheese at the restaurant now) that I wanted to create a dessert that could meld these two ingredients that are traditionally enjoyed together. This beggar's purse is the result, bundling the wine-steeped pears with mascarpone in a bit of crispy pastry. You can adapt it to other fruits, of course, and other sauces, but the key thing, for me, is simply having the long, lovely meal with friends or family beforehand.

Paul Minnillo's cuisine is influenced by three generations of family members who were grocers, butchers, and restaurateurs. A business administration graduate of Miami University, Paul expanded his culinary talents in both New York and London, working with Anton Mossiman at the venerable Dorchester Hotel. Upon his return to Cleveland, he opened the Baricelli Inn, located in a brownstone mansion in University Circle, which showcases his love of the continental dining experience. *Gourmet* chose the Baricelli Inn "One of America's Best 50 Restaurants," and *Food & Wine* named it among "America's Top 50 Hotel Restaurants."

Robert Helstrom APPLE TART WITH BROWN-BUTTER CUSTARD AND CRÈME FRAÎCHE

In third or fourth grade everyone learns the story of Johnny Appleseed, the guy with the saucepan on his head who planted apple trees. But we lived a mile and a half from his grave site in Ft. Wayne, Indiana, and we'd even visit once in a while.

So maybe it was some of Johnny's own seeds that became the apple orchard at the end of our block. As orchards go, Mr. Shambaum's was comparatively small—maybe two dozen trees that produced small, green apples—Pippins probably. In the late summer, my friend Greg and I would venture onto his property to do some serious tree climbing. Apple trees are the ideal size for eight- and nine-year old boys: the branches are low enough, there are plenty of places to sit, and you're not that high up, after all.

We'd haul ourselves up into the largest tree's canopy and just hang out there, telling stories, looking for the best and biggest apples to sample, talking about all kinds of things, including our hopes that old Mr. Shambaum wasn't home.

Eventually we would be spotted. *"Get out of my trees!"* he'd yell through the window.

We'd hear the porch door slam, and we'd leap from the trees, running in utter panic for the safety of our own yards.

I don't think we ever saw Mr. Shambaum, but we knew he was after us. And we'd tell all our friends, too, maybe embellishing the story a little: "And then, then this old man and his German shepherd attack dog come out of the house, and he had a double-barreled shotgun loaded with rock salt, and he started shooting at us." We had to run for our lives, we'd say, and our other friends would have to acknowledge our bravery.

Mr. Shambaum's house was a hundred yards from the trees, so we had a pretty good buffer zone. Still, I remember the feeling of adrenaline pumping as we tore out of his orchard, that feeling of your legs not working as fast as you needed them to.

This was an annual event. One time, aside from eating a few apples in the trees, we got the idea that it would be the coolest thing if Mom could bake an apple pie with these apples. So we brought along a sack, filled it halfway, and brought it home. My mother didn't seem all that concerned, but my dad, a very straitlaced fellow, pretty much viewed this as common thievery—that is, until the apple pies came out of the oven and the subject was dropped.

My mother made great apple pies. She was a great cook, generally, and she loved

APPLE TART WITH BROWN-BUTTER CUSTARD AND CRÈME FRAÎCHE Serves 10

For the pastry

1 1/2 cups all-purpose flour, plus extra
   for rolling

1/4 cup almond flour (finely ground
   almonds)

1/4 cup sugar

10 tablespoons unsalted butter, cold,
   cut into small cubes

2 large egg yolks

1 teaspoon vanilla extract

1 Mix together the flours and sugar in a food processor fitted with a steel blade. Add the cold butter and process for 15 seconds. In a small glass, mix the yolks and vanilla together and add to the flour. Continue to process until the pastry just begins to come together. Place the dough in a large bowl and quickly finish combining the dough with your hands, finally pressing it into a disk shape. Wrap the dough in plastic wrap and refrigerate for 1 hour or overnight.

2 Unwrap the dough and roll the pastry into an 11-inch circle on a floured surface. Transfer it to a 10-inch tart pan with a removable rim. Gently press the pastry into the pan and along the edges. Poke some holes into the bottom of the pastry with a fork. Refrigerate the tart shell for 30 minutes.

3 Preheat the oven to 350°F.

4 Place the tart pan on a baking tray and bake for 20 minutes or until the dough is very lightly browned. Remove the tart from the oven and cool.

For the filling

12 tablespoons (1 1/2 sticks) unsalted butter

4 large eggs

1 cup sugar

6 tablespoons all-purpose flour

1 teaspoon ground cinnamon

1/2 cup crème fraîche

to experiment with recipes she'd find, despite the fact that my father would have none of it. She'd offer up some mystery casserole, and my dad would be served his own meal: one and a half salami-and-white-bread-with-butter sandwiches, ice water with four ice cubes, and some radishes. He'd be as happy as can be with that. And while he did love her apple pies ("Why would anyone bother with cherries?" he'd ask) or her pecan pies, anything else was too "experimental."

Perhaps it's my Ft. Wayne ancestry that keeps apples among my favorite things to

5 medium tart green apples, peeled, cored, and sliced

Whipped cream, optional

5 For the filling, place the butter in a small saucepan over medium-high heat. Stir the butter gently until it starts to brown. Remove from the heat immediately and set aside.

6 In a small nonreactive bowl, whisk together the eggs and sugar. Add the flour, cinnamon, and crème fraîche. Mix in the brown butter until thoroughly incorporated.

7 Arrange the sliced apples in concentric circles in the prebaked crust.

8 Pour the egg mixture evenly over the apples and bake for 25 to 30 minutes or until the custard is set. Remove from the oven and cool on a wire rack.

✤ To serve, remove the sides of the pan and cut the tart into the number of desired wedges. Offer plain whipped cream on the side if desired.

Robert Helstrom began his culinary career washing dishes at the age of fifteen and has worked in more than thirty-five kitchens since then. Author of *Contemporary Italian*, he joined the Kimpton Group in 1987 and served as executive chef for twelve years at Kuletto's, San Francisco's favorite Northern-Italian restaurant. He is now corporate chef for the Kimpton Group, which has more than thirty restaurants in major cities across the nation.

cook. Anytime I do a pork loin on a rotisserie, I have to have baked apples with grappa, balsamic vinegar, and honey. I love a dessert of caramelized apples in puff pastry. And this dish, with the browned butter custard, is certainly a salute to my mother's pies, old Mr. Shambaum, and Johnny himself.

Stan Frankenthaler
TWO BAVARIANS

I've loved cooking for as long as I can remember. The presents I received as a kid were omelet pans and kitchen gadgets. My grandmother gave me her Dutch oven, and I'd lug that on scouting trips. (My father, a great eater, was one of three scout leaders, and another dad was a great cook, so our scouting adventures included lots of cooking. We made biscuits, stews, and cobblers and hauled a lot of kitchen equipment into the woods.)

I used to come home for lunch from elementary school (we had nearly an hour and a half), and my mother and I would watch *Jeopardy!* and then *The Galloping Gourmet*

VANILLA BAVARIAN WITH GINGERED STRAWBERRIES

Serves 8

----

1 1/4 cups whole milk

1 vanilla bean, split and seeds scraped
 and reserved

1/2 cup sugar

6 large egg yolks

3 3/4 teaspoons unflavored granulated
 gelatin

1 cup heavy cream

1 large egg white

Pinch of salt

1 recipe Gingered Strawberries

1 Combine the milk, vanilla bean pod and seeds, and sugar in a saucepan and bring to a gentle simmer (do not boil).

2 Beat the egg yolks in a large mixing bowl and slowly whisk in the hot milk infusion.

3 Return all to the saucepan. Stir gently and constantly until the sauce thickens (do not boil). Remove from the heat and set aside.

4 Soften the granulated gelatin in 1/3 cup cold water for 3 minutes and then add it to the hot custard, stirring until dissolved. Strain the custard into a large mixing bowl and place over an ice bath. Stir occasionally. When completely cooled, cover the surface with plastic wrap to prevent a skin from forming.

5 In a medium bowl, whip the cream until it forms soft peaks.

6 In a second bowl, beat the egg white with a pinch of salt until it forms soft peaks.

7 Gently fold the whipped cream into the custard and then fold in the beaten egg whites.

8 Pour the custard into eight 1/2-cup molds or one 1-quart mold. Refrigerate.

✛ To serve, unmold and serve with Gingered Strawberries.

VARIATION: TANGERINE BAVARIAN

Instead of simmering the vanilla bean in the milk, replace it with the following ingredients: 1/2-inch piece fresh ginger, smashed; 4 star anise, broken into bits; and the freshly grated zest of 2 tangerines. Proceed as directed.

while we ate fried bologna sandwiches. Graham Kerr made everything about cooking—*cooking!*—seem fun.

Family get-togethers at my paternal grandmother's house in the Hudson Valley always centered around food. Though I liked playing flashlight tag with my cousins, I loved helping with the big meals, chopping or stirring or just bringing the things to the table until I was old enough to start cooking. (When, a few years later, our family moved to Georgia to start a new business, I did cook three or four dinners each week—simple pastas, fried chicken, flank steak—and sometimes frogs' legs, which would also involve taking a flashlight outside and scouting around the ponds near our house for the bullfrogs that I'd gig and cook up inside.)

That side of the family, my father's, cooked German dishes: sauerbraten, braised beef roulade, spaetzle, braised cabbage, potato dumplings, roasted ducks. My great-grandmother put out relish trays, cheeses, chopped liver. And, of course, desserts. My favorite thing to eat—and to carry to the table—was my great-grandmother's Bavarian: it wiggled! It looked so beautiful, popped free of her Bundt pan mold. It was a creamy white castle with turrets all around it and little dark flecks from the vanilla bean she'd scraped. (It was from her I learned that vanilla wasn't only a little bottle with the brown liquid.) It was such a lush dessert, as creamy as ice cream but even better. And all around the Bavarian, like a moat, she'd place bright red strawberries that were kind of crushed and sprinkled with sugar.

I was lucky to know my great-grandmother until I was eight or nine. When she passed away, it fell to my grandmother to make the Bavarians for our gatherings. We didn't have them as often. And then my mother took over: they appeared at several college Thanksgiving dinners in a row. And now that my mother is gone, too, I make them. (We even celebrated Mother's Day at the James Beard House with a Bavarian.)

I will confess to adding the ginger to the macerated strawberries. And the star anise and tangerine version is my own invention—but I think these earlier keepers of the Bavarian would have enjoyed it.

GINGERED STRAWBERRIES
Makes 3 cups

$1/2$ cup sugar

One $1/2$-inch piece fresh ginger, peeled and finely julienned

2 tablespoons brandy

1 quart fresh strawberries, washed, hulled, and sliced, or frozen organic strawberries)

Combine $1/2$ cup water, the sugar, ginger, and brandy in a small saucepan and bring to a boil. Reduce to $2/3$ cup. Cool and then pour over the berries, allowing them to macerate for 1 to 2 hours in the refrigerator. Use that day.

Stan Frankenthaler, a Culinary Institute of America graduate, honed his craft at Jasper's and Hamersley's Bistro in Boston. His first independent venture was the award-winning Choice Catering Company. In 1991 he became co-owner and chef of the Blue Room, one of *Esquire*'s "America's Best New Restaurants." In 1994, Stan developed Salamander to reflect his passion for elegantly crafted Asian-inspired cuisine. In Cambridge, and then in Boston, Salamander received accolades for its food, decor, and wine list. A frequent teacher, Stan devotes much of his time to charity and hunger-relief events.

Rick Bayless PEACH ORCHARD COBBLER

Some flavors, some dishes are so thoroughly intertwined with a place and a moment that any thought of savoring a mouthful outside those space-time coordinates is nearly unimaginable. Strawberry shortcake at the backyard picnic table on the earliest of summer days. Roast turkey and dressing at Mom's on Thanksgiving. For me the dish is peach cobbler. And the place and time: my grandma Gladys's kitchen in late June.

PEACH ORCHARD COBBLER
Serves 10

For the dough

2²/₃ cups all-purpose flour, plus extra for rolling

¹/₄ teaspoon baking powder

¹/₂ teaspoon salt

¹/₂ pound (2 sticks) unsalted butter, cold, cut into small pieces

6 ounces cream cheese, chilled and cut into small pieces

1 tablespoon apple cider vinegar

For the filling

5 pounds ripe peaches, peeled, pitted, and cut into 1-inch pieces (7¹/₂ cups)

1 to 1¹/₄ cups sugar, plus extra for sprinkling over the crust

5 tablespoons cornstarch

1¹/₂ tablespoons fresh lemon or lime juice

1 teaspoon ground nutmeg or ¹/₂ teaspoon freshly grated

1 teaspoon salt

2 tablespoons unsalted butter, cut into small pieces

1 tablespoon milk for brushing over the crust

For a number of years in the early sixties, red-headed Gladys piled any of her willing nine grandchildren into the formidable,

1 To make the crust, place the flour, baking powder, and $1/2$ teaspoon salt into a food processor fitted with the steel blade. Add the butter and cream cheese bits. Pulse 6 or 7 times (1 second each), until the mixture looks like coarse crumbs. Mix the vinegar with 3 tablespoons cold water. Remove the lid of the processor and evenly drizzle the liquid over the flour mixture. Pulse 6 to 7 times, until the mixture begins to clump together; it will not form a ball. Turn the dough out onto a large sheet of plastic wrap. Press the dough together, gather the plastic wrap over the top, and, with a rolling pin, flatten into a 10-inch square. Refrigerate for 1 hour or overnight.

2 Place a rack in the middle of the oven and preheat the oven to 400°F.

3 Cut off a third of the dough; rewrap and refrigerate it. Dust a work surface with flour and roll the remaining dough into an 18 X 14-inch rectangle. Drape the dough into a 13 X 9-inch glass baking dish. Ease the dough into the bottom of the pan and allow the dough to hang over the edge of the dish. Refrigerate. Roll the remaining third into a 14 X 10-inch rectangle. Cut length-wise into ten 1-inch strips. Refrigerate the strips.

4 In a large bowl, toss together the peaches, sugar, cornstarch, lemon juice, nutmeg, and salt.

5 Fill the dough-lined baking dish with the peach filling. Dot the top of the fruit with bits of butter. Brush the top edge of the dough with water to make it sticky. Lay 4 strips of dough at even intervals lengthwise over the fruit. Create a lattice by placing the remaining 6 strips of dough at even intervals across the first strips of dough. Press the ends of each strip into the moistened edges of the bottom crust. Trim off any overhanging dough. Brush the lattice with the milk and sprinkle with sugar.

6 Bake for 15 minutes. Reduce the temperature to 350°F and bake an additional 30 to 40 minutes or until the fruit filling is thick and bubbling and the crust is brown. Cool for 10 minutes before serving or cool completely and rewarm.

pointy-tailed Cadillac and headed south from Oklahoma City toward Ardmore. She'd heard through the *Eastern Star* network that the peaches were ready and which "U-pick" orchard had the greatest abundance. The drive wasn't long—less than two hours—and it always involved a stop, usually at Stuckey's, for pecan logs and gas.

Picking peaches is relatively easy work compared to the blueberry, cherry, and raspberry picking that is an occasional summer outing around Chicago, where I live now. My cousins, my grandma, and I climbed homemade ladders, hung the handles of half-bushel baskets on top of the rails, and began the choosing process. *Only blushing golden globes, no green at the stem. Mouthwatering aroma, but no soft spots. Not too many in the basket, or the bottom ones will get crushed.* A dizzying giddiness overtook me up there in the tree, shaded from the blistering Oklahoma sun, breathing air so saturated with the perfume of peaches.

It was the same perfume that permeated the car on the trip back, though my giddiness eventually gave way to drowsiness.

The next two or three days were dedicated to capturing the summer's essence in jars of peach jam, peach butter, pickled peaches, and, the real purpose of our adventure, peeled peach halves canned in light syrup. Those jars provided a year's worth of peach cobblers. Those peach-filled envelopes of tender pastry anchored our family meals.

Grandma Gladys made a cobbler crust that was nicely flaky but a little bit cakey, too—perfect for soaking up the delicious peach juices. Grandma's gone now, as is her crust recipe. I've chosen a delicious cream cheese version that's *almost* as good as I remember hers being. —RB

Rick Bayless is an award-winning chef-restaurateur, author, and television personality who is credited with changing the image of Mexican food in America. Among his books are the classic *Authentic Mexican: Regional Cooking from the Heart of Mexico*, *Rick Bayless's Mexican Kitchen: Capturing the Vibrant Flavors of a World-Class Cuisine*, and *Mexico—One Plate at a Time*, the companion to his first public television series. His Chicago restaurants, Frontera Grill and Topolobampo, have garnered innumerable distinctions, including two Beard Awards: National Chef of the Year and Humanitarian of the Year.

Seth Bixby Daugherty
MULBERRY CRUNCH

In 1987 five hundred citizens from the United States and what was then the Soviet Union marched from Leningrad to Moscow in hopes of raising the awareness of

MULBERRY CRUNCH

Serves 12 to 14

----

8 tablespoons (1 stick) unsalted butter,
cold, cut into $1/2$-inch pieces, plus
2 tablespoons for pans

3 pounds mulberries, picked over and
cleaned, or other fresh or frozen berries

$1^1/2$ cups sugar

Freshly grated zest and juice of 2 lemons

$1/2$ cup packed light brown sugar

4 ounces cream cheese

2 cups all-purpose flour

$1^1/2$ cups quick-cooking oats

Freshly grated zest of 1 medium orange

2 cups whipping cream

$1/2$ vanilla bean, split

1 Preheat the oven to 375°F. Grease two 9 X 6-inch pans with 1 tablespoon butter each. (Alternately, use one larger baking dish that holds the fruit at a depth of about 1 inch.) 2 Toss the berries, 1 cup of the sugar, the lemon zest, and juice together in a mixing bowl. Set aside.

3 Combine the remaining 8 tablespoons butter, remaining $1/2$ cup sugar, the brown sugar, cream cheese, flour, oats, and orange zest. Rub the mixture together between your hands until it resembles a coarse meal.

4 Place the berries in the prepared pan(s). Cover the fruit with the crumble topping. Bake for 20 to 25 minutes or until the topping is golden brown and the berry juice is bubbling and thick. (If longer cooking is needed, watch that the top does not brown too quickly; if it does, cover with aluminum foil.) Remove from the oven and allow to cool slightly.

5 Whip the cream until it forms soft peaks. Scrape the seeds from the vanilla bean and fold them into the cream.

❖ Scoop a portion of the crunch onto individual plates and top each with a dollop of whipped cream.

---

the potential nuclear holocaust that existed between the two countries. A year later, a second march was organized, with 250 citizens of each country gathering near Washington, D.C., for a fifty-eight-day trek across the States.

After graduating from the Culinary Institute of America, instead of seeking my next restaurant job, I found this chance to volunteer, and there aren't that many times in your life when you're offered the opportunity to utterly contribute. I signed on as cook for the march; looking back, I see how much that blessing has provided.

The rest of the march's culinary "staff" had no kitchen skills. They were all well-meaning hippies—like me—that the peace movement had brought together.

Two weeks before the rest of the marchers arrived, the fifty organizers gathered at a large park in Maryland. Our main objective was to practice setting up and breaking down camp, and we moved the campsite from one spot to another in the same park every day for two weeks, improving our efficiency and speed. In addition to tents for five hundred, we had a silver Airstream for our kitchen, two domed tents for prep work, two emptied school buses for storage, twelve school buses for transporting marchers, and four gigantic U-Hauls for our belongings.

Maryland summers can be brutally hot.

And this "exercise" was not exactly keeping peace. We got tired and anxious. The air was so humid you could almost taste it.

Late one afternoon I found a tree near our campsite filled with ripe mulberries. The park was full of them—that was part of the smell, these berries ripening and even fermenting in the heat. I asked these two women to hold this blue tarp under the mulberry, and I climbed into the branches and shook the tree until berries covered the tarp. Then one woman helped me weed out all but the plump, juicy ones. Our fingers were stained for days.

When I brought this warm mulberry crunch to the table, everyone was blown away. Not just *dessert*, but a *warm, delicious dessert . . .* made out of the very air! And I think we all sensed

a certain coming together over that dessert—giving up our cranky, hot, exhausted feelings from the previous week. We knew we were going to be family for the next fifty-eight days. And we knew we'd be welcoming 450 more family members in the coming days, 250 of whom the world had been trying to estrange us from over the last seventy-five years.

That dessert changed my life and all my expectations. It helped me understand that the good energy I put into making food is transferred to the finished dish and then into the people who share it. Cooking has brought me everything I've ever wanted in my life, including my wife, who was the woman who helped me sort the mulberries.

The march took us to Baltimore, D.C., Delaware, Philly, and Pittsburgh. Then from Indianapolis to Rock Island, Illinois, where we hiked twelve straight days to Des Moines. From there we flew to California and walked Highway 1 from Los Angeles to San Francisco, where the march ended with a big benefit concert.

Along the journey our basic supplies were supplemented with donations. One day a food co-op donated a hundred pounds of granola. Another day we had fifty gallons of rice milk. Whatever showed up, I figured out how to use. At six one morning, I made fresh blueberry syrup for a hundred loaves of cinnamon bread a bakery had delivered. What a treat to present that surprise to everyone at breakfast.

Less of a treat was preparing a thousand sandwiches for lunch every day for fifty-eight days.

I barely slept that summer. Passion kept me awake. All day I'd hike or prepare food, and then I'd stay up till four in the morning talking and talking, and then, at seven, begin breakfast prep. Most of the Soviet marchers spoke English, we had many interpreters, and, besides that, 97 percent of language is nonverbal. As is the fellowship of sharing food.

Seth Bixby Daugherty, a graduate of the Culinary Institute of America, worked for many years with the Four Seasons Hotel Corporation in Washington, D.C., and New York City. For three years he cooked with Gilbert Le Coze at Le Bernardin, and for three years he served as chef at D'Amico Cucina in Minneapolis. Currently executive chef at the Le Meridien hotel in Minneapolis, Seth lives in Eden Prairie, Minnesota, with his wife, Karen, and children, Emma and Cole.

Ann Amernick and Frank Ruta CLEVELAND PARK CREAM CAKE

Frank worked as a chef at the White House for eleven years, and I joined him there for a year, starting in December 1979. We were both part of so many memorable events there—especially Frank: from intimate dinners like the first social, rather than political, visit from Princess Di and Prince Charles, to huge affairs like the celebration of the astronauts after the first space shuttle flight.

One event we both shared and will never forget was the return in 1979 of the fifty-two hostages held captive at the American Embassy in Iran.

At the time there were five chef positions in the kitchen: Henry Haller, executive chef; Hans Raffert, executive sous-chef; Roland Mesnier, the pastry chef; and then Frank and me. Roland was particularly honored and thrilled—as were the rest of us—to be creating food for an event that was the resolution of 444 days of anxiety. This was the first accomplishment of Reagan's presidency, and the hostages' release on the very day of Reagan's inauguration was a political triumph, a release of a kind for everyone in America.

The hostages themselves—the dozen or so who were fit enough—attended a special luncheon along with many invited guests and diplomats.

Roland liked to create dishes specific to each event; he was restless that way, rarely repeating himself. His desserts could be adapted or designed to reflect a holiday, a theme, or a visiting dignitary's native

PASTRY CREAM Makes 2 1/4 cups

2 cups whole milk

Seeds from 1 vanilla bean

1/2 cup sugar

6 large egg yolks

2 tablespoons cornstarch

1 Combine the milk and vanilla seeds in a small nonreactive saucepan and bring to a simmer. Remove from the heat and rest for 10 minutes.

2 In a heavy nonreactive saucepan, quickly whisk the sugar into the yolks. Add the cornstarch and mix until well blended. Add the hot vanilla-infused milk and cook over medium heat, stirring the entire time. Cook to 170°F until the cream is very thick. Remove from the heat and pass through a fine-mesh strainer into a glass or stainless-steel bowl. Cover the surface with plastic wrap and refrigerate. The cream can be prepared 1 or 2 days in advance.

CLEVELAND PARK CREAM CAKE Makes fifteen 3-inch cakes

----

10 large eggs, separated

2 cups sugar

4 cups cake flour

5 teaspoons baking powder

1 pound plus 4 tablespoons (4$\frac{1}{2}$ sticks)
   unsalted butter, melted

2 teaspoons vanilla extract

1 recipe Pastry Cream

1 recipe Preserved Orange Slices, diced

1 recipe Crème Anglaise

1 recipe Chocolate Sauce

1 Preheat the oven to 350°F. Fill fifteen 3-inch-diameter muffin tins with large paper liners.

2 Beat the yolks and 1 cup of the sugar in the bowl of an electric mixer until a ribbon forms. In a separate bowl, sift together the flour and baking powder and add this to the eggs along with the melted butter and vanilla. Mix until smooth.

3 In the bowl of an electric mixer, beat the egg whites with the remaining 1 cup sugar until stiff and shiny. Gently fold the egg whites into the cake batter. Pour the batter into the paper liners so that each cup is two-thirds full.

4 Bake for 20 minutes, until the cakes are golden or a toothpick poked in the middle of the cakes comes out clean. Cakes can be made 1 or 2 days in advance and stored in an airtight container.

5 When ready to assemble, release the cakes from the paper liners and slice them into thirds horizontally. Place the largest layer on the serving plate and cover with a large spoonful of Pastry Cream. Place the second round over the cream and cover with a heaping tablespoon of chopped Preserved Oranges. Place the final round over the oranges. Pour Crème Anglaise around the bottom of the cake. Cover the top of the cake with Chocolate Sauce, allowing it to run down the sides and into the Crème Anglaise.

country. But for this homecoming Roland knew that he wanted to do something less French, less classical . . . we needed something utterly American.

Roland bustled around the kitchen, assigning tasks, preparing batter, pastry cream, chocolate sauce. He considered a few variations but settled on this delicate pound cake, sliced into thirds, filled with custard and preserved orange slices, then topped with thick chocolate. I suppose Boston cream pie was his inspiration or

PRESERVED ORANGE SLICES
Makes 1 quart

----

4 navel oranges

1 cup sugar

3 tablespoons fresh lemon juice

3 tablespoons Grand Marnier

1 Cut the oranges (perpendicular to the segments) into thick slices. Place the slices in a nonreactive saucepan with cold water to cover. Bring to a boil; lower the heat to medium and cook for 1 hour. Drain.

2 Combine 1$\frac{1}{4}$ cups cold water, the sugar, and the lemon juice in the same pot. Cook over medium heat, stirring, until the sugar dissolves. Add the oranges and cook over medium heat for 1 hour or until the slices are very tender but not falling apart. Remove from the heat and allow the oranges to cool in the syrup. Add the Grand Marnier. Refrigerate the oranges and syrup in a covered glass or stainless-steel container. The oranges can be stored this way for several months.

CRÈME ANGLAISE Makes 2 cups

----

2 cups whole milk

Seeds from 1 vanilla bean

3 tablespoons sugar

4 large egg yolks

1 Combine the milk and vanilla seeds in a small nonreactive saucepan and bring to a simmer. Remove from the heat, cover, and let rest for 10 minutes.

2 In a heavy nonreactive saucepan, whisk the sugar into the egg yolks. Add the hot vanilla-infused milk and cook over medium-low heat, stirring the entire time, until the sauce thickens and coats the back of a spoon. Do not allow the liquid to simmer or boil (this will scramble the eggs). Pass the sauce through a fine-mesh strainer into a glass or stainless-steel bowl. Cover the surface with plastic wrap and refrigerate. The Crème Anglaise can be prepared 1 or 2 days in advance.

CHOCOLATE SAUCE
Makes about 2$\frac{1}{4}$ cups

----

1 cup heavy cream

$\frac{1}{2}$ pound bittersweet chocolate, chopped

$\frac{1}{4}$ cup half-and-half

In a small saucepan, bring the cream to a boil, then remove it from the heat. Add the chocolate and stir until smooth. This step can be done several days in advance. When ready to serve, warm the sauce with the half-and-half to thin the sauce, which should run down the sides of the cakes but also cover the top.

starting point. Once the first dessert was assembled, he announced to the rest of the kitchen, *"pâtisserie des otages,"* "cake for the hostages." Tears came to more eyes than mine. While Roland often named his desserts (they'd be written in calligraphy on the menus at each guest's place), just hearing him proclaim those words connected us to the joy and relief in the day's occasion.

More than twenty years have now passed. Frank and I have our own restaurant, Palena, and we serve the same cake. We call it Cleveland Park Cream Cake, after our neighborhood here in D.C., but I always add *des otages* myself.

Ann Amernick and Frank Ruta are the co-owners of both a restaurant, Palena, and a bakery, Amernick, in Washington, D.C. Ann became assistant pastry chef at the White House shortly after launching her career and subsequently worked at Jean-Louis at the Watergate, Cashion's Eat Place, Citronelle, and Red Sage. She has written two books, *Special Desserts* and *Soufflés*. Frank has worked in the restaurant industry for more than twenty-five years, including chef positions at Provence Restaurant, River Club, and Yannick's. For eleven years he served as first family chef/assistant chef and executive sous-chef at the White House.

Gary Danko PORT-ROASTED FIGS WITH LICORICE ICE CREAM

Upstate New York is an unlikely area of the world to grow up developing a fondness for figs. But mine came from my mother's mother, who lived in Louisiana. We visited her at Easter, and I played under her fig trees when the fruit was hard and unripe; I always wondered how these green "bullets" became the mason jars filled with fig preserves that we'd receive in the mail every fall. Grandma was an experienced farmer who excelled at making preserves. Her fig jam was an exotic delight spread on toast or, warmed, spooned over vanilla ice cream.

I had seen dried figs from Greece and California in the stores and even commercially grown fresh figs at the markets of Montreal (the largest city near our town of Massena). Generally figs shipped to remote markets have the texture and flavor of milkweed pods. It wasn't until I moved to California in 1977 that I experienced figs picked and eaten right from the tree when they're sun-warmed and dripping with sap. There's no more sensuous or delicious food than that.

Years later I worked at Beringer Vineyards with Madeleine Kamman. We were

PORT-ROASTED FIGS Serves 10

1 cup packed light brown sugar

3 pints ripe Black Mission figs, stems removed and halved vertically

$1/2$ cup port

1 recipe Licorice Ice Cream

1 Preheat the oven to 350°F.

2 Sprinkle the brown sugar in a shallow baking pan that will hold the fig halves snugly. Lay the halves cut side down on the brown sugar.

3 Roast the figs until they release their juices, dissolving the sugar to form a light syrup, about 15 minutes.

4 Pour the port over the figs and continue to cook for 5 minutes. Remove from the oven and cool. Set aside or cover and refrigerate until ready to assemble the dessert. (The figs can be prepared ahead of time and reheated in a 350°F oven for 5 to 7 minutes.)

✤ To serve, place a spoonful of the warmed figs in a dessert bowl and serve with small scoops of the ice cream. Drizzle the port syrup over the top.

VARIATION: PEARS OR PEACHES

You can substitute pears or peaches for the figs. Choose 6 to 8 pieces of ripened fruit; peel, core, halve, and place in the brown sugar. Pears should be roasted for 25 to 40 minutes or until tender. Peaches should be roasted for 25 to 30 minutes or until tender. Increase the port to $3/4$ cup because of the longer roasting time. Otherwise, follow the directions for roasting the figs.

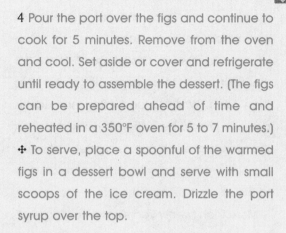

LICORICE ICE CREAM Makes 3 pints

----

3 cups heavy cream

1 1/2 cups whole milk

1/2 vanilla bean, split and seeds
   scraped free

3/4 cup shredded or chipped licorice root
   or 10 to 12 five-inch licorice root sticks,
   rinsed and grated (available at health
   food stores)

10 large egg yolks

1 cup plus 2 tablespoons sugar

Pinch of kosher salt

1 Combine 1 1/2 cups of the cream, the milk, and the vanilla bean in a large heavy saucepan. Place over medium heat and heat just to the point of simmering. Remove the pan from the heat, add the licorice root, cover, and steep for 20 to 25 minutes.

2 Whisk the egg yolks, sugar, and salt together in a heavy nonreactive saucepan. Strain the milk mixture into the egg mixture and whisk to combine.

3 Cook the custard over medium heat, stirring constantly, until the mixture is lightly thickened and coats the back of a spoon. Remove from the heat and whisk in the remaining 1 1/2 cups cream. Strain the custard into a bowl and cool over an ice bath. Cover the cold custard with plastic wrap and refrigerate overnight.

4 Freeze the licorice custard in an ice cream machine according to the manufacturer's directions. Store in a covered container in the freezer until firm, about 2 hours.

brainstorming over a dish to accompany the delicious port wines of those vineyards. Madeleine was reminiscing about the pungent black licorice of her childhood, and I recounted the fig preserves of mine . . . and together we came up with this idea. Initially Madeleine wanted to use licorice drops from Europe; being pressed for time, we couldn't locate any. I found chipped licorice root at a nearby health food store. After a twenty-minute infusion in the cream, we had a delicate anise flavor that we married with vanilla beans to create a very exotic blend. Pairing fresh figs roasted with brown sugar with this licorice ice cream proved to be an exceptional match with the port.

This ice cream is subtle, with just the suggestive hint of licorice. You can intensify the licorice flavor by using the licorice drops or candies we'd originally intended to steep.

Just two years ago I purchased an acre of land in Napa, and although that region can grow the largest walnuts I've ever seen, as well as oranges, pomegranates, persimmons, and even Meyer lemons, the first trees I planted were Black Mission figs. —GD

A protégé of culinary icon Madeleine Kamman, Gary Danko attended the Culinary Institute of America, worked for four years at Chateau Souverain, and opened the new Ritz-Carlton in San Francisco. He helped to launch Viognier in San Mateo and in 1999 opened Gary Danko, the restaurant, in San Francisco. At each of these venues Gary has received *Esquire* magazine's coveted Best New Restaurant award. His achievements include two Beard Awards for Best Chef/California and for Best New Restaurant and three *Mobil Travel Guide* five-star ratings.

Charlie Trotter DYLAN'S CHOCOLATE–PEANUT BUTTER GANACHE TART

My son Dylan is one selective eater! He certainly challenges me when it comes to dinner time. I would say his favorite meal is pasta with butter and chicken with no skin. I am slowly getting him to make the addition of Parmesan cheese.

My mother thinks this is funny, not only because I'm a chef but also because Dylan is as opinionated as I was at his age. (My mother prepared all our meals at home, with traditional midwestern recipes. Thanksgiving, for instance, always had the same dishes that everyone loved. One year I made Thanksgiving and didn't prepare one traditional thing. Need I say more than this: the next year my mother prepared the Thanksgiving meal.)

But one area where I can never go wrong is chocolate and peanut butter: Dylan loves it! Reese's Peanut Butter Cups are the classic, of course, and this dessert captures the idea—and even the shape—of those little crimped-edge treats and produces one large, entirely decadent pie. We often make it together. Dylan happens to be a master chocolate chopper—but I often catch him snacking on the chocolate pieces that are supposed to go in the filling.

Every year I invite Dylan's whole class to the restaurant for lunch. The students design a five-course menu and choose the beverages as well. They all suggest dishes for the possible menu, and then we take a vote. It's a fun program, and it's interesting to see how diverse these kids' palates are. Last year I hosted Dylan's fifth-grade class. The menu they arrived at, after proposing such

DYLAN'S CHOCOLATE–PEANUT BUTTER GANACHE TART Makes one 9-inch tart

----

For the tart shell

6 tablespoons unsalted butter at room temperature

$1/2$ cup sugar

1 large egg

$3/4$ teaspoon vanilla extract

$1/2$ teaspoon salt

$1/3$ cup sifted Dutch-process cocoa powder

$3/4$ cup all-purpose flour, plus extra for rolling

For the ganache

12 ounces bittersweet chocolate, chopped

1 tablespoon unsalted butter

$1^3/4$ cups heavy cream

1 cup chunky peanut butter

$1/4$ cup confectioners' sugar

Dutch-process cocoa powder for dusting

1 To prepare the tart shell, cream together the butter, sugar, egg, vanilla, and salt in a large bowl, either by hand or with a mixer. When smooth, add the cocoa powder and mix well. Add the flour and mix again until just incorporated.

2 Transfer the dough to a lightly floured work surface and shape it into a ball. Cover with plastic wrap and press the dough into a flat disk. Refrigerate for 1 hour.

3 Preheat the oven to 375°F.

4 Roll out the dough to a thickness of $1/8$ inch on the lightly floured work surface. Line a 9-inch tart pan with the dough, trimming and discarding any excess. Prick the dough several times with a fork and bake for 15 to 20 minutes or until the crust is set around the edges. Cool completely.

5 To make the filling, place the chocolate and butter in a medium bowl. Bring the cream to a boil in a medium saucepan over medium heat and strain the cream through a fine-mesh strainer over the chocolate. Let the chocolate mixture stand for 3 minutes and then whisk until smooth. Let cool for 30 minutes.

6 Place the peanut butter and confectioners' sugar in a mixing bowl and combine until the sugar is fully incorporated. Carefully spread the peanut butter in the bottom of the tart shell. Place the tart shell on a small baking sheet. Pour the chocolate mixture over the peanut butter to the very top of the tart. Refrigerate for 3 hours or until firm. Dust the tart with cocoa powder.

things as Asian chicken salad, something with lamb, and chicken noodle soup, consisted of sushi, Caesar salad, macaroni and cheese, barbecued ribs, and, of course, Dylan's Chocolate–Peanut Butter Ganache Tart. (The dessert works equally well with less adventurous meals.) —CT

Charlie Trotter is the author of eight cookbooks and the host of a PBS series, *The Kitchen Sessions with Charlie Trotter.* Beyond his culinary accolades, Chef Trotter is very involved in philanthropic activities, including the Charlie Trotter Culinary Education Foundation, which has raised over $300,000 for individuals seeking careers in the culinary arts. Charlie Trotter's, his restaurant, has dedicated itself to excellence in the culinary arts for the last sixteen years, receiving national and international commendations, including five stars from the *Mobil Travel Guide*, five diamonds from AAA, *Wine Spectator*'s America's Best Restaurant award, and seven Beard Foundation awards.

Index

cheese blintzes, 50
classic Swiss fondue, 48
crespelle of mountain taleggio and
    prosciutto, 54
panko-crusted goat cheese with tomato and
    asparagus salad, 214
ricotta gnocchi with contessa sauce, 101–2
semolina crêpes stuffed with homemade
    ricotta and prosciutto, 104
roasted beef and cranberry salad, 216–18
cheesecake, almond, with champagne-honey
    sauce, 266
Chiarello, Michael, 91–94
chicken
    Bombay chicken with curried tomatoes,
        171–72
    chicken meatball soup, 89
    the devil's chicken with potatoes, leeks, and
        mustard bread crumbs, 168–69
    in home-style clay pot, 120
    honey-fried, with minted cream sauce and
        spicy sweet potato puree, 164–65
    old hen pastina brodo, 92
    roasted Amish chicken and shrimp with Asian
        noodle salad, 122–23
chiles
    ancho chile sauce, 98
    green curry paste, 162
    pork and potatoes with orange juice and
        Coca-Cola, 199
    smoky dill pickles, 229
chive and potato soup, chilled, with gingered
    potato salad, 74
chocolate
    beet brownies, 218
    chocolate applesauce cake with jacked-up
        caramel apple sauce, 259–61
    chocolate-dipped custard-filled éclairs,
        243–44
    chocolate doughnuts, 57
    chocolate mayonnaise cake, 263
    chocolate-peanut butter ganache tart,
        Dylan's, 291
    coconut chocolate macaroon towers, 248
    fudge sauce, 264
    hidden kisses, 90
    mint chocolate chip meringues, 249
    peanut-butter-cup ice cream, 263

sauce, for Cleveland Park cream cake, 286
chorizo, yuca chorizo knish with cilantro
    crema, 45
chow chow, 228
cilantro
    chicken meatball soup, 89
    cilantro crema, yuca chorizo knish with, 45
citrus vinaigrette, 123
clams, Ipswich, fried, with fried lemons, 128–29
clay pot, home-style, 120
Cleveland Park cream cake, 284–86
cobbler, peach-orchard, 278–79
Coca-Cola
    pork and potatoes with orange juice and, 199
    Texas pinto beans, 234
coconut
    coconut chocolate macaroon towers, 248
    coconut crème anglaise, pineapple upside-
        down cake with, 256–57
    coconut cupcakes, 254
cod, Goan pan-roasted, with kanji and pickled
    mango, 141–43
coleslaw, celeriac, 202
conch salad with salsa de vida, 29–30
Condron, Tom, 144–47
contessa sauce, ricotta gnocchi with, 101–2
cookies
    coconut chocolate macaroon towers, 248
    hidden kisses, 90
    Hungarian pecan cookies, 248
    mint chocolate chip meringues, 249
    raisin squares, 246
corn. See also polenta
    blue cheese grits, marinated trout with
        mushrooms and, 153–54
    in chow chow, 228
    corn bread, 87
    fried-corn sauce, crab cakes with, 32
    hominy, posole de Perlita, 97–98
côte d'agneau with globe artichokes and
    oven-roasted tomatoes, 190–91
crab(s)
    cakes, with fried-corn sauce, 32
    gumbo-style risotto, 113–14
    soft-shell, Weezie's, with New Bay seasoning,
        126
    soft-shell crab soup, 64
cranberry and roasted beet salad, 216–18

SOS SHARE OUR® STRENGTH

It Takes More Than Food to Fight Hunger

"All of us have diverse strengths we can share. The challenge lies in creating vehicles that enable each distinctly talented person to do so, especially that vast majority who may not think of themselves as community activists, civic leaders, or social entrepreneurs. It's not just about volunteering or trying to be a better person. It's about making your community a better place."

—Bill Shore, executive director

Though America is the wealthiest nation on earth, thirty-three million of our citizens cannot maintain a healthy, productive life because they are chronically or intermittently hungry. Many experience sustained bouts of profound hunger, while others endure monthly or weekly periods of poor nutrition. Some have no access to sources of healthy foods. Some have no ability to prepare meals, some no kitchen or cooking equipment, some no transportation or local grocers. Roughly half of these individuals work. Nearly 40 percent of those suffering are children.

Share Our Strength is a national organization that taps into the strength of individuals and corporations to find new and lasting sources of revenue to invest in the fight to end hunger. It mobilizes thousands of individuals from every walk of life—chefs, restaurateurs, coaches, civic leaders, writers, corporate leaders—and organizes their talents and resources into a powerful antihunger force. Share Our Strength raises funds in creative, innovative ways and then grants that money to the most effective nonprofits in America and abroad.

Under Share Our Strength's leadership, there are several unique fund-raising programs: **Taste of the Nation®,** presented by American Express and Jenn-Air, is the largest culinary benefit to fight hunger in the United States; for more than fifteen years 100 percent of all Taste of the Nation® ticket sales have been invested in the national and local antihunger efforts. **The Great American Bake Sale®** teams Share Our Strength with *PARADE* magazine to encourage people of all ages to host bake sales in neighborhoods all across the country to fight childhood hunger. **Taste of the Game®,** Share Our Strength's newest program, is a multisport event that enlists the nation's top athletic coaches to provide an impassioned sports experience by teaching families something of what they know and love about the game.

For the last decade, Share Our Strength has also provided direct service in the area of nutrition education: **Operation Frontline®,** nationally sponsored by Tyson Foods, Inc., mobilizes volunteer chefs, nutritionists, and financial planners to teach six-week courses in healthy cooking and food budgeting to individuals at risk of hunger. Today classes run in more than ninety communities across thirteen states and the District of Columbia.

Since its founding in 1984, Share Our Strength has distributed more than $68 million to more than one thousand antihunger, antipoverty programs worldwide. To find out how you, too, can share your strength, please visit www.strength.org, or write to Share Our Strength, 733 15th Street N.W., Suite 640, Washington, DC 20005.